ADOBE® PHOTOSHOP® 6

Advanced Digital Images

Prentice
Hall

Upper Saddle River, NJ 07458

Library of Congress Cataloging-in-Publication Data

Adobe Photoshop 6.0: Advanced Digital Images/Against The Clock.
    p.   cm. -- (Against the Clock series)
ISBN 0-13-091484-3
1.Computer graphics. 2. Adobe Photoshop. I. Against The Clock (Firm)
II. Series.
T385.A35834 2002
006.6'869 — dc21

                  2001021019

Executive Editor: Elizabeth Sugg
Developmental Editor: Judy Casillo
Supervising Manager: Mary Carnis
Production Editor: Denise Brown
Director of Manufacturing and Production: Bruce Johnson
Manufacturing Manager: Ilene Sanford
Editorial Assistant: Lara Dugan
Formatting/Page Make-up: Against the Clock, Inc.
Prepress: Photoengraving, Inc.
Printer/Binder: Press of Ohio
Cover Design: LaFortezza Design Group, Inc.
Icon Design: James Braun
Senior Design Coordinator: Miguel Ortiz

The fonts utilized in this training course are the property of Against The Clock, Inc., and are supplied to the legitimate buyers of the Against The Clock training materials solely for use with the exercises and projects provided in the body of the materials. They may not be used for any other purpose, and under no circumstances may they be transferred to another individual, nor copied or distributed by any means whatsoever.

A portion of the images supplied in this book are Copyright © PhotoDisc, Inc., 201 Fourth Ave., Seattle, WA 98121. These images are the sole property of PhotoDisc and are used by Against The Clock with the permission of the owners. They may not be distributed, copied, transferred, or reproduced by any means whatsoever, other than for the completion of the exercises and projects contained in this Against The Clock training material.

Against The Clock and the Against The Clock logo are trademarks of Against The Clock, Inc., registered in the United States and elsewhere. References to and instructional materials provided for any particular application program, operating system, hardware platform, or other commercially available product or products do not represent an endorsement of such product or products by Against The Clock, Inc. or Prentice Hall, Inc.

Photoshop, Acrobat, Adobe Type Manager, Illustrator, InDesign, PageMaker, Premiere, and PostScript are trademarks of Adobe Systems Incorporated. Macintosh is a trademark of Apple Computer, Inc. Macromedia Flash, Generator, FreeHand and Director are registered trademarks of Macromedia, Inc. CorelDRAW! and Painter are trademarks of Corel Corporation. FrontPage, Publisher, PowerPoint, Word, Excel, Office, Microsoft, MS-DOS, Windows, and Windows NT are either registered trademarks or trademarks of Microsoft Corporation. QuarkXPress is a registered trademark of Quark, Inc. TrapWise and PressWise are registered trademarks of ScenicSoft.

Other products and company names mentioned herein may be the trademarks of their respective owners.

Prentice Hall International (UK) Limited, London
Prentice Hall of Australia Pty. Limited, Sydney
Prentice Hall Canada Inc., Toronto
Prentice Hall Hispanoamericana, S.A., Mexico
Prentice Hall of India Private Limited, New Delhi
Prentice Hall of Japan, Inc., Tokyo
Pearson Education Asia Pte. Ltd., Singapore
Editora Prentice Hall do Brasil, Ltda., Rio de Janeiro

10 9 8 7 6 5 4 3

ISBN 0-13-091484-3

Contents

PURPOSE

The Against The Clock series has been developed specifically for those involved in the field of computer arts and now — animation, video, and multimedia production. Many of our readers are already involved in the industry in advertising and printing, television production, multimedia, and in the world of Web design. Others are just now preparing themselves for a career within these professions.

This series of courses will provide you with the skills necessary to work in these fast-paced, exciting, and rapidly expanding fields. While many people feel that they can simply purchase a computer and the appropriate software and begin designing and producing high-quality presentations, the real world of high-quality printed and Web communications requires a far more serious commitment.

THE SERIES

The applications presented in the Against The Clock series stand out as the programs of choice in professional graphic arts environments.

We've used a modular design for the Against The Clock series, allowing you to mix and match the drawing, imaging, and page-layout applications that exactly suit your specific needs.

Titles available in the Against The Clock series include:

Macintosh: Basic Operations
Windows: Basic Operations
Adobe Illustrator: Introduction and Advanced Digital Illustration
Macromedia FreeHand: Digital Illustration
Adobe InDesign: Introduction and Advanced Electronic Mechanicals
Adobe PageMaker: Introduction and Advanced Electronic Mechanicals
QuarkXPress: Introduction and Advanced Electronic Mechanicals
Microsoft Publisher: Creating Electronic Mechanicals
Microsoft PowerPoint: Presentation Graphics with Impact
Microsoft FrontPage: Designing for the Web
MetaCreations Painter: A Digital Approach to Natural Art Media
Adobe Photoshop: Introduction and Advanced Digital Images
Adobe Premiere: Digital Video Editing
Macromedia Director: Creating Powerful Multimedia
Macromedia Flash: Animating for the Web
File Preparation: The Responsible Electronic Page
Preflight: An Introduction to File Analysis and Repair
TrapWise and PressWise: Digital Trapping and Imposition

FOR THE STUDENT

On the CD-ROM, you will find a complete set of Against The Clock (ATC) fonts, as well as a collection of data files used to construct the various exercises and projects.

The ATC fonts are solely for use while you are working with the Against The Clock materials. These fonts will be used throughout both the exercises and projects and are provided in both Macintosh and Windows format.

A variety of student files have been included. These files, necessary to complete both the exercises and projects, are also provided in both Macintosh and Windows formats.

FOR THE TRAINER

The Instructor's CD-ROM includes various testing and presentation materials in addition to the files that come standard with the student books.

- **Overhead Presentation Materials** are provided and follow along with the course. These presentations are prepared using Microsoft PowerPoint and are provided in both native PowerPoint format as well as Acrobat Portable Document Format (PDF).

- **Extra Projects** are provided along with the data files required for completion. These projects may be used to extend the course, or may be used to test the student's progress.

- **Finished Artwork (in PDF format)** for all projects that the students complete is supplied on the CD-ROM.

- **Test Questions and Answers** are included on the instructor CD-ROM. These questions may be modified, reorganized, and administered throughout the delivery of the course.

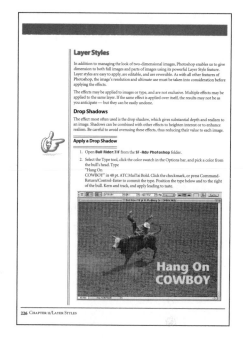

Chapter openers *provide the reader with specific objectives.*

Sidebars and hands-on activities *supplement concepts presented in the material.*

Project assignments *allow you to use your imagination and your new skills to satisfy a client's needs.*

Step-by-step projects *result in finished artwork — with an emphasis on proper file-construction methods.*

In addition to explanatory text and illustrations, Against The Clock course materials have been constructed with two primary building blocks: exercises and projects. Projects always result in a finished piece of work — digital imagery built from the ground up, utilizing photographic-quality images, vector artwork from Adobe Photoshop, and type elements from the library supplied on your student CD-ROM.

This course, *Adobe Photoshop 6.0: Advanced Digital Images*, uses step-by-step projects on which you will work during your learning sessions. There are also open-ended project assignments immediately preceding the two reviews. You will find images of the step-by-step projects you will complete by the end of the course displayed on the inside front and back covers of the book. Here's a brief overview of each:

PROJECT A: JUST SHOOT ME

While an image may be adequate as shot, careful examination of such a photograph will point out to the experienced eye areas where color needs correction, and even the lines of the photo itself need enhancement using Photoshop's color-correction capabilities. For *Just Shoot Me*, you will begin by analyzing the image. You will then skew the image, imitating the skewing produced with a view camera, correct a color shift, and add drama to the photo using a variety of techniques. Your work will transform an adequate photograph into a strong photograph.

PROJECT B: BABY SHOWER INVITATION

In this project, you will work with selection tools and paths, and bring selections from one photo to another. You'll have an opportunity to work with layer-transformation tools, and to alter the color of images. You'll also work with layer masks to create realistic effects for each of the 14 layers you create. In addition, you'll use Photoshop's type tools and layer styles, and merge layers to conserve RAM.

PROJECT C: RETOUCHING THE JONES FAMILY PORTRAIT

At first glance, the Jones family photograph doesn't look bad, however it could be improved. Retouching it means modifying the positions of feet and legs to enhance the overall composition of the photo. It also involves colorizing an element using Hue/Saturation. Finishing touches on this project include removing unsightly blemishes and adjusting the overall look of the photograph to give it a professional touch.

PROJECT D: THE FIX IS IN!

This damaged grayscale photo not only needs repairs, but also colorizing. You'll use the Pen tool to create selections, and then use those selections in a number of ways. You'll manufacture missing elements and create detail where there is none, using the Clone Stamp tool. You will colorize the image primarily with adjustment layers using Hue/Saturation. Along the way, you'll discover a number of tricks to put in your personal bag.

PROJECT E: MAKEOVER

As we grow older, we develop wrinkles, lose some of our dash, and sag here and there. This project takes a middle-aged woman from what the photograph says she looks like to what she is inside (and what most people see when face to face). You'll soften some features, remove a few imperfections, put the glimmer back in her eyes, and give her a facelift using Photoshop's tools. Then you'll bring some light to bear so that her beautiful face fairly glows.

PROJECT F: PHOTOMAT

You may have the best-looking images in the world, but they'll look even better if they're displayed well. In this project you will create a textured matte in which to display your photographs, or photos provided in the student files. In addition, you'll add some shadows and embossing to the matte to make your images pop.

Acknowledgments

I would like to give special thanks to the writers, illustrators, editors, and others who have worked long and hard to complete the Against The Clock series.

Thanks to the dedicated teaching professionals whose comments and expertise contributed to the success of these products, including Janet Frick of Training Resources, Doris Anton of the Wichita Area Technical College, Debbie Rose Myers of the Art Institute of Ft. Lauderdale, and Carin Murphy of the Des Moines Area Community College.

Thanks to Terry Sisk Graybill, senior editor and final link in the chain of production, for her tremendous help in making sure we all said what we meant to say.

A big thanks to Judy Casillo, developmental editor, and Denise Brown, production editor, for their guidance, patience, and attention to detail.

— Ellenn Behoriam, February 2001

OUR HISTORY

Against The Clock (ATC) was founded in 1990 as a part of Lanman Systems Group, one of the nation's leading systems integration and training firms. The company specialized in developing custom training materials for such clients as L.L. Bean, *The New England Journal of Medicine*, the Smithsonian, the National Education Association, *Air & Space Magazine*, Publishers Clearing House, the National Wildlife Society, Home Shopping Network, and many others. The integration firm was among the most highly respected in the graphic arts industry.

To a great degree, the success of Lanman Systems Group can be attributed to the thousands of pages of course materials developed at the company's demanding client sites. Throughout the rapid growth of Lanman Systems Group, Founder and General Manager Ellenn Behoriam developed the expertise necessary to manage technical experts, content providers, writers, editors, illustrators, designers, layout artists, proofreaders, and the rest of the chain of professionals required to develop structured and highly effective training materials.

Following the sale of the Lanman Companies to World Color, one of the nation's largest commercial printers, Ellenn embarked on a project to develop a new library of hands-on training materials engineered specifically for the professional graphic artist. A large part of this effort is finding and working with talented professional artists, writers, and educators from around the country.

The result is the ATC training library.

ROBIN MCALLISTER

Robin McAllister has been speaking and writing about creating effective pages since before desktop publishing was invented. In the process of teaching others, he has written various "how to" guides and training manuals. Rob is a contributing editor for Hayden Books' FreeHand Graphics Studio Skills, and is the author of a series of eight books for Delmar Publishers on a variety of desktop-publishing topics.

Rob is the team leader for America Online's Applied Computing Community. Rob is also a technical editor for *Electronic Publishing*, a contributing editor for *Printing News*, and senior project manager for Against The Clock.

WIN WOLLOFF

Win Wolloff is the president and founder of The Photo Shop, a digital imaging and retouching center in Tampa, Florida. Win holds degrees as Master Photographer and Photographic Craftsmen from the Professional Photographers of America, the nation's largest and most respected trade organization.

Among Win's recent assignments was the position of Digital Director of Eagle Photographics, a Tampa-based commercial color lab. Currently, Win brings his 25+ years of real-world experience to the classroom, where he instructs art students at the International Academy of Design in Tampa.

Platform

The Against The Clock series is designed to apply to both Macintosh and Windows systems. Photoshop runs under Macintosh, Windows 98, and Windows NT. There are separate student files for Macintosh and Windows students.

Naming Conventions

In the old days of MS-DOS systems, file names on the PC were limited to something referred to as "8.3," which meant that you were limited in the number of characters you could use to an eight-character name (the "8") and a three-character suffix (the "3"). Text files, for example, might be called *myfile.txt*, while a document file from a word processor might be called *myfile.doc* (for document). On today's Windows systems, these limitations have been, for the most part, overcome. Although you can use longer file names, suffixes still exist. The Macintosh does not rely on the file extension at all. You see the characters as part of the file name. Whether you see them or not is another story.

When your Windows system is first configured, the Views are normally set to a default that hides these extensions. This means that you might have a dozen different files named *myfile*, all of which may have been generated by different applications and consist of completely different types of files.

You can change this view by double-clicking on *My Computer* (the icon on your desktop). This will open the file. Select View>Folder Options. From Folder Options, select the View tab. Within the Files and Folders folder is a checkbox: Hide File Extensions for Known File Types. When this is unchecked, you can see the file extensions. It's easier to know what you're looking at if they're visible. While this is a personal choice, we strongly recommend viewing the file extensions. All the files used in this course have been named using the three-character suffix.

Key Commands

There are two keys generally used as *modifier* keys — they do nothing when pressed, unless they are pressed in conjunction with another key. Their purpose is to alter the normal functions of the other key with which they are pressed.

The Command (Macintosh) or Control (Windows) key is generally used when taking control of the computer. When combined with the "S" key, it functions to save your work. When combined with "O," it opens a file; with a "P," it prints the file. In addition to these functions, which work with most Macintosh and Windows programs, the Control key may be combined with other keys to take control of specific functions in Photoshop.

Another special function key is the Option (Macintosh) and Alt (for alternate) (Windows) key. It, too, is a modifier key, and you must hold it down along with whatever other key (or keys) is required for a specific function. The Option and Alt keys are often used in conjunction with other keys to access typographic characters having an ASCII number higher than 128. Under Windows, they are used in conjunction with the numeric keypad.

The Macintosh and Windows access context-sensitive menus in similar but different ways. On the Macintosh, holding down the Control (not the Command) key while clicking the mouse button will bring up context-sensitive menus. Under Windows, this is accomplished by clicking the right mouse button (right-clicking). We generically call accessing the context menu "context-clicking."

The CD-ROM and Initial Setup Considerations

Before you begin using your Against The Clock course book, you must set up your system to have access to the various files and tools to complete your lessons.

Student Files

This course comes complete with a collection of student files. These files are an integral part of the learning experience — they're used throughout the course to help you construct increasingly complex elements. Having these building blocks available to you for practice and study sessions will ensure that you will be able to experience the exercises and complete the project assignments smoothly, spending a minimum of time looking for the various required components.

In the Student Files folders, we've created sets of data. Locate the **SF-Adv Photoshop** folder and drag the icon onto your hard disk drive. If you have limited disk space, you may want to copy only the files for one or two lessons at a time.

We strongly recommend that you work from your hard disk. However, in some cases you might not have enough room on your system for all the files we've supplied. If this is the case, you can work directly from the CD-ROM.

Creating a Project Folder

Throughout the exercises and projects you'll be required to save your work. Since the CD-ROM is "read-only," you cannot write information to it. Create a "work in progress" folder on your hard disk and use it to store your work. Create it by context-clicking, while at your desktop, then selecting New Folder (Macintosh) or New> Folder (Windows). This will create the folder at the highest level of your system, where it will always be easy to find. Name this folder "Work in Progress".

System Requirements

On the Macintosh, you will need a Power PC 604 processor or above, running the 8.5 operating system or later; 64 MB* of application memory (with Virtual Memory on); 125 MB of available hard-disk space (after install); a monitor with a resolution of at least 800 × 600 or greater; and a CD-ROM drive.

On a Windows operating system, you'll need a Pentium II or faster processor; Windows 98/NT 4.0, or Windows 2000† or higher; 64 MB* application memory; 125 MB of available hard-disk space (after installation); a monitor with a resolution of at least 800 × 600 pixels; and a CD-ROM drive.

*128 MB required to run Photoshop and Imageready concurrently
† NT Service Pack 4, 5, or 6a required

Preferences

We recommend that you throw away your Preferences file before you begin the lessons in this course. The "Adobe Photoshop 6 Preferences" file may be found inside your Adobe Photoshop 6.0>Adobe Photoshop Settings folder.

Prerequisites

This book assumes that you have a basic understanding of how to use your system.

You should know how to use your mouse to point and click, and how to drag items around the screen. You should know how to resize a window, and how to arrange windows on your desktop to maximize your available space. You should know how to access pull-down menus, and how checkboxes and radio buttons work. Lastly, you should know how to create, open, and save files.

If you're familiar with these fundamental skills, then you know all that's necessary to utilize the Against The Clock courseware library.

Notes:

INTRODUCTION

The concepts and organization of this book make certain assumptions about your knowledge and experience. You should be familiar with Photoshop's tool set, and with the concept of channels, layers, and the variety of selection techniques available to you.

Photoshop is a robust program, with exciting features that go well beyond photo manipulation. There are dozens of books about Photoshop, and each one can teach you something new and useful about the program.

While Photoshop is capable of producing a wide variety of effects, each successive version of the program has made creating them easier. What this means for the creative professional is that time can be spent designing a dynamic piece for print, the Web, or multimedia, instead of executing tedious details. For the design professional, it means increased productivity.

It has been our goal, in creating exercises and projects, first to help you see that you can create "cool stuff" quickly and easily, using Photoshop's built-in features; you can then make those images even more interesting by employing additional effects. While becoming expert in Photoshop is hard work, it should also be fun and fulfilling.

As you progress through this course, we encourage you to pay attention not only to the details — how to execute the tasks associated with the exercises and projects — but also to the principles behind them. While there are some projects and exercises that demand absolute attention to each detail, many give you more latitude. In many parts of this course, we encourage you to experiment with similar effects, rather than limit you to ideas that the authors find interesting. We hope you will do so, and expand your creative vision.

Most important, we encourage you to look at the big picture — what you're actually creating — and make decisions based on that reality, rather than establishing a blanket rule for production.

The goals of this course are to:

- Build on your existing knowledge.

- Expand your toolbox of creative techniques.

- Temper creative possibilities with production reality.

- Explore advanced uses of Photoshop.

This course is slanted toward design and design-related techniques and functions, and also explores practical realities. The course touches on color correction, but does not immerse itself in the details that are needed for high-end color adjustment. It also touches Web creation and design, together with animation, while not delving deeply into those subjects. If your need lies in these areas, consider additional courses following the successful completion of this material.

CALIBRATING YOUR SYSTEM

CHAPTER OBJECTIVE:

To develop a basic understanding of color calibration by learning the intricacies of the process of fine-tuning your system to achieve acceptable output. In Chapter 1, you will:

- Learn how to predict output color and compensate for the many variables involved in the printing process.

- Understand factors that affect color display, such as ambient lighting, monitors, video cards, the ability of the scanner operator, and other variables that can affect the printed piece.

- Become familiar with how to use the gamma program to compensate for the visual difference in your perception of the monitor's color and the colors it actually displays.

- Discover how critical gamma correction is to visualizing how an image will reproduce.

- Learn about setting profiles to synchronize your monitor with other input and output methods and with specific printing processes.

PROJECTS TO BE COMPLETED:

- Just Shoot Me (A)

- Baby Shower Invitation (B)

- Retouching the Jones Family Portrait (C)

- The Fix Is In! (D)

- Makeover (E)

- Photomat (F)

WYSIWYG is an acronym for "What You See Is What You Get," meaning that what you see on your computer screen bears a strong resemblance to what the job will look like when it is printed.

You can use the three major color modes in the industry (RGB, CMYK, and CIE L*a*b) to view different areas of the color spectrum. Understand that each one of these modes can only represent a confined area of the spectrum, and none of these modes can represent all of the colors that your eye can see.

Phosphors produce the red, green, and blue color on the screen.

Calibrating Your System

Monitors, desktop printers, graphic arts service providers, and printing technologies have evolved dramatically over the past ten years, but you can still not completely trust what you see on your monitor. It's easy to trust what we see — after all, our eyes are our primary connection with the world around us. Because of this, we tend to believe our eyes instead of relying on the information Photoshop gives us through the Info palette. Calibrating your system ensures that what you see on your monitor fairly represents what you're going to see when your project is printed, or viewed on the Web.

What is Calibration?

Often, what you see on your screen or from your printer isn't anywhere close to what is output by the service provider. There are many reasons for this, which we'll explain. The important thing to know is that there is something you can do about it.

Calibration is the process that brings the image that a monitor displays closer to what is produced on the printed page. We'll never get an exact match; the idea is to create a consistent working environment from which you can reliably predict output color, as well as to compensate for differences in printing methods, personal interpretation, and other factors.

These differences are more than just a case of the monitor not matching the printer. Many elements affect a person's perception of color.

- **Your physical and mental condition.** Your mood, age, level of tiredness, and the medications you take all affect the way in which you see color.
- **Lighting systems.** If the lighting changes constantly or adds color casts, there is no consistent basis from which to begin calibration. A stable lighting system that does not skew the ambient color of the room may be the most important factor in color calibration.
- **Clothing and the color of the room.** Clothing and the color of the room reflect onto the monitor, giving an image a color cast. In many shops, color specialists wear neutral gray smocks to minimize the effect of reflected color.
- **The monitor you use.** Every monitor, including monitors of the same make and model, is different. A monitor that has not warmed up produces a different display than one that has been on for a while. Phosphors — the substance that monitors use to represent colors — vary between screens, and deteriorate over time.
- **Video cards and driver sets.** These cards and driver sets can produce different sets of colors.
- **The scan itself.** Scans of the same image made on different scanners contain different image information. In addition, there are vast differences in scan quality between scans of reflective material, such as photographic prints, and scans of transparencies, such as slides.
- **Individual color perception and the ability of the scanner operator.** Since everyone's perception of color is different, one area where the color consistency equation can break down lies within the ability (or lack of ability) of the scanner operator who will adjust your scans.

- **The calibration capabilities of the software application**. Software programs have differing calibration abilities, ranging from excellent, as in Photoshop, to none, as in older versions of PageMaker. The available color management systems are good, but they're not perfect. These systems attempt to present a unified view of color on screen to be matched to various output devices.

- **The output device**. All output devices are different. To further complicate matters, two identical printers may have different output characteristics — printing darker, bluer, etc. Many printing devices have their own color control systems (RIPs, color correction software, etc.) that can also affect color consistency.

- **The paper stock on which an image is printed**. The color, density, absorption quality, grain, and finish of the paper stock used all affect output quality and color.

- **The material on which the image is output**. The properties of the different materials used to output Photoshop images can vary greatly between manufacturers. In addition, many manufacturers offer more than one grade of their ink, toner, or film, and the hue usually varies from one grade to another. Impurities in inks or toners, as well as the photosensitive material (emulsions) used in film, can cause the same image to appear differently. That makes it impossible to match colors exactly between two sets of inks or film.

Steps to Calibration

There are many factors to deal with when attempting to calibrate your computer and/or applications to produce consistent output results. Photoshop has many tools that will allow you to work closer with whatever printing device or outside vendor you choose.

The calibration process takes quite a bit of time and would be difficult to experience within a classroom environment. The basic steps to calibrate a computer system and monitor are listed below:

- **Stabilize the lighting system**. Fluorescent lights having 5000°K (Kelvin) color temperature (also called "full spectrum" lighting) don't add color casts to documents the way other light sources can.

- **Calibrate when you're alert and the monitor is warmed up** (at least 30 minutes). If the home or office has windows, either calibrate with shades closed, or calibrate at the same time of day in consistent lighting conditions.

- **Adjust the monitor with the panel controls**. Adjust the brightness and contrast, and if the monitor is so equipped, pick an appropriate color temperature. If it has individual controls for color, adjust according to the manufacturer's specifications. When the monitor is looking good, tape down the controls so they won't be changed accidentally.

- **Use the Adobe Gamma utility to calibrate the monitor and define the RGB color space that the monitor can display**. This utility should have been automatically installed during the installation of the Photoshop application. The monitor must be calibrated if it is to accurately display colors. Once the monitor is calibrated, Photoshop will compensate for differences between the color space in which the image resides and the color space in which the monitor displays images. Setting the Adobe Gamma will be discussed later in this chapter.

Raster Image Processor (RIP) is a device or program that translates files into a format that an output device can produce.

On the Macintosh, Adobe Gamma is located in the Control Panels, which can be accessed from the Apple menu. On Windows-based systems, it is either located in the Control Panels folder or in the Adobe Calibration folder (found by selecting Program Files>Common Files>Adobe Calibration folder).

Color cast occurs when an entire image exhibits too much of a specific color. Often this is introduced by the type of film used. For example, Ektachrome tends to give images a blue color cast. Gray balance is the condition in which grays are neutral — they do not exhibit a color cast.

Adobe Gamma panel

- **Obtain a CMYK color or grayscale proof and compare it with the screen image.** Additional adjustments may need to be made to the Gray Balance to remove unwanted color casts or compensate for *dot gain*, in which a halftone dot grows larger on the press, darkening one or more of the CMYK primaries in your image.

- **Repeat until the results are satisfactory.**

That is all most people use for basic color management with Photoshop, and it may be all you need. Advanced color management features are available within Photoshop, and we'll discuss them later in the chapter.

Using the Gamma Program

Gamma is defined as the contrast between midtones. The purpose of the gamma program is to compensate for the difference between the way we see images and the way the monitor displays an image; it also corrects color casts — hints of blue or green visible in most monitors. Even if other calibration tasks are skipped, gamma correction is critical to accurate reproduction of images.

When Macintosh users correct gamma, the correction affects all applications. When Windows users correct gamma, the correction affects Photoshop only.

Replace the Preferences File

1. If Photoshop is open, exit the application.

Macintosh Users:

2. Locate and open your System folder.

3. Open Preferences>Adobe Photoshop 6 Settings>Adobe Photoshop 6 Prefs.

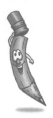

The Color Setup dialog box allows you to match the parameters of your output devices or the output devices of the printing vendor that you are using.

4. Drag the Prefs file to the trash can.

5. That's it! Relaunch Photoshop; it will take a little longer than normal to load while the program builds a new preferences file.

Windows Users:

2. Locate and open your Photoshop application folder.

3. Open Windows>Application Data>Adobe>Photoshop>6.0>Adobe Photoshop 6 Settings.

4. Drag the Adobe Photoshop 6 Prefs.psp file to the Recycle Bin, and empty it.

5. That's it! Relaunch Photoshop; it will take a little longer than normal to load while it builds a new preferences file.

Set Your Monitor

One way to calibrate a monitor is by using the Adobe Gamma Wizard. This program takes you through the calibration procedure step by step. There are some minor differences between Macintosh and Windows setup screens. (Not all screens are shown.)

We're going to make the assumption that your room lighting is at the level in which you wish to calibrate regularly, that your monitor has been turned on for at least 30 minutes, and that your display is set to a neutral gray.

1. Launch the Adobe Gamma utility by selecting Apple menu>Control Panels>Adobe Gamma (Macintosh) or Program Files>Common Files>Adobe>Calibration>Adobe Gamma.cpl (Windows). Alternately, this utility may be in the Control Panels folder under Windows.

2. The first screen allows you to select the method of calibration. The Adobe Gamma Wizard gives the option of either a step-by-step method (by using the Adobe Gamma Wizard), or using the Adobe Gamma panel (as previously shown). We will use the Wizard.

Replace the Preferences file to start Photoshop with a clean slate, automatically removing any user preferences that may be undesirable.

![Adobe Gamma dialog box. This control panel will allow you to calibrate your monitor and create an ICC profile for it. Which version would you like to use? ● Step By Step (Assistant) ○ Control Panel. This ICC Profile will be compatible with ColorSync™ on Macintosh and ICM 2.0 on Windows. Buttons: Cancel, Back, Next.]

3. The first step is to describe the profile. Accept the default description for your monitor.

4. Your next step is to adjust the monitor to the maximum setting. Change the Contrast control to the highest setting, and adjust the Brightness control to make the center box as dark as possible (but not black), while keeping the frame around it a bright white.

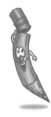

5. The next step will set the Phosphors. Phosphors vary between different manufacturers. The Gamma Wizard will attempt to measure phosphor levels. If this setting is incorrect, obtain the correct setting from the monitor's owner's manual and record it on this screen.

If the Control Panel launches instead of the Wizard, click the Assistant button at the bottom of the dialog box.

Different monitors may produce different defaults than those shown here.

Adobe Gamma Assistant

The red, green, and blue phosphors in a monitor can vary from one manufacturer to the next.

Your current monitor profile indicates that your monitor uses the following phosphors. If you know this to be incorrect, please choose a different setting.

Phosphors: [Trinitron ▼]

[Cancel] [Back] [Next]

6. To set the midtone levels, adjust the midtone level inside of the gray box until the center solid gray box fades into the pattern box. Then choose the proper gamma for the monitor (Macintosh, Windows, or Custom). Deselecting the View Single Gamma Only option allows for the adjustment of the midtone levels for the red, green, and blue phosphors.

Adobe Gamma Assistant

The gamma setting of your monitor defines how bright your midtones are. Establish the current gamma by adjusting the slider until the center box fades into the patterned frame.

☑ View Single Gamma Only

Now choose the desired gamma.

Gamma: [Macintosh Default ▼] [1.8]

[Cancel] [Back] [Next]

You can deselect the "View Single Gamma Only" option, and adjust your midtone levels for the red, green, and blue colors independently.

7. The next step is to determine whether the monitor is using a warm or cool white point. As with the previous steps, the Wizard will determine what it measures as the current temperature at which it believes the monitor is representing the color white. If this is incorrect, reset it.

Adobe Gamma Assistant

The white point of your monitor determines whether you are using a warm or cool white.

The hardware white point of your monitor is shown below. If you know this to be incorrect, choose a different setting or click on Measure to visually estimate it.

Hardware White Point: [9300°K (cool white) ▼]

[Measure...]

[Cancel] [Back] [Next]

8. If you choose to measure, you will be presented with three squares; you need to continue choosing the one with the most neutral gray (left or right). When the square that appears most neutral gray is in the center, click to select it, then click Next.

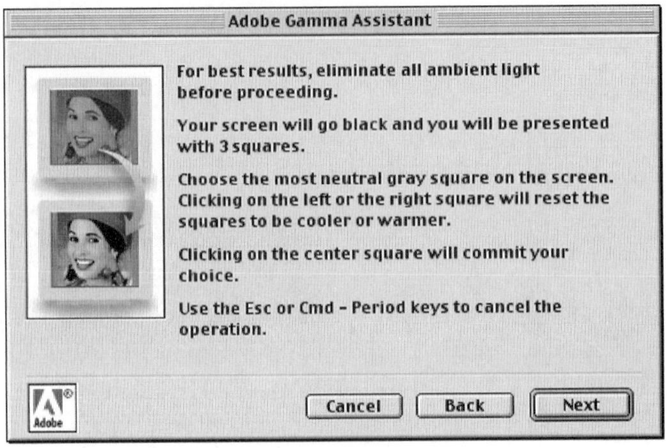

Adobe Gamma Assistant

For best results, eliminate all ambient light before proceeding.

Your screen will go black and you will be presented with 3 squares.

Choose the most neutral gray square on the screen. Clicking on the left or the right square will reset the squares to be cooler or warmer.

Clicking on the center square will commit your choice.

Use the Esc or Cmd – Period keys to cancel the operation.

[Cancel] [Back] [Next]

9. If you wish to work at a different white point (temperature) than your monitor's setting, you can select that temperature in the next Wizard panel. Click Next.

Adobe Gamma Assistant

You can choose to work at a different white point than your monitor's hardware setting. The current adjusted white point is shown below. If desired, choose a new value.

Adjusted White Point: [Same as Hardware ⬍]

[Cancel] [Back] [Next]

10. When you have completed setting up the monitor's gamma, you have an opportunity to compare Before and After settings. Clicking the Before and After buttons will allow you to see the difference of any changes you have made in the thumbnails to the left. Click Finish.

Adobe Gamma Assistant

You have now completed the Adobe Gamma Assistant. To view your screen prior to these changes, compare the results of the following options.

○ Before
● After

To save your settings, click on Finish.

[Cancel] [Back] [Finish]

11. After completing these settings through the Wizard, save them. This will allow you to recall them if it becomes necessary to adjust them or change their settings. They will be saved to the appropriate folder.

Advanced Color Management

Using Photoshop's advanced color-management features allows you to set up a fully managed color workflow, from input device through output device. You can use Adobe's predefined color settings or create custom settings that pertain to the equipment you use. All color settings can be set using the Color Settings dialog box.

Color Settings with Advanced Settings shown.

Predefined Color Management Settings

Included in the Settings grouping are a number of predefined settings for common publishing workflows such as standard press workflows, emulations of various Photoshop workflows, and a ColorSync workflow (Macintosh only). Color management may be turned off if desired.

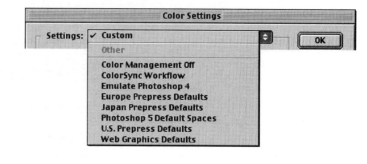

- **Color Management Off**. This workflow considers working space profiles when converting colors between color spaces, but does not tag documents with profiles. This is the option of choice for content that will be output as video, for on-screen presentation, or for the Web. It is also the recommended profile when working with a GASP, and you do not have output device profiles for the printers and other devices the GASP will use to output your files.

- **ColorSync Workflow (Macintosh OS only)**. This workflow uses the ColorSync color management system with profiles chosen from the ColorSync control panel. This is an ideal solution for managing workflows using Adobe and non-Adobe applications, since the color management is at the Macintosh system level.

- **Emulate Photoshop 4**. This emulates the color space of Photoshop for Macintosh versions 4 and earlier.

- **Europe Prepress Defaults**. Use this workflow when you will be printing with press conditions common to Europe.

- **Japan Prepress Defaults**. Use this workflow when you will be printing with press conditions common to Japan.

- **Photoshop 5 Default Spaces**. This emulates the default color space of Photoshop 5. It should be used when attempting to match images prepared using that color space.

- **U.S. Prepress Defaults**. Use this workflow when you will be printing with press conditions common to the United States.

- **Web Graphics Defaults**. This workflow manages color for images that will be published on the Internet.

Choose the proper Setup window, depending on the color mode in which you are going to work, by selecting File>Color Settings. If your monitor is not listed, obtain the specifications from the monitor manual or the manufacturer. The target gamma is usually 1.8 if you deal mainly in print media, or 2.2 for video. If your monitor is listed, the default gamma, which can be as high as 2.5, should be fine.

Working Spaces

If you are using a color-managed workflow, each color mode must have a space with which it is associated. This is called the "Working Space." There are a number of color profiles that Adobe recommends for most workflows; these profiles appear in the Working Spaces menus. If, however, you are working with devices that do not appear in the menus, you may create custom profiles to match the devices from which you obtain images or to which you will output. The working space acts as the color profile for all documents created in Photoshop and for all images imported into Photoshop that are not pretagged with a profile.

Working Spaces		
RGB:	ColorSync RGB – Generic RGB Profile	Load...
CMYK:	U.S. Web Coated (SWOP) v2	Save...
Gray:	Gray Gamma 2.2	☑ Preview
Spot:	Dot Gain 20%	

RGB Space

RGB working space is used by scanners, monitors, and system-wide color spaces, such as ColorSync, Apple RGB, Adobe RGB, and others. All images saved from Photoshop in RGB format will include the RGB working space that you specify. System-wide color spaces include the following:

- **Monitor RGB**. This is the color space of your monitor.
- **ColorSync RGB.** This space uses the RGB profile specified in the ColorSync Control Panel. (Macintosh only.)
- **Adobe RGB**. This RGB color space became the Photoshop standard in 1998.
- **Apple RGB**. This color space is a standard used in earlier versions of Adobe Photoshop as well as other desktop publishing applications. This is the best choice for images that will be displayed only on Mac OS systems.
- **Color Match RGB.** This color space is for Radius monitors.
- **sRGB IEC61966-2.1**. This standard RGB color space is a default space for many scanners and low-resolution color printers.
- **Other.** These other working spaces include NTSC (1953) (for standard television), SMPTE-240M (for high-definition television), Custom, and color spaces for a number of scanners and monitors.

CMYK Space

Use the CMYK work space to define the CMYK color space for a variety of inks, paper stock, and color-management profiles. This setting affects the way in which RGB documents are converted to CMYK. If an ink set runs heavy in magenta, for example, the program takes that into consideration when converting the document. Collaborate with your service provider to choose an appropriate CMYK color space.

- **ColorSync CMYK**. This work space maps the RGB color to the profile you have defined as your standard CMYK ColorSync color space. (Macintosh only.)
- **Euroscale Coated v2 and Euroscale Uncoated v2**. Use these working spaces when you will be printing with conditions and inks common to Europe.
- **Japan Standard v2**. Use this working space when you will be printing with conditions and inks common to Japan.
- **U.S. Sheetfed Coated v2 and U.S. Sheetfed Uncoated v2**. Use these working spaces when you will be printing coated or uncoated stock on a sheetfed press in the United States.
- **U.S. Web Coated (SWOP) v2 U.S. Web Uncoated v2**. Use these working spaces when you will be printing coated or uncoated stock on a web press in the United States.

Gray Space

Use the Gray work space to define how grayscale images onscreen will translate when the image is printed.

- **ColorSync Gray**. This is the profile you have designated as the ColorSync standard for converting monitor space to print. (Macintosh only.)
- **Dot Gain** of varying percentages. This work space is used to compensate for the spread of a halftone dot in a grayscale image.

SWOP is the acronym for Specifications for Web Offset Printing, and is commonly used in the United States. For more information on SWOP, visit the SWOP web site: www.swop.org

- **Gray Gamma**. This allows you to set the monitor's gamma setting to compensate for differences between the monitor's presentation of an image and the actuality of a grayscale image on press.

Spot Space

Spot work space is similar to grayscale work space. However, only dot gains may be specified in these menus.

Color Management Policies

The predefined color-management configurations provide prescribed behaviors for Photoshop for the RGB, CMYK, and Grayscale color modes. The behaviors may be overridden on a case-by-case basis, or the defaults may be changed to better reflect your workflow. The three behaviors are Off, Preserve Embedded Profiles, and Convert to Working Space. They are set separately for each of the three color modes.

Off

- New documents and untagged documents are not tagged with profiles.
- Existing documents that have a profile other than the existing one become untagged.
- Existing documents that have the active profile retain it.
- Color data using the same color model imported into the image retain their exact color definition.
- Colors imported into the document from images in a different color mode are converted into the current document's color space.

Preserve Embedded Profiles

- New documents are assigned the current working space profile.
- Existing documents that have a profile retain the profile with which they are tagged.
- Existing documents with no profile use the current working space, but are not assigned a profile.
- Color data imported within the same color mode between a non-color-managed source and destination retain their color definition.
- CMYK images imported into CMYK documents retain their color definitions.
- All other imported colors are converted to the document's color space.

Convert to Working Space

- New documents and documents tagged with any profile are converted to the current working space and are tagged with the current profile.
- Existing documents with no profile use the current working space, but are not assigned a profile.
- All other imported colors are converted to the document's color space.

Noncompliant Profiles

When the profiles do not match, you can define Photoshop's behavior by selecting the buttons opposite Profile Mismatches and Missing Profiles.

- **Profile Mismatches**. You may leave the buttons untouched, or check one or both, causing Photoshop to Ask when Opening or Ask when Pasting.
- **Missing Profile**. You may choose Ask when Opening, or leave it unchecked.

Conversion Options

The conversion options specify a color-management engine, the rendering intent, and the compensation by which adjustment is made between color spaces. Conversion Options is available only when the Advanced Mode is checked.

Color-management Engine

This option enables you to decide upon the system and color-matching method that will be used to convert between color spaces.

- **ACE**. This is the Adobe Color Engine color management system, and is Adobe's recommendation for most users who choose to use color management.
- **Apple ColorSync**. This method uses the Apple ColorSync engine and its default color-matching methods. (Macintosh only.)
- **Apple CMM**. This method uses the Apple ColorSync engine and the CMM management system. (Macintosh only.)
- **Heidelberg CMM**. This method uses the Apple ColorSync engine and the Heidelberg color management system. (Macintosh only.)
- **ICM.** This method uses the Microsoft ICM engine and its default color-matching methods. (Windows only.)

Intent

- **Perceptual**. This method presents a visually pleasing representation of the image, preserving visual relationships between colors.
- **Saturation**. Use this method for images with high-saturation graphics, such as pie charts and graphs. It concentrates on saturation of color rather than on color accuracy.
- **Relative Colorimetric**. Use this method for accurate representation of colors, using L*a*b conversions. It is especially good when most colors used are in-gamut. This method adjusts for the whiteness of the background media.
- **Absolute Colorimetric**. This method tries to achieve absolute L*a*b conversion, disregarding the base media.

Compensation

- **Black Point Compensation**. When this option is selected, the full range of the source space is mapped into the full color range of the destination space. This method can result in blocked or grayed out shadows, but is most useful when the black point of the source is darker than that of the destination.

- **Dither**. This option is used with 8-bit per channel images. Colors in the destination space are mixed to simulate missing colors from the source space. It can result in larger file sizes for Web images.

Advanced Controls

The monitor does not accurately reflect color that is reflected from a sheet of paper. The reason for this is that light is transmissive, and is subsequently both brighter and more heavily saturated. The advanced controls tend to moderate the differences between transmissive and reflective color.

Desaturate Monitor Colors

This option is useful for visualizing the full range of color and is useful for viewing color gamuts that have colors outside the monitor's range. However, when it is deselected, colors that were previously distinct may appear as a single color, and may print as a single color as well.

Blend RGB Colors Using Gamma

This selection inputs a gamma curve to avoid solid-edge artifacts. A gamma of 1.00 is considered "colorimetrically correct." If the option is deselected, RGB colors are blended using only the document's color space.

Summary

The proper working environment, combined with a calibrated computer system, can be the greatest first step in the production of high-quality Photoshop images. Since many factors can affect the image, Photoshop has included many tools to meet the needs of the graphic design and production professions.

As you have learned from our discussion of advanced image control, managing color is a highly technical aspect of the graphic arts. It is our recommendation that, in general, color management should be undertaken only when performed in conjunction with your service provider.

IMAGE ADJUSTMENT

CHAPTER OBJECTIVE:

To learn about the concept of levels and curves, and how they affect the overall control of the tonal range of your images. To learn how to modify these tools to achieve the best results. In Chapter 2, you will:

- Learn what levels are, and how they affect the appearance of your images.

- Become familiar with how to read a histogram, which provides a visual representation of how an image's tones are balanced.

- Observe the difference between shadows, midtones, and highlights, and learn how these values affect the appearance of your image.

- Learn about the different types of images, and how to adjust levels in an image to improve its appearance.

- Become familiar with how to use levels for other effects, such as cleaning up an image with rough edges.

- Learn about the Curves dialog box and how the graphic it presents relates to various tonal ranges within an image.

- Discover the relationship between curves and levels, and when each technique is most effective.

PROJECTS TO BE COMPLETED:

- Just Shoot Me (A)

- Baby Shower Invitation (B)

- Retouching the Jones Family Portrait (C)

- The Fix Is In! (D)

- Makeover (E)

- Photomat (F)

Image Adjustment

In a perfect world, all photographs would be crisp and clear, and all scans optimally balanced with beautiful, accurate color. The real world is quite different. Digital images come from a variety of sources, and many are far from perfect. To reproduce your images as you want them to appear, regardless of the condition of the original image, you must be able to effectively use the variety of image adjustment tools.

While Photoshop users debate which color correction tool is best, a few facts should be noted. There is no "one perfect tool" for adjusting images. Sometimes, all that is necessary is to modify the brightness and contrast. At other times, you need to make more extensive correction, using the Levels or the Curves command.

Brightness and contrast adjustments affect all channels of the image; these are the most basic adjustments.

Both the Levels and Curves adjustments can be used to affect all channels of the image or only a single channel. If an image only requires an overall adjustment to the brightness, contrast, and gamma settings of a channel, then Levels adjustments will suit the purpose. However, if a greater degree of control is desired, especially in specific areas of grayscale representation of channels, Curves adjustment is the preferred method.

Highlight — the lightest area of the image that still contains definition (a halftone dot).

Shadow — the darkest part of the image.

Gamma — contrast in the midtone range.

Spectral Highlight (also called Specular Highlight) — the bright spots in an image that have no definition at all (pure white).

Images contain four areas of brightness: highlight, midtone (gamma), shadow, and spectral highlights.

The specific controls available for image adjustment are explained in this chapter. Examples are presented to show where each control works best.

Adjusting Brightness and Contrast

The Photoshop arsenal includes many tools for tonal correction and color adjustment. The first step in correcting an image is to adjust brightness and contrast.

What is Contrast?

Contrast is the difference between the lightest and darkest areas of an image. A low-contrast image looks washed out, and lacks detail throughout the image. A high-contrast image lacks detail in the shadow areas and highlights; in some high-contrast images, the midtones are nearly nonexistent.

Adjusting brightness and contrast is a three-step process:

- Determine the highlight areas.
- Determine the shadow areas.
- Adjust the gamma, the contrast in the middle grays or midtones of an image. The gamma adjustment determines the proportion of darker grays to lighter grays.

Tools for Adjusting Brightness and Contrast

There are many methods for brightness and contrast adjustment in Photoshop. The differences between them are mainly a matter of the degree of accuracy and control each adjustment technique can produce. In this chapter we will concentrate on four of these methods.

The Histogram shows the distribution of pixels from the darkest to the lightest portion of the image. This distribution can be shown for the entire image or for each of the individual color channels.

Brightness and Contrast can be used to make gross corrections, changing all the pixels in an image. This is most appropriate for special effects, since you can't adjust the highlight, shadow, and gamma separately.

The Levels adjustment allows you to adjust highlight, shadow, and gamma individually. In addition, you can work either on all the channels in a document at once or on an individual channel. The Levels command uses a *histogram*, a graph of the brightness levels within an image, to allow you to see the distribution of pixels in an image.

The Curves adjustment, while usually used for color correction, can also be used to correct the brightness and contrast of an image. While the Levels adjustment is usually more than adequate for the task, occasionally you'll find a particularly difficult image that needs different midtone adjustments in various ranges of midtone values. For example, Curves enables you to make light midtones darker and dark midtones lighter in each individual color channel. Brightness and contrast for this type of image are usually adjusted while performing color correction, which is covered in the next section.

The Info palette shows the value of the color in a particular point on an image. Photoshop allows you to map two different points on an image. This, as you shall see, assists you in judging the best point to choose for your highlight or shadow area.

Use the Brightness and Contrast Command

1. Open the image **Poolside_GS.TIF** from the **SF-Adv Photoshop** folder. This is an especially low-contrast image.

2. Select Image>Duplicate to make a copy of the grayscale image. Name this copy "Poolside_GS_BC.TIF".

3. Select Image>Adjust>Brightness/Contrast.

4. Move the Brightness slider to the left a little, about -10, to darken the image.

Use the Histogram tool only as a review tool.

Remember, use the Brightness and Contrast tools only for overall correction of an image.

The Levels command gives you the most control over the brightness/contrast and midtones of your image. Use the Curves command for finer correction of midtones.

5. Move the Contrast slider to the right to about 25 to increase the contrast.

Brightness/Contrast

Brightness: `-10`

Contrast: `+25`

OK

Cancel

☑ Preview

While these adjustments have improved the image overall, there is still poor contrast in areas such as the palm fronds at the top. If you adjust the contrast high enough to correct the contrast in the palm fronds, the white around the pool and the shadow areas lose all detail.

6. Play with the Brightness and Contrast sliders until you feel you've achieved the best possible looking image. Notice that while you can make overall brightness and contrast corrections, the highlight and shadow still lack detail. Click OK.

7. Leave both images open for the next exercise.

Use Levels to Adjust Brightness and Contrast

1. Activate the Poolside_GS.TIF image, and select Image>Duplicate again. Name the duplicate "Poolside_GS_Levels.TIF". Activate the Info palette so you can check your readings as you go.

2. Select Image>Adjust>Levels, or Command/Control-L.

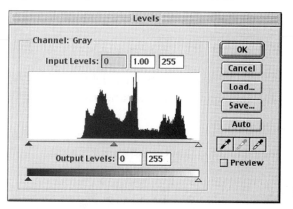

Check the Preview box. This provides you instant feedback as you make changes to the values in the histogram. The histogram (the graph in the center of the dialog box) is typical of a low-contrast image. Most of the image data is bunched together in the middle, indicating a lack of distinct highlights and shadows.

3. The first set of sliders, the Input Levels, are used for increasing contrast and adjusting gamma. The Output Levels are used to decrease contrast in an image. Move the black slider of the Input Levels control bar to the right so that it just touches the rise on the left edge of the graph.

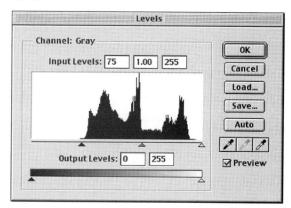

Notice that the first of the numbers listed above the histogram changes as you move the slider. Essentially, any pixel with a brightness value lower than that number (or any pixel to the left of the slider) will be remapped to black.

You can review and revise saved brightness and contrast settings in the History palette.

4. Repeat the process with the white slider. Move the slider to the left until it touches the rise in the graph on the right. The image should now appear similar to the one you corrected using Brightness and Contrast.

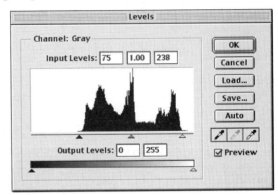

5. The contrast isn't quite high enough. Move the black and white sliders toward the center a little more (but not too far) to increase the contrast. Remember that only the pixels between the two sliders will maintain color; the remainder will turn either black or white.

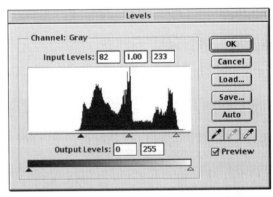

When an image is to be printed, the black point should be 95% and the white point should be 5%. These are areas with definition. They should not print at 100% and 0%, respectively.

6. The slider in the middle is the gamma slider. Moving it to the right increases the distance between the black and gamma sliders, and reduces the distance between the white and gamma sliders. The result is darker midtones, because the ratio of dark pixels (the pixels between the gamma slider and the black slider) is higher. Move the gamma slider left to about 1.30 to lighten the image. Click OK.

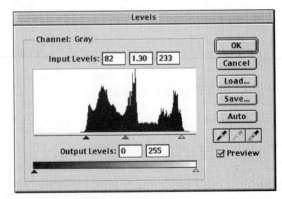

7. Compare this image to the one you adjusted using only Brightness and Contrast. Can you see the difference that adjusting the gamma made? Leave the file open while you proceed to the next exercise.

Choosing Highlights and Shadows from the Image

The result of using Levels in the previous exercise is slightly better than what was achieved using Brightness/Contrast. Generally speaking, most images don't have a contrast problem this severe, and the type of leveling used above is sufficient to achieve excellent depth and results far superior to using Brightness/Contrast.

By moving the black and white sliders in the previous example, you were changing the *black point* and *white point* of the image, the point at which pixels become black or white. Occasionally you'll find an image, such as the one we're working on, that doesn't respond well to leveling according to the histogram. With this type of image it is necessary to pick the black and white points directly from the image.

Setting black and white points manually requires extra thought and care. You could rely on your eyes to find highlight and shadow points, but there's a better way. With the use of the Color Sampler tool and the multiple sampler option in the Info palette, you can determine the black and white points quickly.

Level with Black and White Points

1. Activate the Poolside_GS.TIF image again, and select Image>Duplicate. Name this duplicate "Poolside_GS_ManualLevel.TIF". Click OK.

2. Open the Color Sampler tool in the Eyedropper tool. In the Option toolbar, set Sample Size to 3 × 3 Average.

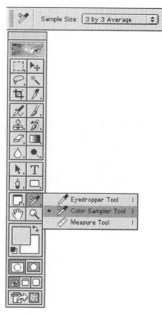

3. Select Image>Adjust>Levels (or Command/Control>L) to activate the Levels dialog box. Preview must be activated in the Levels palette.

4. Hold down the Option/Alt key, and drag the Input (just under the Histogram) Shadow pointer (the pointer on the left) toward the right. The image will turn completely white. As you move to the right, approaching the histogram, the area that becomes visible first is the darkest point in the photo.

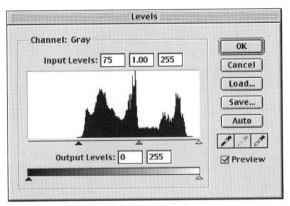

Proper scanning and good originals are very important. No amount of adjusting can pick up detail that wasn't there in the first place.

5. Repeat with the Highlight pointer. That is the lightest part of the image.

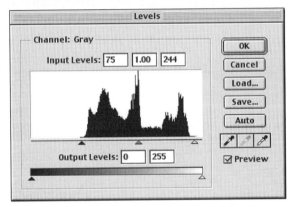

6. Adjust the gamma to 1.30, as you did earlier, to achieve a good midtone. Compare this image with the "Poolside_GS_Levels.TIF" image. It looks a little flatter, but that's fine. This image will print well.

The idea is to find highlight and shadow points that maintain detail. Choosing a point that has no detail will cause the area to turn totally white (highlight) or black (shadow), with no detail reproduced. Look for a good highlight and shadow point; for example, details in the texture of the pool's surface or folds in the bathing suit. These details should be printable, meaning that a halftone dot should be able to distinguish the changes in the grayscale of the image.

Another good location from which to select the shadow dot was in the darker areas of the swimsuits. The woman's shadow was best, with the shadow on the man's suit almost as good. While you're picking and resetting the shadow, pay particular attention to the detail under the left side of the woman's lounge chair. You'll see detail appear and get lost as you pick from different areas.

7. Save the image as "Poolside_GS_ManualLevels.TIF" to your **Work in Progress** folder. Save the rest of the images under their respective names to the same folder.

Using Levels to Adjust Midtones

Levels allows you to adjust the brightness, contrast, and gamma (contrast in the midtones) of an image. Often an image that seems to be lacking in detail is simply a low-contrast image; a quick adjustment of the image brightness levels can drastically improve such an image. You can adjust the contrast of either the entire image or an individual color channel, such as red, green, or blue, in an RGB image. You experienced this with the two leveling exercises that you just completed.

The Levels dialog box is accessible from the submenu found by selecting Image>Adjust> Levels or Command/Control-L.

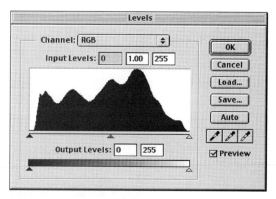

The most dominant feature of the Levels dialog box is the histogram, the graph in the center of the box. The histogram represents the distribution of lighter (or white) and darker (or black) pixels for each channel, or the entire image.

There are two sets of sliders to control Input and Output Levels. Both sets have a black slider for adjusting the shadows in an image, and a white slider to adjust highlights. The Input Levels slider has a gray triangle in the center of the slider bar for adjusting gamma or midtones.

Input and output levels may be changed by moving the slider, entering actual values in the boxes above the slider sets, or by using the eyedroppers to select the brightest and darkest points in the image.

The basic theory behind the Levels sliders is simple: to increase the overall contrast in an image, move the Input sliders toward the center of the slider bar. To decrease contrast, adjust the Output sliders. To adjust the contrast in the midtones of an image, move the gamma slider to the left or right. In the next chapter, we'll discuss using Levels for color correction of individual channels and using the numerical controls. For now, we'll focus on an understanding of the use of the slider.

Identifying the Problem

With a little experience you'll often be able to recognize the adjustments necessary to improve an image. Learning to read the histogram can be useful for identifying a potential problem. Keep in mind that the examples listed are general rules regarding images; sometimes an image is simply, by nature, a low- or high-contrast image, and shouldn't be adjusted at all.

A well-balanced image generally displays a well-balanced histogram. There will usually be peaks or valleys somewhere in the graph, but over all, the distribution of pixels covers the entire brightness range; the histogram is a gradual curve with the majority of the pixels represented by midtones.

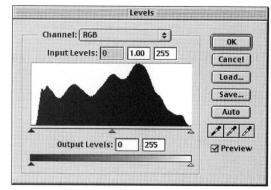

A low-contrast image tends to have all the pixels piled into a smaller range of the graph, usually in a very sharpened curve shape. This is typically the most common problem you'll find when adjusting the brightness and contrast of images.

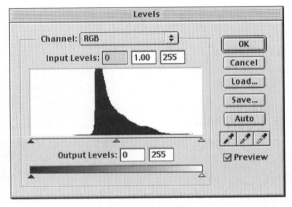

This histogram clearly shows a lack of very dark shadows; there are no pixels on the left side of the graph. In addition, this image lacks highlights — evident by the absence of information on the right side of the graph. Image detail is often defined by highlights and shadows; an image lacking these may appear fuzzy.

The histogram for a high-contrast image may have a spike or two, particularly at the left (in the shadow areas) or far right (in the highlights), but overall, the center area (or midtones) is rather flat.

While this is a rather uncommon profile for an image scanned from an adequate photograph on a properly calibrated scanner, other input devices may not have the contrast controls that photographic film and cameras have. It's a good thing that they're not too common: this type of image can be difficult to correct. Why? To reduce the contrast (by adjusting the Output Levels sliders inward) we have to remove highlights and shadows in the image, and as previously noted, these are usually the components that define detail in the image. Striking a balance between detail and contrast can be difficult. While it is often easier to simply rescan or choose a different image, today's Photoshop user has to be prepared to optimize such images.

Other Image Types

There are many other types of histograms. For example, you may encounter a histogram in which all of the pixels are piled up on the left, indicating a dark and unusually low-contrast image. Some images are very light, which yields a histogram with all of the pixels on the right side of the graph. Be careful when adjusting these types of images; depending upon the subject, an image can be very light or very dark and still be well balanced.

It is quite common to find an image that combines two or more of the basic types. For example, an image could be adequately balanced throughout the highlight areas, and still have a contrast problem in the shadows. A histogram for this type of image would look like this:

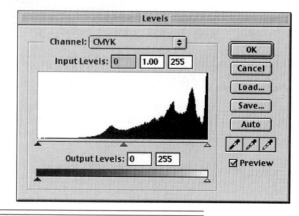

Adjust Image Levels for a Low-contrast Image

1. Open the image **Fishing.TIF** from your **SF-Adv Photoshop** folder.

2. Examine the image. Notice how faded and washed out the image is, and that it lacks detail.

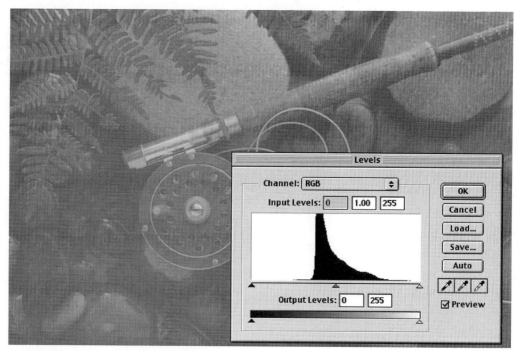

3. Press Command/Control-L to activate the Levels dialog box.

4. Move the black Input slider to the right so that it touches the edge of the beginning of the curve. Move the white slider to the left so that it touches the end of the curve.

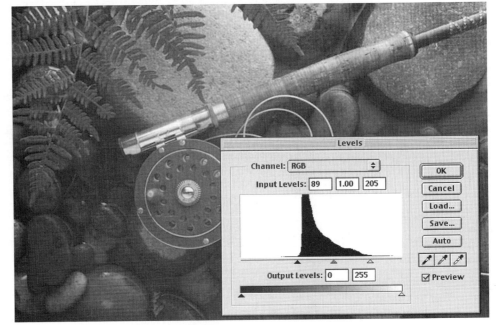

It's looking better already, isn't it?

5. Move the gamma slider to the right until the middle box above the slider bar reads 0.70.

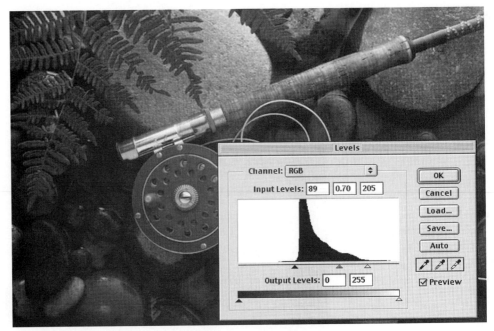

The middle tones of the image are unacceptably darker, but the highlights are not greatly affected.

The gray gamma slider in the center of the image is used to adjust the contrast in the midtones. By moving the gamma slider, you are adjusting the ratio of dark midtones to light midtones. If you move the gamma slider to the right, the distance between the black slider and the gamma slider is greater than the distance between the gamma slider and the white slider, so the ratio of darker shades is higher.

6. Now move the gamma slider to the left to make the distance between the gamma slider and the white slider larger; a setting of about 1.20 should do the trick. Notice the increase in the detail of the image. Click OK.

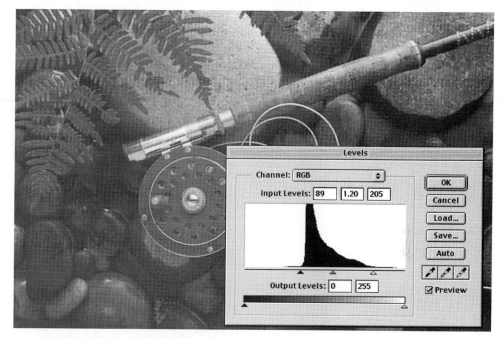

7. Save the image as "Fishing Leveled.TIF" to your **Work in Progress** folder. Close the document.

Adjust Image Levels for a High-contrast Image

1. Open the document **Forest.TIF** from your **SF-Adv Photoshop** folder.

2. Select Image>Adjust>Levels, and view the histogram. As you see, this is a high-contrast image with little variance in the midtones.

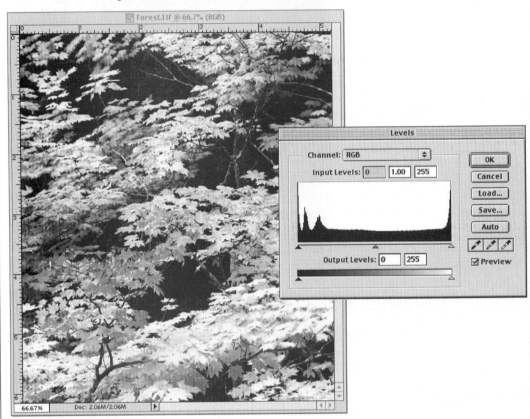

3. The midtones can be enhanced by moving the gamma Input Levels slider to 0.70. Notice how this brightens the image, while it has little or no effect on the highlights.

4. To soften those harsh whites, move the Output Levels highlight slider (on the right) to 230.

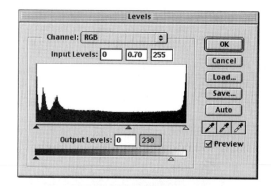

5. Check the histograms of all the channels. Notice that only the Blue channel has any appreciable variation in the midtone area. We're going to use it to enhance the photo.

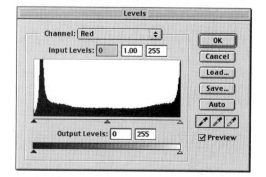

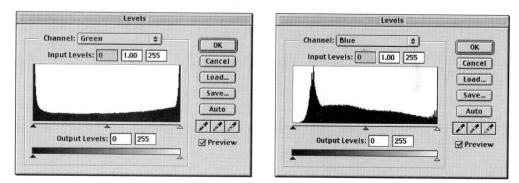

6. Adjust the Input Levels of the Blue channel, giving the shadow a value of 25 and the gamma a value of 1.20. Click OK.

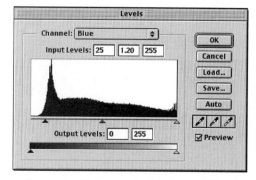

7. Using the History palette, toggle between the first and last instances to see how you affected the image.

8. Save the image as "Forest.TIF" to your **Work in Progress** folder.

Other Uses for Levels

Sometimes the artwork you'll receive will be less than perfect. Sometimes the original art was lost, or a hard disk crashed without a backup, and the only existing copy of a logo is a very nasty enlarged photocopy or faxed document. This type of image tends to have ragged edges, or "jaggies," which greatly reduce the usability of the artwork.

While you might try to rebuild the artwork by hand, you can often recover a large portion of the work using Levels and a few simple techniques.

Clean Up a Simple Bitmap Image

1. Open the file **Bad Logo.TIF** from your **SF-Adv Photoshop** folder. This is an example of a document printed at a small size on a low-resolution printer, enlarged on a copier, scanned at 600 ppi, then converted to grayscale and reduced. Not exactly camera-ready art, is it? Press "D" to return the foreground and background to their default colors.

2. First, clean up any obvious "dirt," the unwanted spots picked up by the scanner. Just circle them with the Lasso or Square Marquee tools, and press the Delete key. Use the Lasso tool to select any large "bubbles" or blobs on the edge of the image, and delete them.

3. Activate the Layers palette. Duplicate the Background layer by dragging the layer name over the Create New Layer icon at the bottom of the palette. Rename the layer "Art".

4. Click on the Art layer and select Filter>Blur>Gaussian Blur. Adjust the blur value so that most of the jaggies disappear. The image will appear quite fuzzy. For our example, we used a value of 7. Click OK.

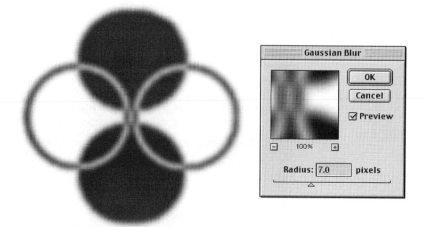

5. Set the blending mode for the Art layer to Difference. You will see a hazy white outline, along with a jagged white outline on a black background.

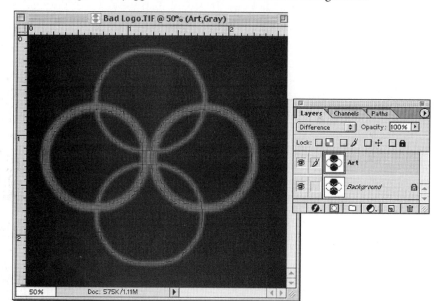

6. Select Image>Adjust>Levels. Pull the black slider to the right and the white slider to the left until most, but not all, of the white disappears. The sliders will be very close together. The white that is remaining is the anti-aliased edge of our new artwork. Click OK.

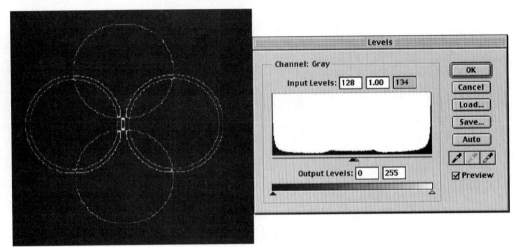

7. Change the blending mode for the Art layer to Normal. If the artwork was mostly curves and began at a high enough resolution, this may be all you need to do to make it a viable graphic.

8. Select Image>Image Size. Make certain that the Resample Image checkbox is checked, allow the method to default to Bicubic, set the Print size height to 1.25 in. (to allow for the background) and the resolution to 200 ppi.

9. Sometimes a little more cleanup is required. You can blur a little more and level again, or use the Lasso tool to clean up the few corners (which should be sharp) and smooth the round edges.

10. Close the image without saving.

Curves

The Curves dialog box is used for brightness and contrast adjustments, changing image gamma, and performing color correction, just as the Levels adjustment does; the difference is in the degree of control available.

Levels allows you to adjust the highlights, shadows, and gamma of an image. Curves, on the other hand, allows you to adjust any gray level in the image; at the same time, you can "lock in" up to 15 values along the line of the grayscale curve.

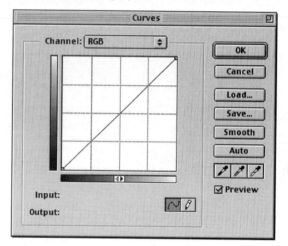

When working on an RGB image, the Curves dialog box works from the darkest grays to the lightest, from left to right (notice the gradient band at the bottom of the dialog box). The diagonal line in the middle of the box is the "curve."

In RGB, raising the curve at any point along the graph lightens the brightness levels that correspond with the gray level shown at that point on the gradient bar. In other words, if you raise the curve beginning at dead center of the diagonal line, you are adjusting the 50% grays within the image. Lowering the curve would darken the image in that range of brightness levels.

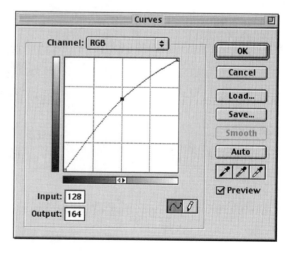

Notice that even though we only wanted to raise the 50% area, the line is remapped into a curve. This prevents abrupt drop-offs in color, allowing gradual transitions between lighter and darker shades of gray.

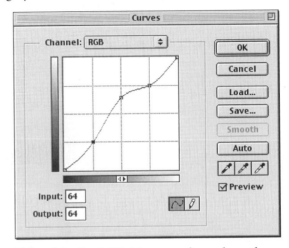

See the point in the middle of the line? Clicking anywhere along the curve adds a point that locks in that level of brightness. For example, if we needed to lighten the shadow areas and midtones without affecting our highlight areas, we could lock the highlights and adjust only the problem areas in the image. Adding more than one point is often required to protect a part of the curve.

Compare Curves and Levels

1. Open the image **Grandpa Joe.TIF** from your **SF-Adv Photoshop** folder.

2. This image is very dark. First, we'll try to adjust it using Levels. Press Command/ Control-L to activate the Levels dialog box.

Bring the black slider to the beginning of the histogram bump; move the white slider to the left until his shirt brightens and the colors become clear.

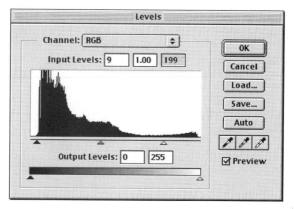

3. Examine the image. Note the lack of detail in the highlights on the left side of his face and hat.

4. Move the white slider back to the right until the highlight details return. Now try to brighten the shirt with the gamma slider. Move the gamma slider to the left to increase the ratio of white in the image.

To bring out the tones in the shirt, the gamma has to be adjusted far enough into the white range that the image appears flat. We're losing the medium-dark shadows in the midtones.

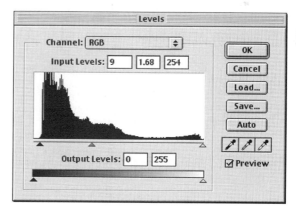

5. Click Cancel, and select Image>Adjust>Curves or press Command/Control-M to activate the Curves dialog box. First of all, we know that it is necessary to preserve the highlights within the image. Click on the curve to add a locking point in the upper-right quadrant of the Curves dialog box.

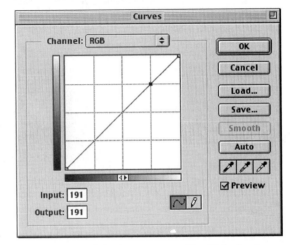

6. We need to lighten the rest of the image overall. Click dead center in the grid and drag a point a little more than halfway up to the next horizontal line. Notice that the Input and Output numbers at the bottom of the dialog box change as you move the cursor. These represent the "before" and "after" of the curve's adjustment, and are shown in a scale of 0, or black, to 255, or white.

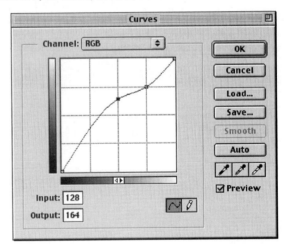

7. The image is getting flat again, just as it did when we adjusted the gamma in the Levels palette. We need to preserve some of the darker midtones and lighter shadows of the image; they need to be lightened, but not as much as the lighter midtones.

Add another locking point near the lower-left quadrant to restore the shadows. (If you accidentally add a point you don't want, simply drag it to any existing point or to either end of the curve.)

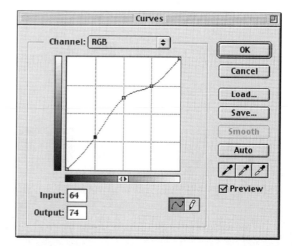

8. Click the Preview checkbox off and on to compare the image before and after curve adjustment. Fine-tune the brightness and contrast until it looks just right to you by moving the points up and down or side to side.

    Click OK to apply the changes to the image.

9. Open the Curves dialog box again, and spend some time adjusting curves up and down to get a feel for how they work.

10. Save the file to your **Work in Progress** folder and name it "Old Man Curves.TIF". Close the file.

Arbitrary Curve Maps

So far, the curves with which we have worked have been very simple. The Curves command is capable of much more, however. *Arbitrary curve maps* are special maps drawn with a pencil directly on the grid. They're extremely useful for special effects.

Create Arbitrary Curve Maps

1. Create a New 5 in. × 5 in. RGB document at 200 ppi. Set the background to white.

2. Press "D" to reset to default colors. Activate the Linear Gradient tool (Press "G"). Set Gradient to Foreground to Background. Draw a gradient from top to bottom while pressing the Shift key.

3. Press Command/Control-M to activate the Curves dialog box. At the bottom of the box are two buttons: one illustrates a curve, the other a pencil. Click on the pencil button.

4. Use the pencil to draw a squiggly line on the grid; any line will do. Watch the different areas in the gradient fill change to banding shades of gray.

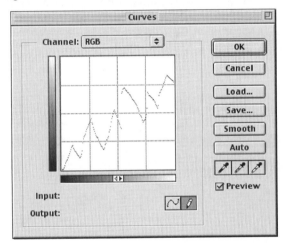

What you are actually doing is remapping one shade of gray to another. For example, the far left of the curve represents the black pixels in the image. By clicking the mouse at this part of the curve at the top of the grid, you will turn all of the black pixels in the image white.

5. The changes are probably pretty abrupt. Press the Smooth button to make the tonal shifts more gradual.

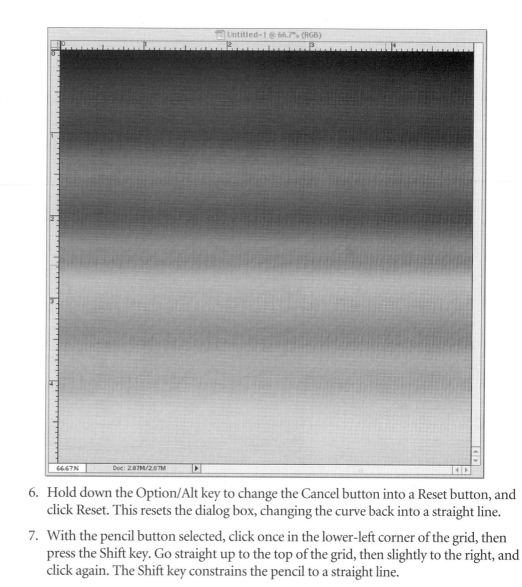

6. Hold down the Option/Alt key to change the Cancel button into a Reset button, and click Reset. This resets the dialog box, changing the curve back into a straight line.

7. With the pencil button selected, click once in the lower-left corner of the grid, then press the Shift key. Go straight up to the top of the grid, then slightly to the right, and click again. The Shift key constrains the pencil to a straight line.

Continue clicking top and bottom until you have a zigzag pattern. The gradient should now look a little like a pile of fabric.

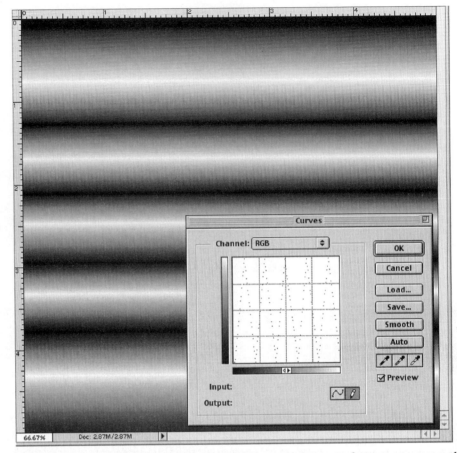

8. Click the Smooth button several times, and watch the curve become more gradual. Eventually it will become a straight diagonal line again.

9. Reset the dialog box again. Select the pencil button. Draw a series of tiny dashes at the top and bottom of the grid. Repeat until the image is entirely made up of thin, rough, black-and-white stripes.

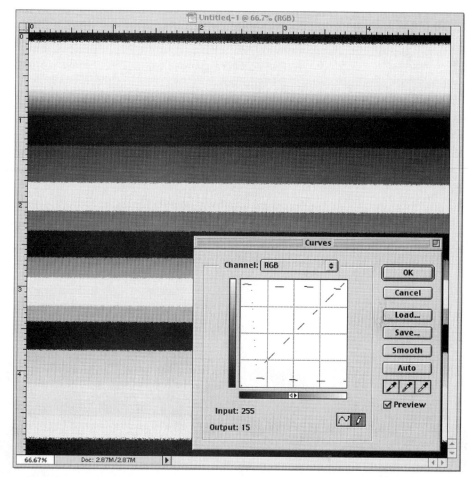

10. Click the Smooth button once, then press the curves button (to the left of the pencil button). The arbitrary map is now converted into a normal curve that can be adjusted point by point.

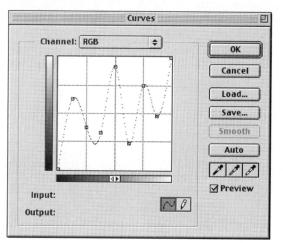

11. Close the file without saving.

Sometimes you want to create a unique effect for type. In the following exercise, we're going to use the functions of Curves adjustment to create type having both inline and outline effects.

Create Inline/Outline Type Using Curves

1. Create a New grayscale document. Make it 5 in. × 1.5 in. at 200 ppi, with a white background.

2. Select the Type tool and type "SALE!" in 96 pt. ATC Mai Tai Bold Italic. Press Command-Return (Macintosh) or Control-Enter (Windows) to commit the type.

3. Select Layer>Rasterize>Type.

4. Select Filter>Blur>Gaussian Blur. Enter a value of 7, and click OK.

5. In the Channels palette, duplicate the Gray channel. The new channel will default to Gray Copy, because there is only one channel in a grayscale document.

6. While in the Gray Copy channel, press Command/Control-M to activate the Curves dialog box. Click the pencil button to activate the arbitrary curve function.

7. Using the pencil, draw little lines at the top and bottom of the grid, as shown below.

 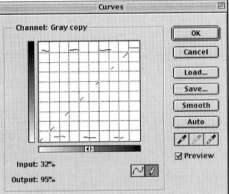

8. Click the Smooth button, then click the curves button next to the pencil. Adjust the points up and down. Moving a point down adds a white stripe. Moving a point up adds a black stripe. Make certain that the far-right point is in the upper-right corner, and the far-left point is in the lower-left corner. These points determine the background color and the color in the center of the text. Click OK.

9. Activate the Gray channel. Choose Select>Load Selection, and choose Gray Copy. Make certain that the Invert box is checked, so that the type is loaded as a selection

rather than the background. Click OK, choose the Gradient tool, then choose then activate Reflected Gradient in the Options toolbar. Select the Foreground to Transparent gradient style. Change Opacity to 50%. Click the Reverse box.

10. Set the foreground color to white. While pressing the Shift key to constrain the gradient to a straight line, make a gradient from the center of the text to the top edge.

11. Deselect to admire your work, then save the file to your **Work in Progress** folder as "Fuzzy Sale.PSD".

Understanding Duotones

A *duotone* is a special type of colorized image made from a grayscale photograph. Essentially, information is added to the image that replaces or augments the black in the image with another color. The color may be a spot or process color.

Duotones are used to enhance a two-color printed piece for artistic effect, or to colorize selected areas of a black-and-white image — they're great for enhancing low-budget print jobs. Duotones used to be painstakingly created using a lithographic camera, but Photoshop gives you the ability to easily create not only duotones, but also tritones (black and two spot colors) and quadtones (black and three spot colors) as well.

Spot colors are chosen from the following preset libraries: ANPA, DIC, Focaltone, HKS, Pantone, Toyo, and Trumatch. You can also custom libraries, if you wish.

Create a Duotone

1. Open the image **Chargit.TIF** from your **SF-Adv Photoshop** folder. This is a grayscale image.

2. Select Image>Mode>Duotone to activate the Duotone Options dialog box. If Type is not set to Duotone, change it now.

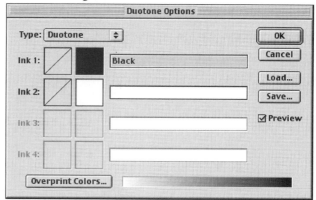

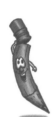

Because the darkest color covers 100% of the range, while the lighter color covers only 0% to 80% of the range, we assign them different curves to enhance specific areas of the image.

3. Click the box with the diagonal line next to Ink 1. The curve and grid are similar to those in the Curves palette, but they work a little differently. Click in the 50% box, and type "40". This will cause every pixel in the image that is at 50% black to display only 40% black. The rest of the curve is redrawn to smooth the transition between gray shades.

4. Click the 80% box, and change the value to 90%. While duotone curves can be adjusted point by point in similar fashion to regular curves, it is often easier to make the initial selection by typing in values, then adjusting if necessary later. Click OK.

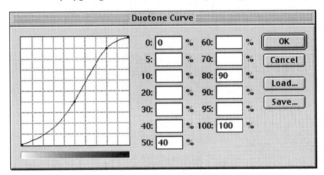

5. Click the second box to the right of Ink 2 in the Duotone Options dialog box to activate the Color Picker. Select the Pantone Coated Book. Type 144 (there's no box to type into) to select Pantone 144 CVC, and click OK. Alternately, you could scroll in the color bar until you find the color you're looking for. If you know the color, type it in and save some time.

You don't have to create your own duotones; many duotones are accessible through the Duotone Options palette. Click Load, which will take you to the Adobe Photoshop 6.0>Presets>Duotones folder. From there, select Duotones, Quadtones, or Tritones.

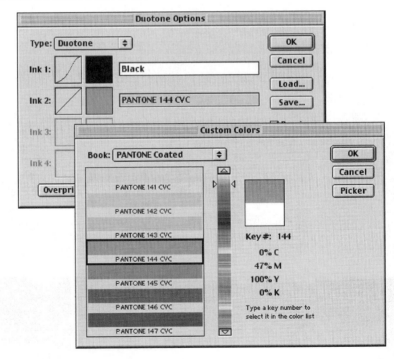

6. Click the Duotone Curve box next to Ink 2. Change 10% to 5% and 100% to 80%. Notice how this brings all the values between 10% and 80% on the graph to well below their normal levels. To pump a little more color into the image, select the 30% box and change it to 30%, which will lock it in at that value. Click OK.

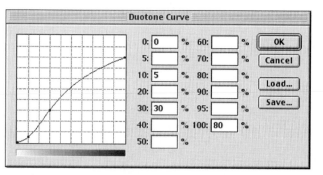

7. Examine the gradient bar at the bottom of the dialog box. Notice the orange-brown shades in the midtone section. The pixels that correspond to these shades in the image will be recolorized. Click OK.

8. To print a duotone properly at a GASP, it must be saved as an EPS file before being placed into a page layout program.

   Choose File>Save As, and select Photoshop EPS as the file type. Change the file name to "Duotone.EPS", and save it to your **Work in Progress** folder. Select Binary Encoding, to keep the file smaller, and a TIFF (8 bits/pixel) preview for accurate on screen viewing in your page-layout program. Click OK.

Summary

Understanding the relationship between brightness and contrast, and how these two values affect the quality of reproduction in digital images, is the first, and possibly the most critical factor in creating a high-quality image. An image that has too much contrast (a "sharp" image) or not enough contrast (a "flat" image) will produce an unsatisfactory print. Photoshop's Brightness/Contrast, Levels, and Curves tools replicate a process that used to take hours in a photographic darkroom and reduces it to minutes on a computer.

Through the Levels and Curves tools, tonal correction that would normally take hours for the photographer or printing vendor is reduced to minutes. Understanding when to use the proper tool will maximize the Photoshop user's time for more creative tasks, such as building duotones.

Notes:

COLOR CORRECTION

CHAPTER OBJECTIVE:

To learn how colors interact or complement one another, and to understand the relationship between the two primary color models — RGB and CMYK. To learn the basic concepts required to correct an image's color tones using Photoshop's tools for color correction. In Chapter 3, you will:

- Become familiar with the theory of complementary and adjacent colors, and learn to use them to adjust the color in an image.

- Discover the difference between additive and subtractive color, and learn why an image can look great on screen but reproduce differently.

- Learn to mix colors.

- Learn about Photoshop's color correction tools.

- Become comfortable with using the Levels command to balance specific color ranges in color images.

- Expand your knowledge of the Curves dialog box, as you see how curves can control the balance of one color with another.

- Learn to use Hue and Saturation to change colors.

- Become familiar with neutrality, and see how balancing the neutral tones in an image is a key to high-quality color correction.

- Learn to adjust an image using Adjustment Layers, so that you're able to experiment with color and effects.

PROJECTS TO BE COMPLETED:

- **Just Shoot Me (A)**
- Baby Shower Invitation (B)
- Retouching the Jones Family Portrait (C)
- The Fix Is In! (D)
- Makeover (E)
- Photomat (F)

Try to use a process color book that matches your job's paper stock (matte, gloss, dull, etc.) and ink type. The absorption qualities (how much ink is absorbed into the paper) and color of the paper stock can greatly affect the final ink color.

In the CMYK model, K (black) is added to the printing process to create a better-quality image. The combination of only C, M, and Y will produce a muddy brown in areas that should appear black. Printing inks contain pigments, which, unlike natural light, contain impurities. Black ink adds definition to the image, compensates for the impurities in the inks used, and enhances the overall contrast of the image. It can also reduce the overall ink coverage when used in GCR and UCR (discussed later in this chapter).

Color Correction

It's not unusual for color in an image to be slightly out of true. No matter what method is used to acquire an image, many factors can influence the color and tonal ranges. Unfortunately — due to the differences in RGB and CMYK color — an image can look terrific on screen, yet when output to film and printed, may contain too much or too little of a particular color. Photoshop has many useful tools to correct these problems in images. Each is suitable for a particular task.

The Color Models

Before starting to color correct an image, you will need to understand how colors interact or complement each other. We use the relationship of the three basic color modes, *L*a*b*, *RGB*, and *CMYK*, to maximize our efforts.

The L*a*b model defines color by its luminance and chromatic components across two axes — the "a" axis ranges from green to magenta, and the "b" axis ranges from blue to yellow. RGB, also known as the "additive primaries," combines the colors of light (all colors added together make white). CMYK, the *subtractive primaries* (*additive secondaries*), combines the pigments cyan, magenta, yellow, and black; when all pigments are removed, white results.

L*a*b

CIE L*a*b was introduced by the Commission Internationale de l'Eclairage, an international standards-making body.

In the late 1920s, as color printing became more prevalent, it was seen that a standard for color description was needed. If two colors appear the same, they should be described in the same manner. For example, we might define "pure red" as R: 255, G: 0, B: 0 using RGB color space; we might define it as C: 0, M: 100, Y: 100, K: 0 using CMYK space. Of course, someone else might call it simply "bright red." In L*a*b color space, it is defined by the numeric positions L: 56, a: 77, b: 73.

In 1931, CIE developed the first widely used independent color space, known as "CIE XYZ," named for the three axes used to describe the location of the colors. The values in this color space are derived from the relative amounts of RGB present in the color, and expressed as a percentage of luminance, together with 256 levels (ranging from −128 to +128) across the two axes. In 1976, CIE XYZ was redefined and renamed "CIE L*a*b." Photoshop simplifies the spelling and calls the color model "LAB."

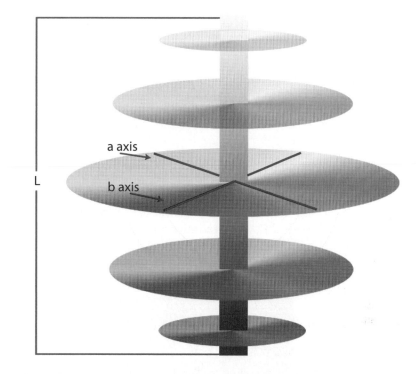

Portions of the L*a*b color model, showing the L, a, and b axes. From "pure" color at the center of the L axis, colors become shades, as they are lower on the helix, and tints as they are higher.

Hue, Saturation, and Lightness

Closely related to the L*a*b color space are the three primary components of color: hue, saturation, and lightness.

Hue is the property we refer to when we call a color by its name: red, purple, or teal, for example. Hue changes as we travel in a circle around the axis of the color wheel. As you see, hue is defined as beginning from red (0°) and travelling counterclockwise around the wheel.

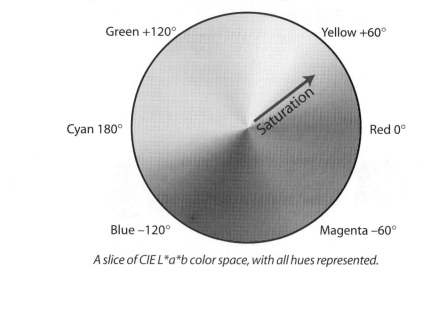

A slice of CIE L*a*b color space, with all hues represented.

Saturation, also called "chroma" or "intensity," is the clarity of the color. Color is dulled by the introduction of elements of the color opposite it in the color wheel. Red, for example, is neutralized by the addition of cyan (blue and green). When the color approaches the center of the wheel, the color becomes a neutral gray.

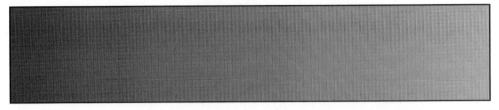

Red and cyan are opposite one another on the color wheel. When they are blended, the point at which there are equal amounts of red and cyan becomes neutral gray.

Lightness, luminance, or *value,* is the amount of white or black added to the pure color. A Lightness of 0 means that there is no addition of white or black. Lightness of +100 is pure white, luminance of −100 is pure black.

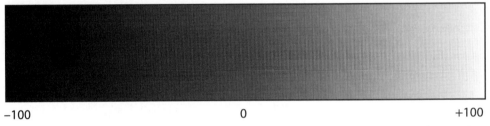

−100   0   +100

The color at its full intensity is represented by a lightness of 0. When lightness is subtracted, shades of the color are introduced. When lightness is added, the color is tinted.

RGB

The RGB color model is capable of displaying the largest area of the color spectrum, with the exception of the entire L*a*b model. Red, green, and blue are known as the "additive primary" colors. When they are all added at full intensity, the result is white light. Where they overlap, they create a version of the additive secondary colors: cyan, magenta, and yellow. RGB colors are the colors of light, and are used by monitors and scanners.

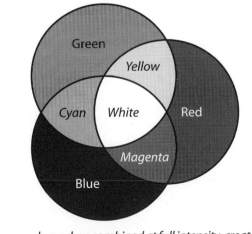

Additive primary colors, when combined at full intensity, create white, with the subtractive primaries created as additive secondary colors.

The RGB color model should be used if documents are to be printed to RGB-savvy printers such as inkjet and laser printers, of if they will be distributed electronically and viewed on monitors such as CD distribution, e-books, or publication on the Internet.

Indexed color is a subset of RGB, and is used to create GIF files. Indexed color is used in drawn images with areas of flat color, but not for photographs. The greatest number of colors that can be contained in an indexed-color image is 256. When creating indexed color images, you should always use the Web-safe palette, and use as few colors as possible, so that the image will paint up quickly.

CMYK

The CMYK model is based on the absorption and reflection of light as opposed to the transmission of light used by the RGB model. A portion of the color spectrum is absorbed when white light strikes ink-coated paper (or any pigment-coated material). The color that is not absorbed is reflected. Cyan, magenta, and yellow are called the *subtractive primary* colors. When all pigments are subtracted from an image, white remains; when they are added, they create black. The subtractive secondaries are red, green, and blue, the additive primaries.

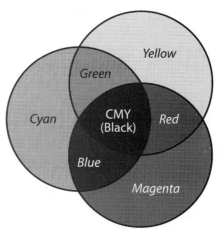

Subtractive primary colors, when combined at full intensity create a theoretical black, with the additive primaries created as subtractive secondary colors.

Theoretically, a mixture of equal parts of cyan, magenta, and yellow would produce black. Pigments, however, as opposed to light, are not pure; the actual result of mixing these three colors is a muddy brown. To obtain vibrant colors (and so that elements such as type can be printed cleanly), we add black to the palette. The CMYK model is also called "Process color."

Process color is used to print documents that contain multiple distinct colors, or that contain color photos. A pattern of dots in varying sizes (called a "rosette") fools the eye into thinking that it is seeing distinct colors, although it is actually seeing cyan, magenta, yellow, and black dots. The resolution of these dots, when used in the printing process, is described in lines per inch.

Let's take a look at how colors work together.

RGB-savvy printers automatically convert RGB values to the values of the inks used in the printing device (usually CMYK, but often up to eight inks).

In school, many of us learned that the primary colors were red, yellow, and blue. What we were working with was paint, which, although it is a pigment, does not have the proper-ties of printing ink. The printing process uses the subtractive primaries: cyan, magenta, and yellow.

The Color Wheel

Clicking on the menu found by selecting Image>Mode will show a long list of different options. Each of these modes has its benefits. For working in color, however, two standard modes are used almost universally: RGB and CMYK. Scanning, inputting, outputting to photographic materials (such as slides and light-sensitive paper), and preparing images for Web publication, are done in RGB. Output for printing is generally done in CMYK. Although they handle color differently, these two color modes are definitely linked. In digital display, RGB colors are directly inverse to CMY colors. Their relationship is the primary basis for all on screen color.

The words "directly inverse" refer to positions on a Color Wheel. To illustrate this concept, let's create one.

Create a Color Wheel

1. Open **Color Wheel Template.TIF** from your **SF-Intro Photoshop** folder.

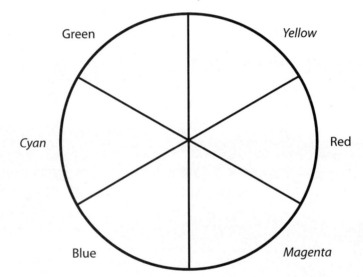

2. Click on the foreground color to open the foreground color picker, and find the box labeled R.

3. Type "255" in the R box. Make certain that the values in both the G and B boxes are 0. Now you have pure red. Click OK.

4. Activate the Paint Bucket tool, and click in the sector marked Red on the color wheel to fill it with the color.

5. Repeat for the blue and green sectors. Type "255" in the B box, and "0" in the R and G boxes, then fill the blue sector with the Paint Bucket. Type "255" in the G box, and "0" in the R and B boxes, then fill the green sector with the Paint Bucket.

   Now you have half of the colors you need to complete your color wheel. It's time to add the CMY colors. Since we're working in the RGB color model, however, we'll create the RGB equivalent of cyan, magenta, and yellow.

The table below lists the different combinations of RGB and CMY primaries and the colors that result.

RGB:

$R = M + Y$

$G = C + Y$

$B = C + M$

CMY:

$C = B + G$

$M = B + R$

$Y = R + G$

Complements:

Red and Cyan

Green and Magenta

Blue and Yellow

While it may seem odd that red and green together produce yellow, it's not as strange as you might think. If you mix red and green paint together, you get an unappealing brown; if you reduce the saturation and lightness of yellow in Photoshop, you get a very similar color.

6. Open your foreground color picker, and type "255" in both the G and B boxes, making certain that the values in the other RGB boxes are set to 0. Click OK.

7. Use the Paint Bucket tool to fill the sector labeled Cyan.

8. Repeat for the magenta and yellow sectors. With the other RGB values set to 0, type "255" into the R and B box to create magenta; mix yellow using red (R) and green (G). Use the Paint Bucket tool to click on the appropriate sector in each case.

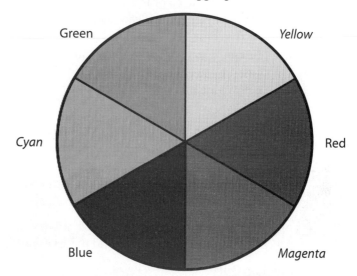

9. You have now completed your color wheel. Save the image to your **Work in Progress** folder as a TIFF file named "Color Wheel.TIF." Keep it open; we'll be using it in the next section.

Understanding the Color Wheel

Now we can refer to the color wheel and use it to understand how the RGB colors relate to the CMY colors. If you take any two colors in a triangle (for example, red and blue from the RGB triangle) and add them together, the resulting color will be the CMY color located between the two RGB points. In this example, red and blue combine to form magenta. This is what we mean when we say the two color modes are "directly inverse." Each CMY color is made up of two RGB colors and vice versa. Vary the proportions of the primaries and add black to the equation and you have the millions of colors in the digital palette.

A *color complement* is the color located directly opposite on the wheel. For example, find green on the wheel. Green is the complement of magenta, because green is the one color in the RGB triangle that is not included when making pure magenta. Adding the complement of a color neutralizes its brilliance, causing the color to become grayish.

Mixing Colors

As you noted when creating the color wheel, red and green, surprisingly enough, make yellow. This seems confusing when you think of mixing red and green paints together. Paint is an example of *subtractive* color. When additional colors are applied to a surface, the amount of light that is reflected to your eye is reduced, or subtracted, from the original light that is hitting the subject.

Since colors made with light are *additive* (meaning that you add colors to produce other colors when the light is transmitted to your eye, the same as with a monitor) red and green together make yellow. Yellow is the CMY primary that the two RGB primaries have in common; red is made of magenta and yellow, and green is made of cyan and yellow. By the same token, magenta is created by adding blue and red, and cyan is created by adding blue and green.

To manipulate color in an image, you need to take advantage of the relationship between color complements. If you want to add a specific color to an image, you have three options: add the color, add equal parts of its constituent colors, or remove some of its complement. For example, to add magenta to an image, you could add magenta, add more blue and red, or remove green. Conversely, this means that to remove a color from an image, you can remove the color itself, equal parts of its constituents, or add its complement.

While it may seem that it would be easiest to add or subtract the color in question, better results may be achieved by adding one color and subtracting another. For example, if an image needs less blue, simply removing blue may cause reds to go pink or cyan to lean toward green. Instead, adding red and green may be a better solution. Subtracting all three colors, or subtracting blue and adding amounts of red and green may result in the best image. Ideally, work with just the primary colors in a given model to achieve best results.

Shortly, we'll be learning how to make these types of corrections in images. For now, it's important that you understand the relationship between colors.

Pop Quiz

Here's a quiz for you to test your color-mixing skills. (It's OK to refer to the color wheel you have open.)

1. To take out red, either remove _____ and _____ or add _____.

2. To add green, either add _____ and _____ or remove _____.

3. To remove cyan, you can add _____ or remove _____ and _____.

4. To increase blue, you may add _____ and _____ or remove _____.

5. To take out yellow, either remove _____ and _____ or add _____.

6. To add magenta, either add _____ and _____ or remove _____.

Close the Color Wheel image.

Answers to Pop Quiz

6. Blue, Red, Green

5. Green, Red, Blue

4. Cyan, Magenta, Yellow

3. Red, Blue, Green

2. Cyan, Yellow, Magenta

1. Yellow, Magenta, Cyan

Can you figure out the bottom two interactions without turning the page upside down and reading the answers?

The Interaction Between Color and Pigment

The "color" of an object is created by the reflection of light waves. When light strikes an object containing pigment, some of the light waves are absorbed and others are reflected. The examples below show how this occurs using several colors.

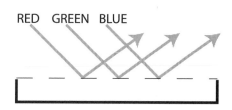

An object that reflects all light from an object appears white.

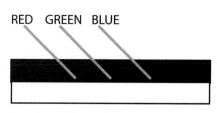

An object that reflects no light from an object appears black.

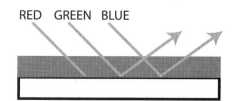

A cyan object reflects green and blue light and absorbs red.

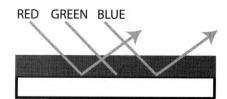

A magenta object reflects red and blue light and absorbs green.

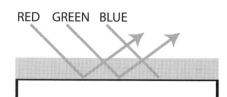

A yellow object reflects green and red light and absorbs blue.

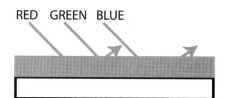

A violet object reflects some red and blue light, and absorbs green, plus some red and blue.

RED GREEN BLUE

What does a green object do?

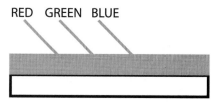

What does a brown object do?

A green object reflects green light, and absorbs red and blue.

A brown object absorbs some of all colors and reflects a portion of the red and green, and sometimes blue.

Full-spectrum Color Wheels

The color wheel we created in the previous section is useful for understanding the relationship between CMY and RGB. There are many more colors than these six, however. A full-spectrum color wheel will allow you to locate the complement of virtually any color.

Create a Full-spectrum Color Wheel

1. Create a New file 5 in. × 5 in. square, RGB Color Mode, Contents White, and 100 pixels/inch.

```
                              New
  Name: Untitled-1                        OK
  ┌ Image Size: 733K ──────────────┐    Cancel
         Width: 5      inches    ⬍
        Height: 5      inches    ⬍
    Resolution: 100    pixels/inch ⬍
         Mode: RGB Color    ⬍
  ┌ Contents ──────────────────────┐
     ◉ White
     ○ Background Color
     ○ Transparent
```

2. From the View menu, select Show Rulers.

3. Select the Elliptical Marquee tool.

4. Position the cross hairs of the Marquee tool exactly in the center of the square (at 2.5 in. on both rulers).

5. Hold down the Option/Alt-Shift keys, and drag from the center until the edges of the circle are just inside the edge of the square.

6. Click the Gradient tool in the Tool palette, and choose the Angle Gradient (the third from the left). Set the Gradient to Spectrum. Make certain that the Reverse option is not selected. Keep the Opacity at 100%.

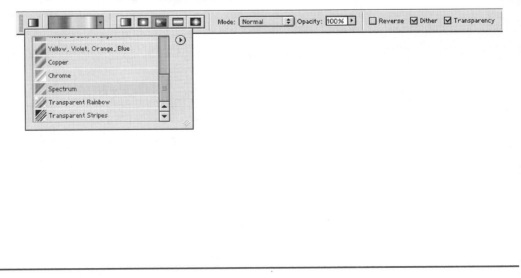

7. Create a blend from the center to the right. Hold the Shift key down while dragging the mouse to the right. When completed, your image should look like a circle of color, with red to the right, and the balance of the colors in a clockwork direction, similar to the color wheel that we made in the first example.

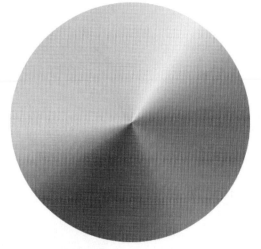

8. Save the image into your **Work in Progress** folder, and name it "Color Wheel 2.TIF".

Using a Full-spectrum Color Wheel

The manner in which the wheel works is quite simple. Imagine a triangle inscribed in a circle, positioned over the color wheel. A point that lies between any two corners of the triangle is the corresponding color in the opposing model. For example, if you add red (one corner of the RGB triangle) and green (the other corner), you get yellow, which is positioned between them on that side of the triangle. Red and blue create magenta, while green and blue create cyan, just as in the simplified version of the wheel we used before.

A full-spectrum wheel, however, allows you to find a complementary color for any color, not just primaries. To clarify things somewhat, let's add a triangle to the color wheel.

Use the Wheel to Determine Complementary Colors

1. If it isn't already open, open the image **Color Wheel 2.TIF** from your **Work in Progress** folder. Press "D" to set the default foreground and background.

2. Choose Image>Canvas, and set the size to 6 in. width and height to allow for additional space around the color wheel.

3. Select File>Place, and place the **Com Pointer.EPS** file, located in the **SF-Adv Photoshop** folder. The EPS file might place slightly off-center from your color wheel, so align the vertical line through the middle of the wheel. Press Return/Enter to finish placing the image.

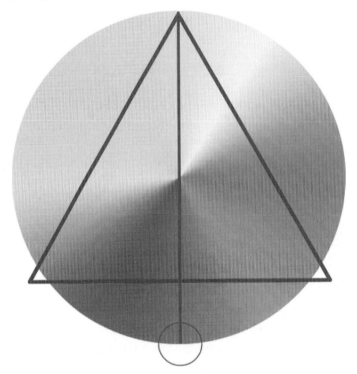

4. The top of the triangle is placed on the color you want to match. The center of the circle at the bottom represents the exact complement, while the entire bottom bar represents closely complementary colors. To find a complement for pure yellow, for example (which lies 30° away from the point at which the triangle is pointing right now), activate the Com Pointer.EPS layer.

5. Make certain that the Info palette is visible. Select Edit>Transform>Rotate. Drag the center point to the center of the color wheel. Drag a handle to rotate the triangle image to the right about 30°, until it is pointing at yellow (or enter 30 in the Rotation dialog box.) Press Command-Return/Control-Enter to finish the rotation.

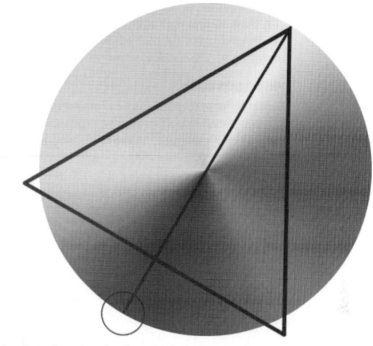

By simply estimating the degree of rotation from its current position to the color you need to match, you can use this tool any time you need to find a color's complement.

6. Save the file as a Photoshop document, and name it "Color Wheel.PSD" before closing.

The Color Correction Tools

Photoshop has an array of color correction tools. You have already worked with some of them — Brightness and Contrast, Levels, and Curves. Selecting and using the right tool for the job will make your use of Photoshop more pleasant and efficient.

Color Balance

Color Balance is the most basic of color correction tools. It's easy to use, but lacks the fine adjustments necessary for proper color correction. The Color Balance adjustment is best used to correct an overall color cast to an image.

You can adjust the highlights, shadows, or midtones of an image. The Preserve Luminosity checkbox ensures that only the colors shift and that the tonal balance of the image is unchanged. Color Balance is fine for special effects such as adjusting artificial textural backgrounds created in Photoshop, but shouldn't be used for everyday color correction.

Hue/Saturation

The Hue/Saturation adjustment can be extremely useful in some situations. For example, an improperly calibrated scanner will sometimes shift the colors around the color wheel, making cyan too green, magenta too blue, and yellow too red. A quick adjustment with the Hue/Saturation command will easily correct this problem. It will also allow you to adjust individual primaries in an image, such as turning a lemon into a lime.

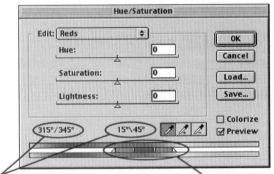

Not only can Hue/Saturation affect an entire image, it can work on specific ranges of color. When working on a specific range of color, Photoshop assigns, by default, a 30° color range, plus a "fall-off" area of 30° to either side of the color defined. So, if red were defined as the color range, the primary range of color would be 345° (–15°) to 15° — 15° on either side of the definition of red, 0°. The two fall-off areas would be 315° to 345° and 15° to 45°. While you can adjust these ranges, you may experience dithering if you adjust the ranges too low.

Fall-off ranges. Colors in these ranges on the color wheel will be affected by changes made.

Range Indicator gives graphic representation of colors affected and allows you to adjust the affected range.

You can also use the Hue/Saturation dialog box to colorize a grayscale image.

Selective Color Replacement

The Selective Color Replacement controls allow you to edit the amount of ink produced in only the neutrals, blacks, whites, or individual primary colors without affecting other components of the image.

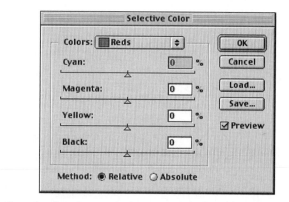

For instance, if a red car looks too magenta, you probably want to remove magenta from the image to produce a truer red. Unfortunately, magenta is a component of blue, as well as a color in its own right. If you reduce the amount of magenta, you might give your deep-blue sky a greenish cast. Selective Color allows you to adjust *only* the red, without affecting magenta, yellow, or any other range of primaries in the image. Though similar to Hue/Saturation with regard to editing a range of colors, Selective Color allows you to adjust the actual ink values, and can isolate and adjust the blacks and whites in your image

Brightness/Contrast

You have already used the Brightness/Contrast adjustment in Chapter 2. As you discovered, this control should be used only to affect the look of the overall image. Brightness/Contrast is good for a quick fix when the entire image needs to be affected.

Levels

While the Levels adjustment allows you to work on individual color channels, and allows you to adjust the gamma, it lacks the control of the Curves palette. It's effective if you're trying to limit your adjustment to midtones, but lacks fine control in highlight and shadow areas. As you have discovered, however, use of its histogram allows you to quickly discover the white and black points of an image, and to visually determine the nature of an image.

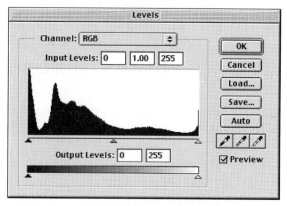

The histogram in the Levels tool allows you to readily see what type of image you are working on, and allows you to modify the gamma, in addition to white and black points.

Curves

The Curves adjustment, on the other hand, gives you exactly the type of precise control you need to adjust every area of the image individually, from the lightest highlights to the darkest shadows. It is the preferred tool for color correction. You can set individual points along the grayscale representation of each color, thereby making more accurate adjustments to an image.

The appearance of the Curves tool can be changed from the standard quarter/ mid/three-quarter-tone look to an even division into ten horizontal and ten vertical divisions by Option/ Alt-clicking on the graph.

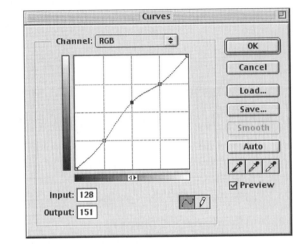

The Curves tool allows almost infinite control of the midtones of an image. Here we have locked the position of the quarter and three-quarter-tones, while modifying the midtones.

Variations

The Variations adjustment is interesting, though not very useful for color correction for offset printing. It enables you to make adjustments based strictly on visible information by showing you the original image, plus the image with every variation of primary color added.

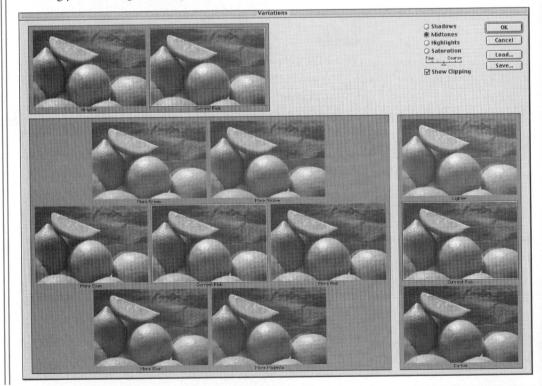

If the upper-right image, which adds yellow, looked better than the center image, clicking on it would move it to the center, then recolor the surrounding images. You could then decide to add some magenta, which would move that image to the center. It's easy and fun, but it lacks the fine control of other correction methods. As you've learned, you can't judge printed output color based on monitor color. Variations also allows adjustment of saturation and brightness. It can be useful for "quick and dirty" correction of RGB graphics, but once you understand adjusting with curves, you'll find them to be more efficient.

Let's see how Hue/Saturation ties in with the color wheel to get started correcting color in Photoshop.

Use Hue and the Color Wheel

1. Open the file **Lemon.TIF** from the **SF-Intro Photoshop** folder.

2. Choose Image>Adjust>Hue/Saturation (Command/Control-U) from the Menu bar.

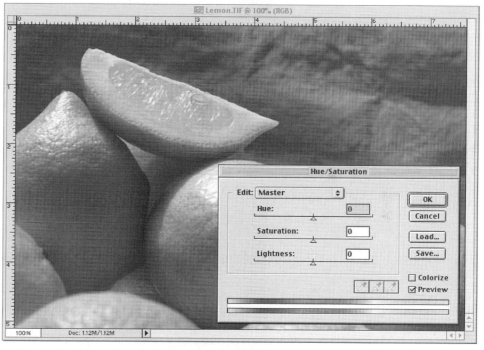

3. Move the Hue slider in the Master option to the far right. All of the colors in the image shift to their complements.

   We've essentially rotated the colors in the image 180° around the wheel.

Moving the Hue slider in either direction actually rotates the color around the color wheel. Notice that the bottom bar of the Hue/ Saturation palette is a representation of the color spectrum, like your color wheel. When you move the Hue slider, this strip will also change, showing you the shift in the color spectrum.

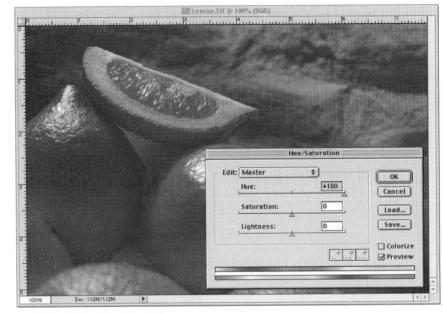

4. Move the Hue slider back to 0.

5. We'd rather not affect any of the other colors in the image except those used in the lemon. Click on the drop-down menu, and scroll down to Yellows (Command/Control-2). Each color, whether in the RGB or CMY palette, has its own controls in the Hue/Saturation window.

6. Reduce Lightness to -30 or so, and drag the Hue slider at the top roughly halfway to the right. Move the slider back and forth until you find a good lime-green.

Notice that the indicators above the color spectrum bar also show the current placement of the selected color in reference to the color wheel. The number represents the areas of fall off. The area between those numbers is the range of color being primarily affected. The range indicator will help you judge the degree of change in relationship to the overall image.

7. Save the file to your **Work in Progress** folder as "Limes.TIF".

Practical Color Correction

Every Photoshop user has found his or her own techniques to minimize the time spent on color correction. With all of the creative tools available within Photoshop, technical tasks, such as color correction, should be streamlined; the Photoshop user can then devote more time to the artistic side of creating high-quality images.

Most Photoshop users do their color corrections in the RGB color mode because:

- The spectrum of colors is greater in the RGB color mode than CMYK.
- A monitor represents and transmits colors in the RGB color mode.
- Quality color conversion software is available through Photoshop and many interpolation and RIP applications.
- Files in an RGB color mode are naturally smaller (only three channels), therefore easier to work with.

This first exercise focuses on finding the best manner to identify the printable highlight and shadow point of an image. Because the quality of the images can vary, using a specific method to establish these points is imperative to color correction. The Histogram, Levels, Color Sampler, and Info palette can make finding the highlight and shadow points easy and painless.

Find the White and Black Point with the Histogram

1. Open the file **Bishop's Harbor.TIF** from the **SF-Adv Photoshop** folder.

The histogram provides a great deal of information about the image. Reading the Mean will tell you if an image is light (over 170), dark (under 85), or normal. At a glance it displays distribution of pixels in the image.

2. Choose Image>Histogram to open the Histogram dialog box. A representation of the overall pixel distribution of the image in a composite (Luminosity) and the individual color channels can be shown.

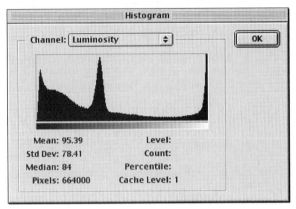

Depending on the resolution of your monitor, the histogram may show substantially different numbers.

3. Use the histogram to view the overall distribution of the pixels from the shadow to the highlight area. High concentrations of pixels are in the darkest and lightest area of the image, with another concentration just to the darker side of the midpoint of the histogram. This shows that even though there are a great amount of detail pixels in the highlight, shadow, and midpoint areas of the image, not too many pixels are in the other areas.

To further review the Histogram dialog box, let's examine the Mean, Standard Deviation, and Median values. The *Mean* is an average point of the brightness values in the image. A Mean of 128 usually identifies a well-balanced image. Images with a Mean of 170 to 255 are light; images with a Mean lower than 85 are dark. The *Standard Deviation* (Std Dev) represents how widely the values vary. The *Median* shows the middle value in the range of color values. As shown above, the image is slightly on the dark side (Mean of 106.23). Close the Histogram dialog box.

4. To determine the proper highlight and shadow points in the image, use the Color Sampler tool and the Info palette. Open the Info palette by choosing Window>Show Info, then select the Color Sampler.

5. With the Info tab selected, click the black triangle drop-down menu, and select Palette Options. Select two separate readouts. For this exercise, use Actual Color or the current color of the image for the First Color Readout, and RGB Color for the Second Color Readout. While two different color modes can be selected, the First Color Readout selection should be the color mode of the image as acquired, and the Second Color Readout selection should be the final color mode to which the image will be output, so that comparisons can be evaluated. Click OK.

The Color Sampler tool is found beneath the Eyedropper tool on the Tool palette.

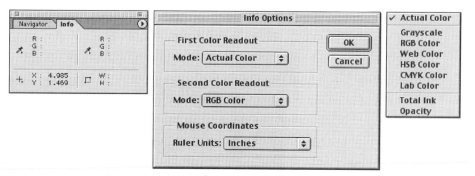

6. Place the Color Sampler tool over a portion of the image that appears to be a light (highlight) area of the image and that has some detail, and then click. A number "1" will appear and the setting for the area will appear in the Info Palette window. Try three other locations on the image. The Color Sampler will record up to four areas on a single image. To remove a point, click on the point, and drag it off the image, or Option/Alt-click the point.

When points are selected in this manner, they can be referenced, then the best solution chosen as the highlight or shadow.

When the mean is 128 (exactly half the 256 available levels), the image is almost always well-balanced.

7. Click each point and drag it off the image. Follow the procedure in Step 6 to determine the shadow area of the image.

8. There isn't a great deal of difference in the shadow area either. Whichever area is selected for the highlight and shadow area will be appropriate.

9. Close the file without saving.

Understanding Neutrality

The purpose of basic color correction is to create truly neutral grays in an image, thereby removing any unwanted color casts.

It is a common misconception that neutral gray is made up of equal parts of cyan, magenta, and yellow inks. As you learned earlier, printing pigments are impure; in other words, the magenta ink isn't an absolutely pure magenta. In addition, different sets of printing inks give the pigments different values — the yellow in Toyo inks, a set of inks quite common in Japan, contains more magenta than SWOP (Specifications for Web Offset Proofing) yellow, which is an industry standard in the U.S. Finally, due to the way in which the human eye perceives color, a gray needs to contain a little more cyan than other colors to be perceived as neutral.

Create Neutral Grays

1. Create a New document, 300 × 300 pixels (no other settings matter) in CMYK mode.

2. Press "D" to reset the foreground and background to their default colors.

3. Photoshop automatically uses gray component replacement (GCR) when you have set your CMYK settings to SWOP coated (the default). To see what really happens with colors, we need to turn this off. Select Edit>Color Settings>CMYK>Custom CMYK.

When selecting highlight and shadow areas, an area with some definition (about 5%) is desirable.

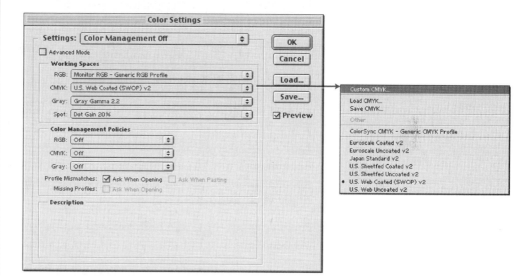

4. Set the Black Generation to None, then click OK. Click OK again to exit Color Settings.

One of the greatest benefits of creating a neutral gray is that when a neutral state has been achieved, color cast is removed, and the image may be color corrected much more easily.

5. Click on the foreground color swatch to display the Color Picker dialog box. Locate the values for CMYK in the lower-right corner of the dialog box. Enter 100 each for C, M, and Y, and set black (K) to 0. Click OK.

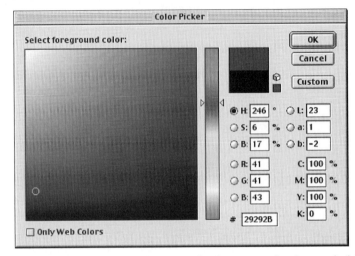

6. Depending on your monitor calibration, the foreground color probably looks fairly black on screen. We're about to demonstrate how deceptive this is. Select the Linear Gradient tool. Draw a gradient from top to bottom with the gradient type set to linear, Foreground to Background.

7. As you can see, the gradient isn't neutral at all. It appears as a warm brownish gray. If your Info palette is not already open, select Window>Show Info. Set the palette options to show RGB and CMYK color. Drag the cursor over the image while watching the numbers change on the palette. Contrary to what the screen seems to be showing you, every shade of gray in the image contains similar amounts of cyan, magenta, and yellow.

8. Select Image>Adjust>Curves. Select Cyan from the Channels drag-down menu.

9. Click and drag the middle of the curve upward to increase the percentage of cyan throughout the image. As you drag, the image becomes more and more neutral.

Notice the Input and Output readings at the bottom of the box. The Input level is the ink percentage before correction, reading from 0 to 100, left to right. The Output level represents the ink percentage after correction. Raising the curve increases this number; lowering reduces it.

Adjust the curve until Input reads 50% (the middle of the graph horizontally) and Output reads about 65%.

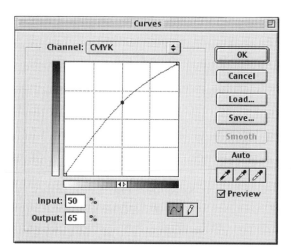

Using GCR, black ink replaces portions of cyan, magenta, and yellow ink in colored areas and in neutral areas. Closely related is UCR (undercolor removal), where black ink is used to replace cyan, magenta, and yellow ink in neutral areas only. UCR uses less ink than GCR, and gives greater depth in shadows. UCR is used for uncoated papers; GCR tends to maintain a better gray balance on press.

10. Again position the cursor over the image and look at the numbers on the Info palette. The first number listed after a color is the ink percentage before correction and the second number is what the new percentage will be if you click OK. The magenta and yellow are unchanged, but the cyan is boosted. Notice that there is a larger percentage increase of cyan in the middle of the image (the midtones) than there is in the highlight and shadow areas.

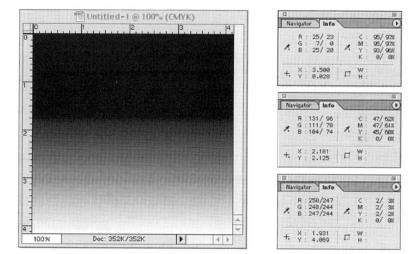

11. Check and uncheck the Preview checkbox a few times to compare the image before and after correction.

12. Click Cancel and close the file without saving.

Adjust an Image

1. Open the file **Poolside2.TIF** from the **SF-Adv Photoshop** folder.

2. Open the Info palette. Open the palette options dialog box. To see the color points in the RGB and CMYK color modes, set the First Color Readout mode to RGB Color and the Second Color Readout mode to CMYK Color. Click OK.

Info Options

First Color Readout
Mode: RGB Color

Second Color Readout
Mode: CMYK Color

Mouse Coordinates
Ruler Units: Inches

OK
Cancel

3. Select the Color Sampler tool in the toolbar, or press Shift>I, and in the Color Sampler Options bar, select 3 by 3 Average.

Sample Size: 3 by 3 Average   Clear

Click and hold the mouse button anywhere on the image. A small dot appears on the curve (which is a diagonal line at this point) in the dialog box. As you move the cursor across the image, the dot is relocated on the curve. This allows you to determine the RGB values of the curve as a whole or channel by channel. If you are in grayscale or CMYK mode, you can determine the ink coverage on the curve channel by channel.

To correct colors in the RGB color mode, and to have it relate directly to CMYK, you will use complementary colors. As described in Chapter 2, the complementary color for red is cyan, green is magenta, and blue is yellow.

4. Carefully examine the image. Notice the yellow cast in the skin tones, and the greenish cast in the sky. It may not be apparent on an uncalibrated monitor, but if you place the Eyedropper tool over these areas, you will find a high proportion of yellow. If you place the Eyedropper tool over the sand in the foreground, you'll find that it is nowhere near neutral. Red is running 215 to 230 (Cyan: 15 to 25%); and Blue is running as high as 185 (Yellow up to 40%).

Navigator   **Info**

R : 230   C : 10%
G : 229   M : 5%
B : 182   Y : 27%
           K : 0%

X : 4.460   W :
Y : 7.120   H :

5. Check the values of both Yellow and Blue values on a few locations in the image. The relationship should be approximately the same.

Navigator   **Info**

R : 231   C : 9%
G : 240   M : 3%
B : 230   Y : 8%
           K : 0%

X : 4.920   W :
Y : 4.880   H :

#1 R : 184   #2 R : 225
   G : 222   G : 226
   B : 201   B : 179

#3 R : 238   #4 R : 233
   G : 236   G : 230
   B : 205   B : 188

6. Choose a point of neutral color in the foreground sand that shows a value between 215 to 230 Blue and between 15% and 25% Yellow values in the Info palette. (We used X:2.760, Y:6.950 as our point of reference.)

7. Select Image>Adjust>Curves. Since we want to remove yellow, activate the Blue channel in the Curves drag-down menu. Make certain that the Preview checkbox is activated.

8. Move that point in the curve to equal the Red value (around 240), or simply click on the curve line and type the Blue value in the Input box and the Red value of that point in the Output box. Notice that the image starts to lose its yellow cast. If we picked the right point, we'll notice that the Red, Green, and Blue values are essentially equal. If not, we'll have to adjust the Red and Green channels as well, because the white will start to wash out.

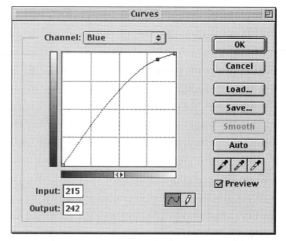

9. When the neutral area is about 240 for all three colors, you'll find that the skin tones have become more natural and the sky and water have lost most of the greenish cast.

10. Save the file as "Poolside Corrected.PSD" in your **Work in Progress** folder, and leave it open for the next exercise.

Once the color cast has been adjusted, you're ready to refine your image adjustment. This is where Photoshop experts stand out from the pack, and you're about to learn the trick that makes them expert.

Refine Image Adjustment

1. With the image Poolside Corrected.PSD still open, open the Curves palette. Set the highlight so that there will be a printable dot. Double-click the Set White Point eyedropper to open the Color Picker, and set C:5, M:3, Y:3, K:0. Click OK.

2. Set the shadow so that it won't turn completely black. Double-click the Set Black Point eyedropper and set C:95, M:82, Y:82, K:80. Click OK.

3. Set the midtone. Double-click the Set Gray Point eyedropper, and set C:62, M:50, Y:50, K:80. Click OK.

   Although you're working with an RGB image, you want to use these CMYK curve values to achieve good translation to the printing process.

4. Find the highlight in the image, and click on it with the Set White Point eyedropper.

5. Find the shadow in the image, and click on it with the Set Black Point eyedropper. Usually, as is the case here, this adjusts the image appropriately, and you can skip to Step 10. The following three steps may be necessary for certain jobs.

6. Adjust the brightness by dragging up or down at the 50% point of the RGB curve, if needed.

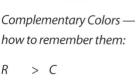

Complementary Colors —
how to remember them:

R > C

G > M

B > Y

The Set White Point and Set Black Point eyedroppers are often referred to as the Highlight and Shadow eyedroppers.

7. Increase contrast by adding up to 10% to the Input in shadow areas and subtracting up to 10% in highlight areas.

8. Flatten the image by subtracting up to 10% to the Output in shadow areas and adding up to 10% in highlight areas.

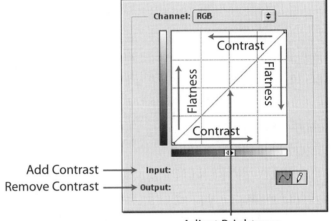

Adjust Brightness

9. Finally, convert from RGB to CMYK. Leave the file open for the next exercise.

In this exercise, we're going to change the time of day from around noon to sunset, or at least make a good start on it. We're going to accomplish this by changing the color of the sky and water.

Color Correct with HSL

1. Open **Poolside Corrected.PSD** from your **Work in Progress** folder.

2. Using the Magic Wand tool, select an area of sky, then choose Select>Similar.

3. Switch to the Lasso tool. While holding down the Option/Alt key, deselect everything below the point where the trees meet the sky.

4. Select Image>Adjust>Hue/Saturation, and change the Hue to +170 and the Saturation to +65. Leave the lightness alone. Click OK.

5. Now select the ocean water, and change its Hue to +170. Leave the saturation and lightness at 0 (zero). Click OK.

6. Select the pool, which is a little trickier. We're going to lighten the hue to +160, and desaturate to −20, with the lightness set at −5.

7. To give the scene the overall setting-sun look, choose Image>Adjust>Variations, and, with the Midtones button selected, click twice on "More Red."

8. To finish the impression, we would lengthen the shadows — but that is outside the scope of this exercise.

9. Close the file without saving.

Setting the white and black points as we have will ensure that there is a printable dot, rather than pure black or pure white. The gray point achieves a neutral tone.

This is where the relationship between the Histogram and the Curves dialog boxes become important. After determining the kind of image with which you're working from the histogram, you can apply steps 7, 8, or 9 with confidence. If you couldn't tell what kind of image you had, you would only be guessing how to handle it.

Adjustment Layers

Adjustment layers are a special type of Photoshop layer. They contain no image data; instead, adjustment layers allow you to apply color adjustments such as Curves, Levels, and Hue/Saturation, to layers or layer groups. The specification for each command may be edited at any time, until the layer is permanently merged into the layers it is affecting.

Each adjustment layer contains a layer mask. You can paint on the mask as you would a regular layer mask or alpha channel. Instead of hiding or showing portions of the image, however, an adjustment layer mask determines which portions of the underlying layers are affected by the color-correction command included in that layer.

Adjustment layers enable you to isolate portions of an image for correction, and adjust that layer separately. They're effective for correcting a color cast in a blue lake, for example, when the blue sky is acceptable without changes. They are also helpful for experimenting with corrections, such as Levels or Curves, without overcorrecting the image. Rather than attempting to reapply new adjustments to a previously modified image, you can edit the existing Levels or Curves Adjustment layer.

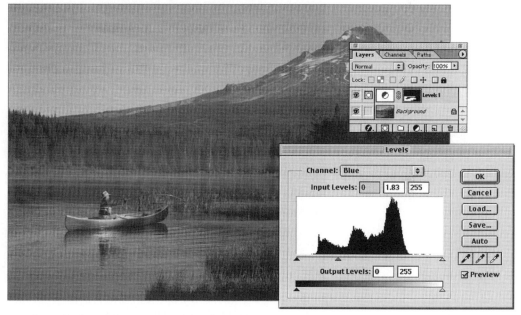

If a selection is active when an adjustment layer is created, the selection is automatically converted to the mask for the adjustment layer. Adjustment layer masks may be saved or loaded just like any mask or alpha channel.

Many of the commands available from the Adjust submenu (Image>Adjust) may be used as an adjustment layer. The exceptions are Autolevels and Desaturate, which may be achieved using Levels and Hue/Saturation respectively; Replace Color and Variations, because they require real-time interaction with the image; and Equalize.

You can change the opacity, order, or blending mode of an adjustment layer, just as you can change a regular layer. You cannot, however, merge one adjustment layer into another.

Selection of the black point, with white and gray points defined, will usually color-correct the image.

Exclamation marks following a number in the Info palette indicates that these values are out-of-gamut, and cannot be achieved using the specified color model.

Use Adjustment Layers

1. Open the image **Lemon.TIF** from your **SF-Adv Photoshop** folder.

2. Create a selection which includes just the lemons, then choose New Adjustment Layer>Hue/Saturation from the Layers palette drag-down menu.

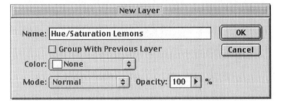

Alternately, you can click the New Adjustment Layer icon at the bottom of the layer palette. If you choose this option, hold down the Option/Alt key if you wish to name the new Adjustment Layer.

3. If necessary, change the name of the layer to "Hue/Saturation Lemons" by Option/Alt-clicking on the name portion of the layer. Leave the other settings at their defaults and click OK.

4. If it is necessary to return to the menu, choose Layer>Change Layer Content>Hue/Saturation. Slide the Hue slider around to recolor the lemons; make them any color that looks fun or interesting to you. Notice that although there is not a selection border visible, only the lemons are changing color. Click OK.

5. Choose Select>Load Selection, and load Hue/Saturation Lemons Mask; click the Invert checkbox.

6. Choose Layer>New Adjustment Layer to add another adjustment layer to the image. Make it a Hue/Saturation adjustment layer named "Hue/Sat Background". Click OK.

7. In the Hue/Saturation dialog box that appears, click Colorize. Colorize the background in a bright color that contrasts well with the lemons. Click OK.

8. Add another adjustment layer. This time base the layer on Curves, and let the name default to Curves 1. Click OK. Adjust the individual color channels in the Curves dialog box so that the color in the image shows some fairly dramatic changes. For example, you could push the red curve much higher and bring the green curve much lower. Click OK.

9. In the Layers palette, drag the Hue/Sat Background layer down below the Hue/Saturation Lemons layer. Nothing changes in the image, because the two layers have no unmasked data in common.

10. Drag the Curves layer below the Hue/Sat Background layer. The colors in the image change, because now the curves are being applied after the hue change.

11. Add a new layer to the document. Position it just above the Background layer, and paint it with some bright colors; the colors won't appear as they do on the swatches because they are being affected by the adjustment layers.

Group the adjustment layers with the new layer by selecting each adjustment layer and then selecting the Group with Previous option from the Layer menu.

12. Notice that Layer 1 is still affected by the adjustment layers, but the lemons have returned to their original hue. Drag Layer 1 into the trash.

13. To see how the image would appear without the results of an adjustment layer, simply click on the visibility icon to the left of the layer thumbnail. Turn off different combinations of adjustment layer views and note the results. Then be sure to reset all adjustment layer views to visible.

14. Adjust the Opacity of the Hue/Saturation layers; notice how the effect changes, the closer the Opacity of the layer is to 0 (zero). Essentially, an adjusted version of the image is being blended with an unadjusted version. Using this method, you can soften the effect of a Curves or Levels adjustment. Return all Opacity sliders to 100%.

15. Double-click the Layer thumbnail (the first icon) in any adjustment layer. A dialog box with your original settings for that command will appear. You can make changes as desired and click OK to change the command specifications. Note that double-clicking an adjustment layer with the Invert command will bring up the Layer Options dialog box, because there are no settings for this command — it's either on or off.

16. Save as Adjustments.PSD. Close the file.

The visibility icon is often referred to as the "eye," or "eyeball" icon.

Points to Remember about Correcting Images

Like many other skills, it takes time and practice with image correction before you can do it with ease and accuracy. Here are some things to remember while gaining experience in color correction:

- Approach all image correction with a plan of attack. Examine the image carefully before correcting, and formulate a logical work path for correction.

- Leveling may be done in either CMYK or RGB mode.

- Leveling removes information from the file. Never level more than once. Make certain that you save an uncorrected copy to which you can revert to, if necessary.

- Perform most color corrections in the color mode in which the image was scanned. Correct in RGB, then make final tweaks after converting to CMYK for images intended for traditional offset printing, or after converting to Indexed, if the image is to be used as a GIF.

- Never convert back to RGB after converting an image to CMYK or Indexed, unless absolutely necessary.

- Realize that some filters and blending modes won't work as expected, or won't work at all, in CMYK mode. For example, the Lighting Effects filter only works in RGB mode, and the Hard Light Blending mode depends upon a 50% RGB gray to define transparent areas.

- If you have to use an image in both forms, such as for both a Web page and a printed piece, do most of your corrections in RGB, then convert a copy to CMYK and fine-tune the color adjustments.

- Make certain that you don't overcorrect images. A sure sign of overcorrection is *posterization,* an image that is divided into distinct areas of color rather than blending smoothly from one to the next. Another way to tell is to examine the histogram for each channel in the Levels dialog box. The more space that there is between the bars in the graph, the less color information exists in the file.

- Not all images need color correction, though most need a levels adjustment.

- It can often take several steps and different adjustments to correct a single image. For example, you may want to level the image, correct color with Curves, then use Selective Color or Hue/Saturation to correct areas of shifted color. Occasionally, you'll need to select an area, such as a sky, with selection tools before correction; that way, you can adjust the blue in the sky without adjusting the blue in water or other blue objects in the image.

- Never trust the monitor when dealing with CMYK color. The only sure way to predict color in output is to use the information on the Info palette and a process color book, which shows swatches of colors printed with various proportions of cyan, magenta, yellow, and black.

- Finally, realize that color correction is a science, dealing with values that are verifiable. With experience, you'll find that you know almost instinctively what adjustments are necessary to produce a beautiful, well-balanced color image.

Summary

Understanding how the additive and subtractive colors works and complement each other is the basic theory behind color correction. Through the use of the color wheel, you can mix colors to achieve the proper blend. Using Adjustment Layers allows you to experiment with the look and feel of the image without having to commit to actual changes until you are happy with the results.

Remember that the combination or deletion of certain colors can determine the total spectrum that is visible to the output and display devices used. As you become more comfortable with the use of the color correction tools, you will gravitate almost instinctively toward the right tool for the task.

Complete Project A: Just Shoot Me

CHAPTER 4

CHAPTER OBJECTIVE:

To learn about Photoshop's ability to perform image transformations; to understand the commands for transforming graphics; to learn to use grids and guides in your artwork. In Chapter 4, you will:

- Discover how to use transform commands, and learn how transformations apply to layers.

- Observe how grids and guides allow you to align images with precision.

- Become familiar with how to scale with Free Transform while maintaining aspect ratio.

- Learn to transform two-dimensional artwork into a three-dimensional object.

PROJECTS TO BE COMPLETED:

- Just Shoot Me (A)

- Baby Shower Invitation (B)

- Retouching the Jones Family Portrait (C)

- The Fix Is In! (D)

- Makeover (E)

- Photomat (F)

Transforming Images

It is good practice to determine the required transformation(s), such as scaling, rotating, and skewing in the page-layout program, and then apply those numbers as Photoshop transformations. You may be able to link directly from the layout application, opening the high-resolution image into Photoshop.

It's often necessary to rotate, skew, scale, or otherwise transform an image. While most desktop-publishing applications have commands to achieve these effects, printing an image transformed in a layout application can slow output, or stop it entirely, since the output device must calculate and execute the transformations of the high-resolution image.

Transformations that are executed in a page-layout program are applied only to the low-resolution preview image that you see on your monitor. The actual commands are stored in the layout as OPI comments, along with the information on the external location of the high-resolution version of the image.

Transform Commands

Photoshop contains commands for transforming graphics. A selected path or even selected points on a path can be transformed. In these cases, the menus change to read Transform Path (or Points). The Transform menu allows you to perform a variety of functions.

OPI (Open Prepress Interface) is an extension to PostScript that automatically replaces low-resolution images, such as the screen representations of images used in page-layout programs, with high-resolution images when the file is printed. Information about the image, such as crops, skews, and scaling from the page-layout program, are attached to the image and the instructions are acted upon by the RIP. OPI is a specific process, and is often confused with Automatic Picture Replacement (APR) which, while replacing the low-resolution image with a high-resolution image, does not contain all the comments of an OPI image.

- **Scale**. This command allows you to resize a layer, a series of linked layers, or a selection, either proportionally or nonproportionally.
- **Rotate**. This command rotates image data in either direction, in 0.1-degree increments.
- **Skew**. This command allows you to lock two or three corners of the image while distorting the remaining points.
- **Distort**. This command allows you to warp an image in any direction, giving you the ability to place image data on a three-point perspective plane.
- **Perspective**. This command twists the image into a one-point perspective.

There are three different ways to use Transform commands. You can access one command at a time, access all commands at the same time using Free Transform, or enter specific values for transformation using Numeric Transform. Whichever method you choose, it's a good idea to perform all transformations on the image at one time, and apply the transformation only once. Otherwise, the image may degrade because Photoshop has to recalculate pixel values for each transformation.

Whichever method you choose, all transformations are available in the Options bar for numeric transformation.

Tool Selected   X/Y Sizes   Width/Height %   Rotation   Skew (H/V)   Abort

| | X: 795.0 px Y: 1527.0 px | W: 100.0% H: 107.1% | ∠ 0.0° | H: 0.0° V: 0.0° | ✕ ✓ |

Reference   Relative   Maintain   Confirm
Point   Reference   Aspect
Location   Position   Ratio

The Transform commands work on any layer except the Background layer when there is no active selection; they work on the Background layer when a selection is active and on a selected portion of a normal layer. If the active layer is linked with one or more layers, the transformation applies to all linked layers.

To convert the Background to a standard layer, you simply double-click on it; it will be renamed Layer 0, by default.

Use the Transform Commands

1. Open **Light Lunch.TIF** from the **SF-Adv Photoshop** folder.

2. Double-click the Background layer, then click OK to let the layer name default to Layer 0.

Layers	Channels	Paths
Normal	Opacity: 100%	
Lock:		
👁 🖌	Layer 0	

3. Select Edit>Transform>Scale. Hold down the Shift key, and drag a handle from any corner. The image is scaled proportionally, maintaining the height and width aspect ratio. If you drag a handle from the center of the top, bottom, or sides, the image will be nonproportionally scaled.

4. Release the Shift key and drag a corner handle. The image is resized again, only this time, the height and width aren't proportional.

When the Shift key is held down while scaling, the object is scaled proportionally (left). When the key is not held down, disproportional scaling distorts the image (right).

5. To return the image to its proper aspect ratio, click the Maintain Aspect Ratio link icon in the Options toolbar.

6. Click the Cancel Transform button to return the image to its previous state, or press the Escape key. Select Edit>Transform>Rotate. Expand the window a bit, then hold the cursor over any handle and drag to rotate the layer. The rotation will display immediately. Double-click on the image, press Return/Enter, or click the Commit checkmark to apply the transformation.

Unless you have increased the Canvas Size dimensions, the corners of the rotated image will be cropped.

Reversing a transformation with another transformation will degrade the image.

Hold down both the Option/Alt and Shift keys to scale the image from the center.

7. Select File>Revert, and double-click on the Background layer to convert it to Layer 0. Then select Image>Rotate Canvas>Arbitrary and enter 45° clockwise to automatically increase the canvas size when you rotate (any degree of rotation will work).

When transforming images, try to perform all the transformations before applying. It will reduce the resulting image degradation. And if you decide that you do not want a transformation, do not use a transformation to reverse the effect. Instead, use the History palette to go back to a stage before the transformation; or revert to the last saved version of the image.

8. Apply Revert to the image again, changing the Background layer to Layer 0, and scale it down to about 50% of its original size (Edit>Transform>Scale). Now rotate the image about 45° by typing the rotation in the Options bar. It has enough canvas room to avoid cropping the corners. Press Return/Enter to accept the transformation.

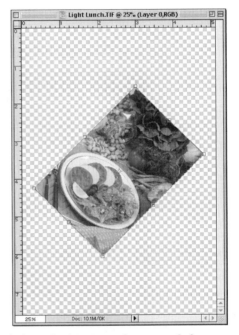

9. With the Move tool, drag the image to the upper-left corner of the canvas. Select Edit>Transform>Skew. Drag the right-center handle down. When dragging any side handle, the two corner points opposite the handle are locked into position.

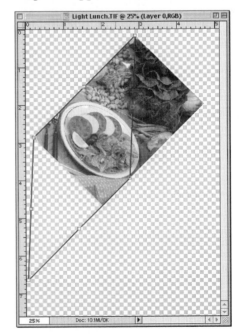

10. Press Command/Control-Z to undo the action. Now drag a corner point; the remaining three corner points are locked into position.

11. Click the Cancel Transform button.

12. Resize to 50% again. Select Edit>Transform>Perspective. Drag the upper-right corner handle to the left. The image is pulled into a one-point perspective. If you drag another handle after the first drag, you're essentially applying a Distort or Skew transformation.

13. Click the Cancel Transform button. Select Edit>Transform>Distort. Pull any handle in any direction. Distort allows you to move any point without constraining the other points around the image.

14. Press Escape, and leave the file open for the next exercise.

Use Free Transform

1. With the **Light Lunch.TIF** image still open, select Edit>Free Transform.

   Scaling with Free Transform is achieved the same way as using the Scale command. Simply drag a handle, holding down the Shift key to maintain aspect ratio.

2. Rotate the layer by positioning the cursor just outside any handle until it turns into a curved two-sided arrow. If you press the Shift key while dragging, the rotation is constrained to 15° increments.

3. Press the Command/Control key, and drag any handle; this is the equivalent of the Distort command. The other handles remain fixed.

4. Press Command/Control-Shift, and drag a handle. The image is skewed just as if you were using the Skew command.

5. Finally, press Command-Option-Shift (Macintosh) or Control-Alt-Shift (Windows), and drag a corner handle; the image is pulled into a one-point perspective.

6. To undo the last adjustment, select Edit>Undo or Command/Control-Z.

7. Press Escape or click the Cancel Transform button to return the image to its original state.

8. Leave the image open for the next exercise.

Press Command/Control-T to access Free Transform.

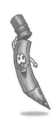

Double-click the image, click the Commit button, or press Return/Enter to commit the image.

Use Numeric Transform

1. Choose Edit>Transform, and select any of the transform options; numeric transformations are available in the Options bar.

2. Using the numeric controls, you may perform any transform except Distort and Perspective.

3. To move the layer within the image, enter values in the X and Y boxes in the Position box. The Relative checkbox, when checked, moves the layer the specified distance from its current position; if unchecked, it moves to absolute points on the ruler. Enter 0.5 in. in both boxes, and leave the Relative triangle checked.

4. Scale allows you to scale the image to specific dimensions or a percentage. Enter 50% in both boxes. If the Maintain Aspect Ratio link is selected, when you enter a number into one box, it is automatically duplicated in the second box.

5. Enter "30" in the Horizontal Skew box and "45" in the Vertical Skew box to skew the image.

6. Enter "20" in the Angle box to rotate the image.

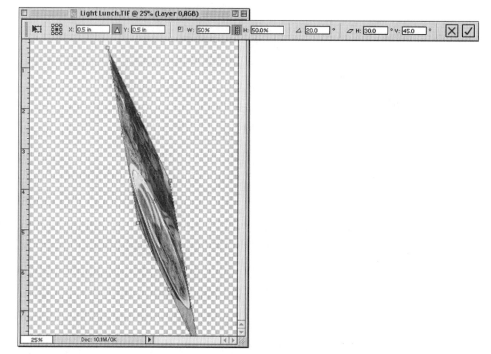

7. Press Escape, and close the file without saving.

Unless there's a reason to play with an image to achieve the effect (because you'll "know it when you see it"), it's usually best to use the Numeric Transform palette. It's most accurate, and all transformations can be performed quickly.

Guides and Grid

The ability to freely drag a portion of an image into another shape is a useful feature. Often, however, a little more precision is required, particularly when using the Distort command. Photoshop allows you to specify a grid and drag out non-printing guides to assist in aligning objects. They're really helpful in precisely positioning items on a page.

By selecting Preferences>Guides and Grid, you may specify, in the dialog box, the spacing between gridlines, the distance between subdivisions within the gridlines and the colors of the grid and guides.

The grid is turned on and off in the View menu. Choosing View>Snap to Grid automatically aligns objects to grid points as you move them, if the grid is visible, and the moved object comes within a few pixels of a gridline.

Guides are created by clicking and dragging from either ruler. The rulers must be visible in order to create guides; once guides are created, the rulers can be turned off. Guides may be moved with the Move tool unless the View>Lock Guides option is checked. When dragging or moving guides, pressing the Shift key while moving causes the guide to snap to whatever ruler tick marks are visible on screen. If the Shift key is not pressed, and the Snap to Grid option is turned on, the guide will snap to the grid if it is near a gridline when released. You can make objects snap to the guides by choosing View>Snap to Guides. To hide guides, select View>Hide Guides.

Using Guides and Grids

1. Create a new RGB document, 5 in. square at 100 ppi. Set Contents to White.

2. If rulers aren't visible on the screen, press Command/Control-R. The Ruler Units are set from the Info palette. Activate the Info palette and click the plus sign in the lower-left corner of the palette, or select Palette Options from the fly-out menu to ensure that the units are set to Inches.

3. Select Edit>Preferences>Guides and Grid. Change Gridline Every to 1 in. and Subdivisions to 8. This will create a grid in ⅛″ increments.

4. The grid and guide colors may be changed by clicking on their respective swatches. For now, leave these at their defaults. You can also specify the type of line used denoting grids or guides. Selecting Lines style displays solid lines and the Dashed Lines style displays a lighter, dashed-line style. These options are available for both grids and guides. The third style choice, Dots, places a dot at each subdivision of every gridline. This choice is less distracting than the others. Change the Grid Style to Dots. Click OK.

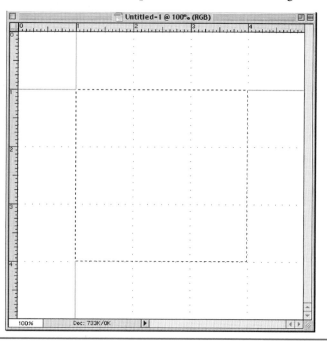

5. If the grid is not visible, select View>Show>Grid, and make certain that the Snap to Grid option is checked.

6. Click and drag the horizontal ruler down into the image area. Release it near a gridline to draw a guide.

7. Click and drag the vertical ruler across the image area; release it on a ruler tick mark.

8. Check that View>Snap to Guides is on. Create a rectangle using the Rectangular Marquee tool; notice how the marquee tends to "stick" to the guides and grid.

If you don't need the snap to function of the grid and guides, turn it off. There's nothing more annoying than an element trying to snap to a point to which you don't want it to snap.

9. Move the selection border; again, it sticks to the guides and grid.

10. Turn off Snap to Grid and Snap to Guides. Now move the selection border again. Though the gridlines and guidelines are still visible, the selection moves freely throughout the image. If you hold down the Shift key, the selection border will stick to the guides, but not the grid. If you hold down Shift-Command/Control, the selection border will stick to both.

11. Activate the Move tool. Click on a guide and drag it to a new position.

12. Close the file without saving.

Create a Cube

1. Open the image **Beach Boy.TIF** from the **SF-Adv Photoshop** folder.

2. If the grid is visible, select View>Show>Grid and uncheck it. If rulers aren't visible, press Command/Control-R. If they are not already set, change the ruler units to inches by clicking the plus sign in the lower-left corner of the Info palette and selecting Inches.

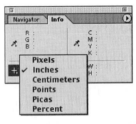

3. Double-click the Background layer, and rename it "Top". Duplicate the layer twice; name one layer "Left" and the other "Right".

4. Select Image>Canvas Size. Resize the image to 2 in. × 2 in., keeping the Anchor located in the center.

5. Double-click the Zoom tool to size the image to 100%.

6. Make certain that Snap to Guides is on. Hold down the Shift key and drag horizontal guides to the following positions: ¼″, ½″, ¾″, 1 ³⁄₁₆″, and 1 ½″.

7. Again, hold down the Shift key and drag vertical guides to the following positions: ⅜″, 1″, 1 ⅝″.

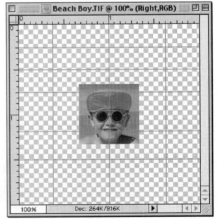

8. Turn off all layers except Left. With the Left layer active, select Edit>Transform>Distort.

Drag the upper-left corner of the image to the intersection of the first vertical guide and the second horizontal guide.

Drag the upper-right corner of the image to the intersection of the middle vertical guide and the middle horizontal guide.

Drag the lower-left corner to the intersection of the first vertical guide and the fourth horizontal guide.

Drag the lower-right corner to the intersection of the middle vertical guide and the last horizontal guide. Press Command-Return/Control-Enter.

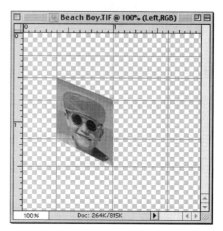

9. Turn off the Left layer, turn on the Right layer, and activate it. Select Edit>Transform>Distort.

Drag the upper-right corner of the image to the intersection of the last vertical guide and the second horizontal guide.

Drag the upper-left corner of the image to the intersection of the middle vertical guide and the middle horizontal guide.

Drag the lower-right corner to the intersection of the last vertical guide and the fourth horizontal guide.

Drag the lower-left corner to the intersection of the middle vertical guide and the last horizontal guide. Press Command-Return/Control-Enter.

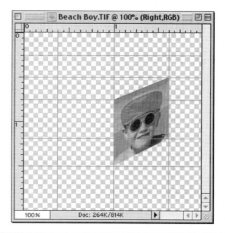

10. Turn off the Right layer, turn on the Top layer, and activate it. Select Edit>Transform>Distort.

Drag the upper-left corner of the image to the intersection of the middle vertical guide and the first horizontal guide.

Drag the upper-right corner of the image to the intersection of the last vertical guide and the second horizontal guide.

Drag the lower-left corner to the intersection of the first vertical guide and the second horizontal guide.

Drag the lower-right corner to the intersection of the middle vertical guide and the middle horizontal guide. Press Command-Return/Control-Enter.

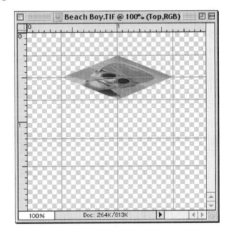

11. Turn on all layers, then save the file as "Beachboy Cube.PSD" to your **Work in Progress** folder.

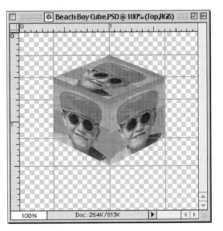

Summary

In this chapter you have learned to use Photoshop's transform tools to rotate, scale, and distort images. You have used both grids and guides as aids to placement of images on the page, taking advantage of the snap-to functions of both. You have learned to create a cube in perspective using the transformation tools in conjunction with appropriate placement of guides.

ADVANCED CHANNEL OPERATIONS

CHAPTER OBJECTIVE:

To build an understanding of how all images use channels to record color information and selections. To understand how density masks are used to create composite images, filter effects, and fades for shadows and reflections. In Chapter 5, you will:

- Discover how to create depth in your images.

- Learn how to create special alpha channels, and how to combine them to create special effects or complex masks.

- Become familiar with the Calculations dialog box, and learn how to use calculations to create special effects.

- Observe how Apply Image blends the image and channel of an image into the active file image.

- Become familiar with the Channel Mixer, and learn how to mix channels of an image.

PROJECTS TO BE COMPLETED:

- Just Shoot Me (A)

- Baby Shower Invitation (B)

- Retouching the Jones Family Portrait (C)

- The Fix Is In! (D)

- Makeover (E)

- Photomat (F)

Advanced Channel Operations

All images use channels to record color information. How much red, green, and blue should appear in each pixel to create the illusion of a red Jeep in a green meadow? Designers and production specialists manipulate the grayscale of each channel to adjust color. They also use channels as a tool to create shadows, smoothly composited images, and effects such as embossed type and 3-D highlights and shadows.

Channels serve two simple purposes. First, they act as a grayscale print of each primary color. When overlaid on screen (RGB), white areas in the Red channel, for instance, display red; black areas display no red. (CMYK is reversed.) An amount of 25% (202) shows as 75% gray, while 60% (102) shows as 40% gray.

Channels can be used to record selections. The selection might be a complex tracing of shapes to isolate them from the rest of the image. This selection/channel could have a hard edge or may include a feather value so that changes blend with unchanged areas. The advantage of channels is that they record what is selected (white), what isn't selected or is masked (black), and what is partially selected (the gray areas) in direct proportion to the gray value.

Using gradient masks is vital in image compositing. Gradient masks allow smooth blends at the edges of both images, soften or fade one into another, or simulate the reflection of one object onto the surface of another.

Channels and Density

The ability to record *density* or grayscale values provides great power and flexibility in the hands of users, enabling them to control how much (light) or how little (dark) an applied effect will have on different parts of the image. A channel containing a gradient from light to dark will have the effect of gradually protecting or hiding pixels in the image that appear where the gradient channel darkens. Density masks are used to create professional compositing, filter effects, and fades for cast shadows and reflections. A good way to learn this concept is through the following exercise that uses a Gradient mask.

Use Gradient Masks

1. With no file open, type "D" to reset the foreground and background color defaults. Open **Pokey.TIF** from your **SF-Adv Photoshop** folder. Select Image>Canvas Size. Anchor the image to the upper-middle box, and crop the canvas to a height of 3.125 in. At the warning box, press Return/Enter to proceed.

2. Select Image>Canvas Size. Double the current height to 6.25 in., and anchor the image to the upper-middle box.

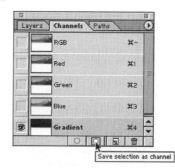

3. Using the Magic Wand tool, select the white area at the bottom of the image. In the Channels palette, click the Save Selection as Channel icon to convert the current selection into a new Alpha channel. Double-click to rename it "Gradient".

4. Working in the Gradient channel, click the Linear Gradient tool, and set it to Foreground to Background. Make certain that white is the foreground color and black is the background color, and that the tool Opacity is set to 100%. Press the Shift key, and drag the gradient from the bottom to the top of the white region of the mask.

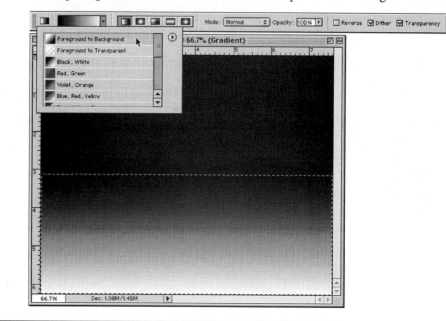

Try this: load the Gradient channel as a selection. Apply a small amount of the Twirl filter to the image — just enough to slightly distort the lower reflected surface. Then, apply the ZigZag filter with the Pond Ripples option. The results are very realistic.

5. Return to the RGB channel. Choose Select>Inverse to select the top scene. Press Command/Control-C, then Command/Control-V to paste a copy of it into a new layer. Choose Edit>Transform>Flip Vertical, and position it at the bottom.

6. Load the Gradient selection mask (Command/Control-click on the Gradient channel). Press Delete, which will delete pixels not protected (white area) by the mask. The result is a smooth fade out in the direction that the mask lightens. These pixels are less protected from being deleted.

When the Gradient channel appears, a selection box will be only half the height you expect. This is the way it should look.

A Gaussian Blur used in conjunction with a density mask will cause strange artifacts to develop.

7. Save the file as "Pokey Reflected.PSD" to your **Work in Progress** folder, then close the file.

Creating Depth Where None Exists

Light defines how we see in the real (non-digital) world. The surface of an object absorbs, reflects, and redirects light according to its shape, giving the object dimension. High points reflect a lot of light — sometimes eliminating detail. These areas are called "specular highlights." Normally, lit areas, called "highlights," give the illusion of raising items off the surface. Indentations and low areas cast shadows.

In the digital world, the direction, hardness, and color of created highlights and shadows affect how a 3-D illusion appears. For an image to appear raised from the surface, shadows are generally placed at the bottom and right sides of the shape or selection. To give the illusion of being depressed into the surface, highlights are used in this position. The edge thickness and fuzziness determines how far the object appears to be from the surface. Thicker and fuzzier shadows make the shape very depressed or embossed, while harder, narrow edges give only the slightest hint of dimension. Consider the colors of both the object and the surface. In real life, shadows and highlights contain a tint of the predominant color(s); they aren't just gray.

This exercise demonstrates how to visually raise a two-dimensional object from a surface. To do this, we're going to learn how to create two types of special alpha channels. One will simulate highlights, and the other will create the shadows.

Create Highlight and Shadow Masks

Highlights, shadows, and midtones comprise the tonal range in an image. So-called "specular highlights" are outside normal tone calculations — they are ignored when determining the brightest point in the image. An example of this might be the sparkle of a diamond. Specular highlights contain no dot on press.

1. Open **Rough Stone.TIF** from the **SF-Adv Photoshop** folder. It's a basic stucco background, perfect for three-dimensional type and artwork.

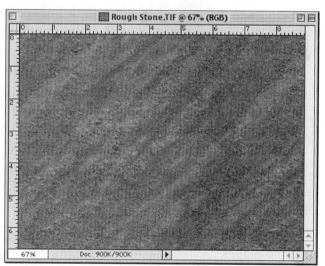

2. Make certain that the Layers and Channels palettes are showing. Choose File>Place. Select **Tropical Interiors.EPS** from the **SF-Adv Photoshop** folder. Click "Place" to place it directly onto a new layer. Resize the image, holding down the Shift key to maintain aspect ratio and position it as shown. When you're satisfied that it roughly matches this visual, press Command-Return/Control-Enter.

"Load" a channel means to click the Load Channel as a Selection icon in the Channels palette, or choose Select>Load Selection. "Activate" a channel means to highlight that channel name in the Channels palette.

3. In the Layers palette, Command/Control-click on the new layer created to move a selection of the layer. In the Channels palette, click the Save Selection as Channel. This turns a selection of the placed graphic into a channel. Double-click its name in the Channels palette, and name it "Type Inside".

4. Copy the channel by dragging it to the New Channel icon. Double-click on this channel to rename it "Type Outside".

5. With the selection still active, choose Select>Modify>Expand. Enter 3 pixels and click OK. This will expand the selection by 3 pixels all the way around.

6. Press "D" followed by "X" to select, then exchange default colors, making the foreground color black. Now press the Delete key to clear the extra regions of the mask.

This expanded outline of the type will contain the shadows and highlights that we're going to create.

If your machine has enough RAM and Adobe Illustrator, you can copy paths from Illustrator and paste them directly into a new layer. If you choose to continue to work with the image as paths, click Paste as Paths in the dialog box that appears when you paste into Photoshop.

7. Duplicate the Type Outside mask by dragging it to the New Channel icon, and name it "Blur Mask". At this point, you should have three additional channels (a total of six in addition to the composite RGB).

8. With the Blur Mask channel active, press Command/Control-D to deselect. Choose Filter>Blur>Gaussian Blur. Use a radius of 2.5 pixels to soften the edges of the mask.

9. Duplicate the Blur Mask channel; name it "Highlights". Choose Filter>Stylize>Emboss. Set Angle: –45°, Height: 3 pixels, Amount: 100%. Click OK when you're done.

When something is truly embossed, it's raised from the surface but maintains a sharply defined, flat surface with soft shadows on the slope. This exercise creates that effect with a more sophisticated result than the Photoshop Emboss filter.

10. Duplicate the Highlights channel. Rename the new channel "Shadows".

11. Activate the Highlights channel by clicking on it once. Press Command/Control-L to activate the Levels dialog box. Select the Set Black Point eyedropper tool.

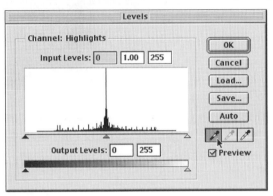

12. With the black-point eyedropper tool, click anywhere on the gray image area. This will set 50% gray as the darkest tone in the image, resulting in all of those areas turning black. The upper-left edges of the type objects retain their tonal values, thus creating the highlight mask. Click OK.

13. Activate the Shadows channel. Select Image>Adjust>Invert or press Command/Control-I to create a negative or tonally opposite mask. What was light is now dark and vice versa.

14. Press Command/Control-L to repeat the Level adjustment executed in Step 12 (set the black point by clicking on a gray area of the image). Since the image was inverted before selecting the black point, the highlights have been reversed — we now have a shadow mask. Click OK.

15. Make sure that the Background layer is active. If it's not, the next steps won't work. This also activates the RGB composite.

16. Now we'll use these channels as selections to highlight and shadow the pixels in the actual color image. In the Channels palette, Command/Control-click the Highlights mask to load it as a selection. Press Command/Control-L to open the Levels dialog box. Lighten the shadow tones in the Highlight selection area by sliding the white (right) Input Levels slider to achieve a white point of 143. Click OK.

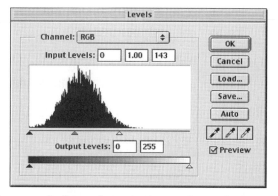

17. Load the Shadows mask channel. Again, in Levels, set the black (left) Input Levels slider to achieve a black point of 88. This will darken the selection to create the shadows. Click OK and deselect.

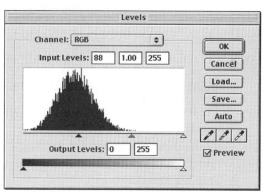

You can invert the tonal map of an image by simply pressing Command/Control-I. This eliminates the mouse clicks needed to activate the menu selection.

18. Save the file as "3D Text.PSD" to your **Work in Progress** folder, and leave it open for the next exercise.

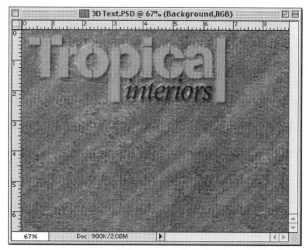

Practicing Complex Techniques

This same basic technique with minor modifications can create a range of different effects. Once you're familiar with the concept of creating highlight and shadow masks, practice the technique until you can repeat it without thinking. Complex yet commonly required techniques, such as this one, should be as natural as writing your name so that you can apply them automatically when creative inspiration strikes.

Sometimes, it helps to list the steps for a complex technique in order of execution. To create highlight and shadow masks, you would:

a. Load or create the background.

b. Place or create the artwork.

c. Create and save the "inside" mask.

d. Duplicate and expand.

e. Blur and Emboss.

f. Duplicate twice — name one channel "Highlights" and the other "Shadows".

g. Set the black point of Highlights to 50% gray with the Levels command.

h. Invert the tone map of Shadows, and set the black point to 50% gray.

i. In the composite image, load/lighten highlights, then load/darken shadows.

Many variations are possible with this technique. For example, on a high-resolution file, the embossed channel can be made *tighter* (with smaller, more defined edges). The technique can also be used to sharpen edges by loading the inside mask into the blur channel and filling it with 50% gray. You can also use the channels to add noise, and other effects.

Using Channel Calculations

The Image>Calculations command allows alpha channels to be combined in unusual ways to create special effects or complex masks. Channel calculations are similar to the blending modes used with layers and painting tools. The difference is that they work on channels rather than layers, and the calculation results are saved as a new channel, an active selection, or into a new document.

Channel calculations can seem pretty confusing at first. Your best bet is to experiment with different channel operations, then, when you achieve a pleasing effect, write it down! Depending on the document, the Calculations dialog box can generate thousands of different possibilities. One small setting change will generate an entirely different effect. Keep a record of the changes to duplicate the effect later.

The Calculations dialog box is divided into four sections: Source 1, Source 2, Blending, and Result.

Make certain that the Background layer and the Layers palette are active, or the tonal adjustments you're making to create the highlights and shadows will be executed on the transparent portion of the Type layer, and it won't work.

Almost all these channel effects can be more easily accomplished using Layer Styles. So why bother learning to do them the hard way?

In the real world, you're liable to have to work on an image created before Layer Styles were available, and unless you understand how it was built, you won't know how to fix it.

Calculations

Source 1: Untitled-1
Layer: Background
Channel: Red ☐ Invert

Source 2: Untitled-1
Layer: Background
Channel: Alpha 1 ☐ Invert

Blending: Multiply
Opacity: 100 %
☑ Mask: Untitled-1
Layer: Background
Channel: Alpha 1 ☐ Invert

Result: New Channel

OK
Cancel
☑ Preview

- **Source 1** and **Source 2**. These sections specify which channels will be included in the calculations. Source channels may be from any open document (specified in the Source drag-down list), provided the channels are the same height and width in pixels. You can use color channels (i.e., Red), an alpha channel (created or saved from a selection), or an existing selection. When using a color channel, you specify from which layer the channel should be extracted or if it should come from all layers Merged. Be sure to invert the channel before calculating if the channel is to be inverted.

- **Blending**. This section determines how the Source 1 image/channel will be combined into the effect; in it you choose a Blending mode and Opacity value. In addition, you can apply a mask to confine the contribution of Source 1 using a channel as a density mask. You may also invert the Mask.

- **Results**. This section specifies where the results of the calculation should be saved. You should choose to save in the current document as a new channel, in another document having the same dimensions, or as an active selection that can be used or additionally altered.

Create Type Effects Using Calculations

1. In the open document, 3D Text.PSD, duplicate the Type Inside channel so that we can blur and offset it. Name the channel "Offset Mask".

2. Choose Filter>Blur>Gaussian Blur, and blur the channel 2.5 pixels.

3. Press "D" to change the background color to black. With the Tropical Interiors.EPS layer and the Offset Mask channel active, choose the Move tool and use the arrow keys to move the mask 3 pixels to the right and 3 pixels down.

4. Choose Image>Calculations. Make certain that Preview is checked.

5. Make the following settings:

   Source 1: 3D Text.PSD, Layer: Merged, Channel: Offset Mask, Invert box checked.
   Source 2: 3D Text.PSD, Layer: Merged, Channel: Type Inside, Invert box unchecked.
   Blending: Add, Opacity: 100%, Offset: 0, Scale: 2, Mask box unchecked.
   Results: New Channel.

Channels are also useful for color correcting portions of an image. For example, if you need to pull green out of all parts of an image except the grass, you can create a channel that excludes the grass and then apply curves to the image.

6. Click OK. A new channel, "Alpha 1," has been created.

7. Choose Image>Calculations again, and make the following settings:
   Source 1: 3-D Text.PSD, Layer: Merged, Channel: Alpha 1, Invert box unchecked.
   Source 2: 3-D Text.PSD, Layer: Merged, Channel: Offset Mask. Invert box unchecked.
   Blending: Difference, Opacity 100%, Mask box unchecked.
   Results: New Channel.

8. Click OK. A new channel, Alpha 2, appears.

9. With Alpha 2 active, choose Select All and then copy to the clipboard.

10. Back in the Layer palette, activate the Background layer and turn off (or hide) the Tropical Interiors Logo.EPS layer. Select Edit>Paste to paste to a new layer.

11. Change the blending mode for the layer to Hard Light.

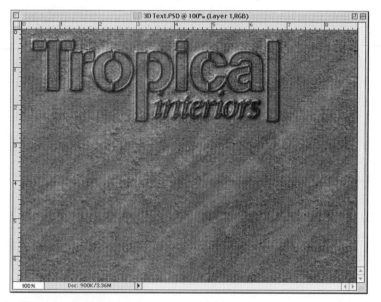

12. Save the file to your **Work in Progress** folder as "3D Text_2.PSD" and close it.

Using Apply Image

Apply Image is somewhat different from Calculations. It blends the image and channel of an image into the currently active file image. It can blend from the source file any combination of a layer and channel or merged layers and composite channel. While it provides the same blend features as Calculations, Apply Image offers the ability to apply the effect to composite channels; Calculations does not. If desired, the result can utilize a mask from either of the documents from any layer or channel. The source image and the slave mask can be inverted as well. The result is often splashy and wild, but with certain blend modes it produces a haunting ghost or embossed effect of the image's texture using light and shadow.

The Calculations command adds, subtracts, and multiplies the numeric values of the specified pixels, altering the image accordingly. So if you use the Multiply mode, for example, the pixels increase in number and the image become darker. Higher numbers create darker colors.

Using Channel Mixer

This dialog box provides yet another method to adjust and play with colors in an image based on the existing color information. In the Channel Mixer, you choose the primary color to work with and add to the image. Sliders for each color channel are the means with which to do this. For example, if Red is chosen in the pop-up menu, red is added or subtracted (cyan added) to the image, regardless of which slider is changed. Dragging the Green slider would add or subtract magenta using the Green channel as a density mask. It would be like telling the monitor to shoot more or less red phosphors through the Green channel or printing magenta ink through the cyan negative. (If you're in CMYK mode, the choices and sliders are C, M, Y, K.) Dragging sliders to the right (positive) adds color up to twice (200%) the current amount, to the left (negative) subtracts color and adds its complement.

The Contrast slider heightens or subdues the effect created by other adjustments. Checking Monochrome converts the image so that it appears to be grayscale (all color channels will end up the same). This works well for creating density masks which isolate backgrounds or contrasted objects in the image.

The following exercise, using both of these features, provides opportunities for experimentation.

Mix Channels of an Image

1. Open **White Vanda.TIF** from the **SF-Adv Photoshop** folder. Choose Image>Duplicate to create a temporary copy of the file with which we can play. Open the Channels palette so it can be viewed while the Channel Mixer is open.

2. Choose Image>Adjust>Channel Mixer. Check Preview, and using the description below and some creativity, play with the controls. Use Red as the Output channel, and observe the lower leaf on the left. Changing the Green slider makes it very red, but changing the Blue slider doesn't change it as much. That's because the leaf contains green throughout, but blue in only a small patch. Observe the Channel icons in the palette to monitor how adjustments affect the image. The Constant adjustment adds or subtracts red all over.

3. Now that you have a feel for how the controls work, make the following settings:

Output Channel: Red, Source Channels: Red: +127%, Green: –20%, Blue: 0%, Constant: 0%, Monochrome unchecked.

Output Channel: Blue, Source Channels: Red: 0%, Green: +96%, Blue: –8%, Constant: 0%, Monochrome unchecked.

Sometimes the + sign will display and sometimes it won't. We indicate it in the instructions to differentiate it from a –% entry. It is not necessary to enter the "+" sign.

Channel Mixer

Output Channel: Red

Source Channels
Red: +127 %
Green: -20 %
Blue: 0 %

Constant: 0 %

☐ Monochrome

OK
Cancel
Load...
Save...
☑ Preview

Channel Mixer

Output Channel: Blue

Source Channels
Red: 0 %
Green: 96 %
Blue: -8 %

Constant: 0 %

☐ Monochrome

OK
Cancel
Load...
Save...
☑ Preview

4. Click OK. Return to the original file and make another duplicate. With Copy 2 active, again choose Image>Adjust>Channel Mixer. This time we'll use it to create a mask of the flowers. Check "Monochrome", and use the following settings:

Output Channel: Gray, Source Channels: Red: +200%, Green: +86%, Blue: +20%, Constant: 0%.

Channel Mixer

Output Channel: Gray

Source Channels
Red: 200 %
Green: 86 %
Blue: 20 %

Constant: 0 %

☑ Monochrome

OK
Cancel
Load...
Save...
☑ Preview

When using Monochrome in the Channel Mixer, notice that all color channels end up the same in the document. The image is still in RGB but appears grayscale. When using the Channel Mixer for this purpose, work on a duplicate file and drag one of the color channels back to the original document to use it as a channel mask.

5. Click OK. With the Magic Wand tool, click in a white area inside the flower shape. Choose Select>Inverse (or Command/Control-Shift-I).

6. Press "D" for default colors, then Option/Alt-Delete (fill with black). This creates a mask through which only the flowers show or can be selected. Drag the Blue channel from Copy 2 into the window of the original document. It will be saved in the Channels palette of the original as Alpha 1. Close the window of Copy 2 (black-and-white image) without saving.

7. Two document windows should be open: the original unchanged image and the copy whose color we changed (White Vanda copy). Activate the copy. Open the Layers palette, and drag the Background layer to the New Layer icon to copy it. With that layer active and with no selection, choose Filter>Stylize>Find Edges. Set this layer to Soft Light mode.

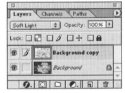

8. Activate the original image file with the RGB Composite channel active, and choose Image>Apply Image. With Preview checked, start with the settings displayed, then experiment with the blending modes and try inverting the source file to see its effect. The settings indicated in the graphic below will apply a composite (RGB) of the duplicate to the original. This composite will have both layers (Merged), and will be

Apply Image works only when both documents are in the same color mode and have the same pixel dimensions.

If you are using Apply Image on a layer of the active or target document that has transparent areas, click on Preserve Transparency to prevent the image being blended from appearing in those areas.

at 50% Opacity in Screen mode. Using the Alpha 1 mask means that only the flower section of the duplicate image will be applied.

The final image looks like this, but in color.

9. Save the image to your **Work in Progress** folder as "White Vanda Merged.PSD".

Managing Channels

Channels are effective and versatile, but can consume large amounts of RAM and bloat file sizes when you work with large images. These two related strategies can help. Just as in the preceding exercise, when we dragged a channel from one image to use in another, we can borrow a channel from one document to use in another document if images are the same pixel dimensions. This can be accomplished by referencing the channel, without having to drag it from document to document.

Channel Libraries

A document doesn't need to contain an image in order to have channels, and thus serve as a scrapbook or library. To create such a channel library, you simply create a document of the same pixel dimensions and drag channels into it. You then save it as a TIFF, if you're using

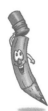

If a document contains many channels from which you want to make a library, just apply Save a Copy to the file. You then delete the RGB or CMYK color channels (to reduce file size), and save it as a TIFF.

Before converting Duotones to Multichannel, make certain that you're satisfied with all of your adjustments. Multichannel images can't be converted back to Duotone mode to alter the ink coverage.

RGB or CMYK mode, or save it as a Photoshop DCS 2.0 if you're using Multichannel mode or outputting the file.

To use the library without dragging channels from it, open the library file and the image file. When you need a channel, choose Select>Load Selection from the image file. In the Document pop-up menu, choose the file name of the library file, and select which channel to load. To save selections directly to the library, choose Select>Save Selection and choose the library file name in the Document pop-up menu. Channel libraries are most efficient if you convert them to Multichannel mode (Image>Mode>Multichannel).

Multichannel Mode

A multichannel image has no composite because none of its channels are assigned to RGB or CMYK. While such an image cannot be printed in color, it is useful for several purposes. Since it contains only channels, it's perfect for a channel library. Remember that channels must be the same pixel dimensions as the target image.

In addition to creating a channel library, you can use this mode to create special effects such as swapping the cyan and magenta channels of an image. You just convert the image to Multichannel, reorder the channels in the palette, then convert it back to CMYK mode. Another way to use the Multichannel mode is to improve duotones. Once you have completed your adjustments in Duotone mode, convert the image to Multichannel. You can then adjust each color channel tonally using curves or levels. Be sure to save Multichannel files as Photoshop DCS 2.0 or in native Photoshop format (PSD).

Transparency as a Channel

Conservation of channels is often important when file size grows. Saving every selection may not be necessary, especially when elements are on separate layers. The transparency of a layer acts as an automatic selection; you just Command/Control-click on the layer name to get a hard-edged selection of what's on that layer. You can even use a layer in the dialog box accessed by choosing Select>Load Selection.

A layer can also act as its own channel mask. For any layer, just click on Preserve Transparency to create a channel around the elements on that layer. Areas that are currently transparent become masked so that painting, pasting, applying a filter, and other channel operations affect only non-transparent areas; the edges and empty areas are protected.

Combining Channels

Another way to be minimize the number of elements in your Photoshop document is to use combinations of channels. If you save the building blocks of selections, you can later use them in tandem — adding them together, subtracting one from another, and even using their intersections. You can combine channels either through the Load Selection dialog box or through keyboard shortcuts used while clicking on the name of each channel.

The following exercise provides a simplified example of how a few channels can be used together to enhance an image.

Work with Library Channels

1. Open **Wine.TIF** from the **SF-Adv Photoshop** folder. Open the Channels, Layers, and Swatches palettes. Notice that three channels (other than RGB) already exist in this file.

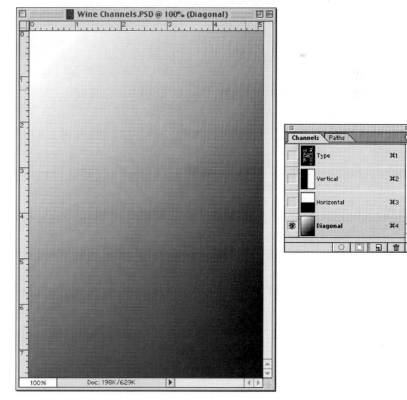

We'll use these to create a Library channel file. Choose Image>Duplicate and name it "Wine Channels.PSD".

2. In this Library file, we don't need the RGB image. Convert it to Multichannel mode (Image>Mode>Multichannel), then delete the Cyan, Magenta, and Yellow channels. (They automatically change from RGB to CMY.)

3. We need to add a Gradient channel to the library. Click the Create New Channel icon, press "D" for default colors, and choose the Linear Gradient tool. Set the options to Foreground to Background. Drag the tool from left to right at a slight angle to create this gradient, and name it "Diagonal".

We save Library Channels with no composite because we're not going to print them. If a file is to be printed, it should be saved in one of the options with a composite preview.

4. Save the file to your **Work in Progress** folder in Photoshop format, and leave the window open off to the side. Return to the original Wine.TIF file.

5. The channels that we duplicated to the Wine Channels.PSD library file are still in the original Wine.TIF file. We'll see how to combine them here with the channels in the library. Change the foreground color to cyan and the background color to magenta.

6. Command/Control-click on the Vertical channel to load it. Command-Option/Control-Alt-click on the Type channel to subtract it from the current (Vertical) selection. Press Shift-Delete/Backspace to open the Fill dialog box. Set Use: Foreground Color (cyan) and Opacity: 50%. Click OK.

7. Command/Control-click on the Vertical channel again. This time, choose Select>Inverse to select the other side. Command-Option/Control-Alt-click on the Type channel to subtract it from the current selection. Press Shift-Delete/Backspace, but this time choose the background color (magenta) at 50%.

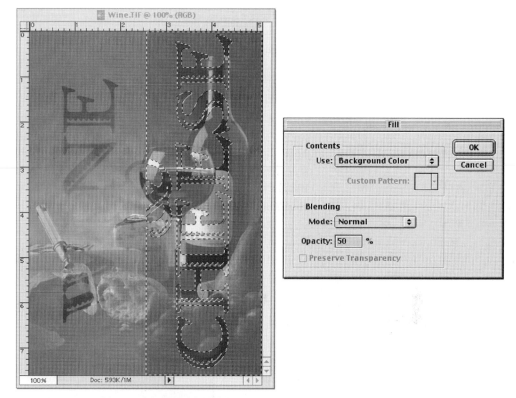

8. Command/Control-click on the Type channel, then choose Select>Load Selection. Choose Wine Channels.PSD from the Document pop-up menu and Diagonal from the Channel pop-up menu. Click the button to apply Intersect with Selection to the current selection. Click OK.

The keyboard shortcut to intersect a new selection with the current selection is Command-Shift-Option/ Control-Shift-Alt-click on the name. To add a selection, Command/ Control-Shift-click on the name.

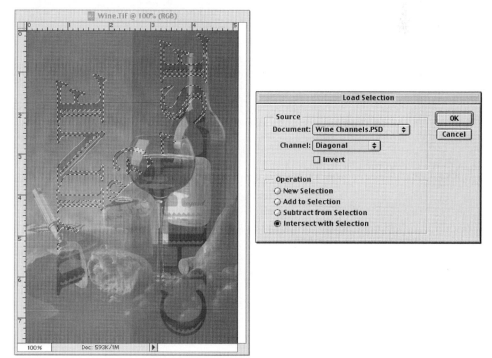

9. Press Shift-Delete/Backspace and fill with the background color (magenta) at 40%.

10. Repeat steps 8 and 9, but this time check Invert in the Load Selection dialog box to bring the lower-right part of the type through the gradient mask, and fill with the foreground color. Deselect.

11. We won't need the Type, Vertical, or Horizontal channels any longer; they are stored in the Wine Channels file. Delete them here to save memory for a larger image.

12. Choose File>Place and place **Banana Boat BW.EPS** from the **SF-Adv Photoshop** folder. Position it in the lower-left corner, clearing the type. It is placed on a new layer once you press the Return/Enter key. In the Layers palette, duplicate the Banana Boat BW.EPS layer, then click the visibility icon to hide the layer just created (Banana Boat BW.EPS copy), and activate the Banana Boat BW.EPS layer, which should be just above the Background layer.

13. We're going to use color from this layer to colorize the logo on top of it. Press Command-Delete/Control-Backspace to fill with the background color. The result is that the entire layer is filled. That's not what we want. Press Command/Control-Z to undo.

14. In the Layers palette, click the Lock Transparent Pixels button. Press Command/Control-Delete again. Now it fills just the area occupied by the logo.

The Delete key fills a layer with transparency, Command/Control-Delete fills it with the background color.

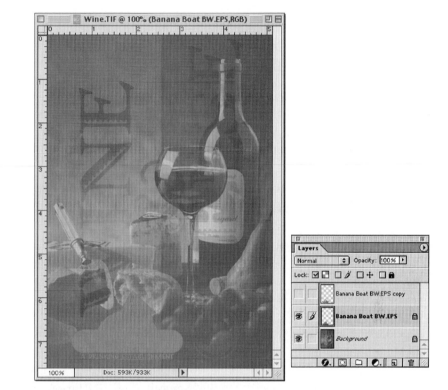

15. With the Banana Boat BW.EPS copy layer active, click the visibility icon on the top layer to show it, and set its mode to Screen.

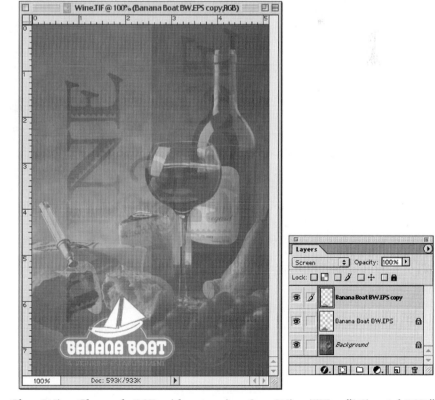

16. Close Wine Channels.PSD without saving. Save Wine.TIF as "Wine Ad.PSD" to your **Work in Progress** folder and close the file.

Special Purpose Channel Modes

With Photoshop, you use the unique capabilities of channels to work with duotones (although it does not display a visible channel for them), bump plates, varnishes, and spot color. Using spot channels and Multichannel mode to edit the pixels of spot color images can open up a variety of possibilities and effects for certain segments of the print industry, such as printers of boxes and screen printers, to apply to their art. Making these special effects work isn't difficult, but requires attention to the procedure and to saving files correctly for output.

The following two images will provide a chance to apply some special channel effects. Adding varnish or a fifth color to a printed image can make the difference between just a picture and something good enough to eat.

Create a Bump Plate

A bump plate is used to enhance the color of the original, through the addition of spot color, or by creating another application of an underlying CMYK color or colors.

1. Open the file **Berries.TIF** from the **SF-Adv Photoshop** folder. Among the blueberries are a few raspberries that we need to pop off the page.

2. With the Magic Wand tool (Tolerance: 32, Anti-alias on), click on a bright area of one of the raspberries. Choose Select>Similar, then choose Select>Grow, then Select>Modify>Smooth: 4 pixels. This provides a distinct selection of the Raspberry shapes. Choose Select>Save Selection so we can reuse it. Name it "Raspberries".

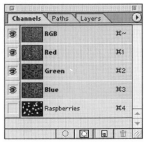

3. Adding a spot red this way would blot out most of the dimple detail. We'll temper it by using the information contained in the Red channel to boost, not obliterate, those juicy berries. Duplicate the Red channel by dragging it to the New Channel icon (next to the trash can). Double-click on the Red copy channel name to see Channel options. Choose Spot Color to change this to a Spot Channel. Click the swatch, and then click the Custom button to choose the Pantone Coated color Red 032. Click OK. The channel is automatically renamed. Change Solidity to 25%. Click OK.

The name of the channel will appear on the negative to indicate which spot color ink should be used to print.

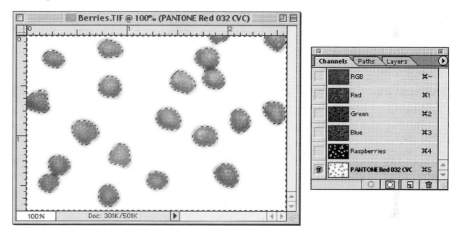

4. Everything on this channel that is black will print in the Red 032 ink. But we don't want to print red over the blueberries. With the Pantone Red 032 CVC channel active, choose Select>Load Selection>Raspberries, and check Invert to select everything but the raspberries. Feather the selection 2 pixels, and press Option-Delete/Alt-Backspace (Fill white).

5. Often a bump plate is most effective as a highly contrasted image. With this channel active, choose Select>Inverse to return to the raspberries, then change the Levels setting to a black point of 45 and a white point of 159. Click OK.

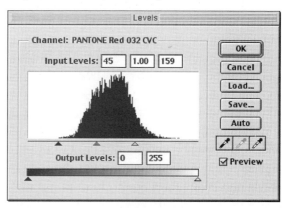

6. Click on the RGB channel to see the color image, then click the visibility icon next to the spot channel on and off to witness the effect.

7. Deselect and save the file as a Photoshop file to your **Work in Progress** folder as Berries.PSD. Leave it open for the next exercise.

Varnishes can be used in a variety of ways. They can be used to completely cover a page or apply spot coverage just over the shape of certain subjects in the image. Gloss and dull varnishes can be used creatively as drop shadows to images, or even as patterns and logos that overprint the entire page in clear varnish for a subliminal effect.

Create a Varnish Plate

1. In the open file, make Raspberries the active channel. Select Command/Control-I to invert the channel.

2. Double-click on the name of the channel, and rename it "Varnish". Choose Spot color to change it into a Spot channel. Click the swatch to define its color as anything in contrast to the image so that it can be distinguished from the image. Set the Solidity to 20%. Return to this dialog box, and reset it to 0% once you are convinced the position is correct — varnish has no color.

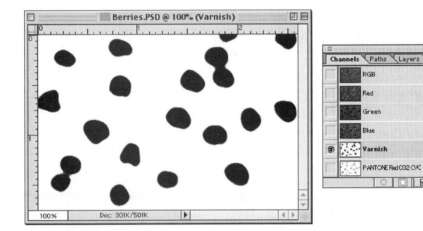

3. Convert the image to CMYK, and save it as "Berries.EPS" to your **Work in Progress** folder using the Photoshop DCS 2.0 file format. In the DCS 2.0 Format dialog box, set Preview: TIFF (8 Bits/Pixel), DCS: Single File with Color Composite (72 Pixel/inch). This enables you to retain the spot channels so that you can place the image in a page-layout program. (DCS: Multiple Files with Color Composite may be required for your output procedure).

4. Save and close the file.

When using spot channels, always save to a DCS 2.0 file format and output to a PostScript level 2 or higher RIP. Use a Single or Multiple file, depending on your procedures. Macintoshes usually use Binary encoding, while output devices driven by Windows prefer ASCII. If problems occur, try ASCII anyway. Due to their encoding, ASCII files take longer to print.

We have set the file up with TIF preview and ASCII encoding, since these settings allow the image to be viewed and output correctly on either Macintosh or Windows-based computers.

Spot Color Images

Spot channels make it possible to create original images in Photoshop or convert images from vector art while maintaining the separation of colors and viewing the composite. The image on a spot channel can be created in virtually any way in which other images are generated in Photoshop, including using filters, as long as the desired "ink" channel is active.

Create a Spot Color

1. Open **Spot.EPS** from the **SF-Adv Photoshop** folder. It contains paths, copied from Adobe Illustrator, which will be used to screenprint a repeating pattern on ceramics and textiles.

2. Open the Channels, Paths, and Color palettes. If they are combined, drag each tab to a separate position. The image itself is blank. With the Paths palette active, load the Gold 15% tint path as a selection by clicking on the Load Paths as Selection icon.

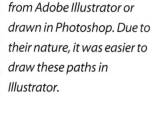

Paths may be imported from Adobe Illustrator or drawn in Photoshop. Due to their nature, it was easier to draw these paths in Illustrator.

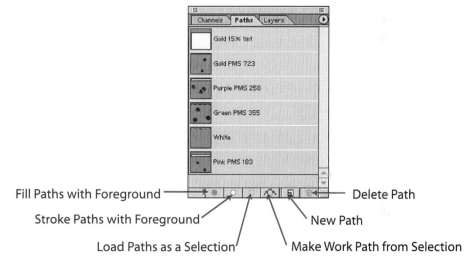

Fill Paths with Foreground ——— Delete Path

Stroke Paths with Foreground ——— New Path

Load Paths as a Selection ——— Make Work Path from Selection

3. From the Channels palette menu, choose New Spot Channel. Click on the swatch, then click Custom, and type "723" to define the ink that this channel will print and display. Click OK. You may need to type the name of the channel, Pantone 723 CVC. Change Solidity to 75% to simulate opaque inks. Click OK.

New Spot Channel

Name: Pantone 723 CVC   OK

Ink Characteristics   Cancel

Color: Solidity: 75 %

Photoshop sometimes remembers the name of the last channel selected manually for a spot color channel (in this case, it may be Varnish).

The selection is automatically filled with 100% color and is deselected. But this area will be a light background for the pattern, only a 15% tint of Pantone 723.

Spot channels listed at the bottom of the Channels palette appear to cover those listed above. In reality, all channels overprint solid images (they don't automatically knock out anything).

4. With the Pantone 723 CVC channel active, reload the Gold 15% path, and press Delete (white). Change the foreground color to 15% (black) via the Color palette. Press Option-Delete/Alt-Backspace to fill with the foreground color. Then revert the colors back to their default by pressing "D".

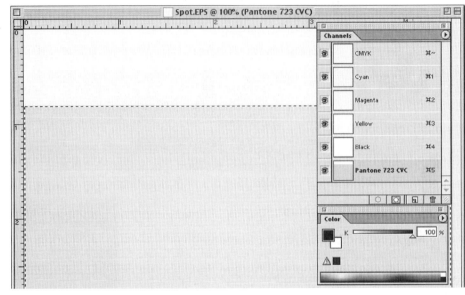

5. With the Pantone 723 CVC channel active, load the path labeled Gold PMS 723 as a selection. Press Option-Delete/Alt-Backspace to fill with 100% color. While this channel is active, everything created will print in gold. Deselect.

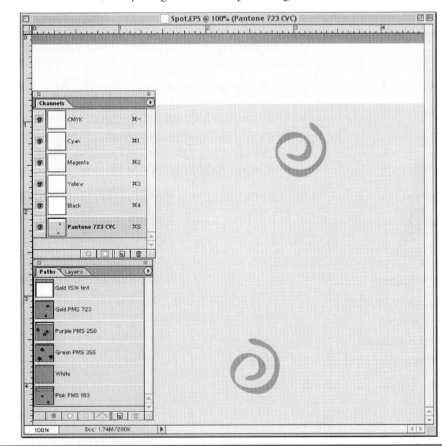

6. Again choose New Spot Channel from the Channels palette menu. This time select Pantone 258 CVC (Purple) as the ink color. Leave the solidity at 75%. Alter the channel name as needed.

7. At the top of the Paths palette, Command/Control-click on the path named Purple PMS 258 to make it a selection. Press Option-Delete/Alt-Backspace to fill it with color; it should appear purple on top of the gold. Deselect.

When creating type for spot color channels, use the Type Mask tool. The regular Type tool will add color to the RGB or CMYK channels.

8. Repeat this process for a Green spot channel (Pantone 355 CVC). Fill the selection made from the Green PMS 355 path with 100% color. Then create a White spot channel. Since Pantone doesn't list white, use any light color, but be certain to rename it "White" so that it appears on the negative (Cool Gray 1 CVC is a good choice.). Use the White path to fill small circles around the green squiggle. Create one more spot channel for Pink PMS 183, and use the Pink path. When you're finished, the image and channels should look like the ones that follow.

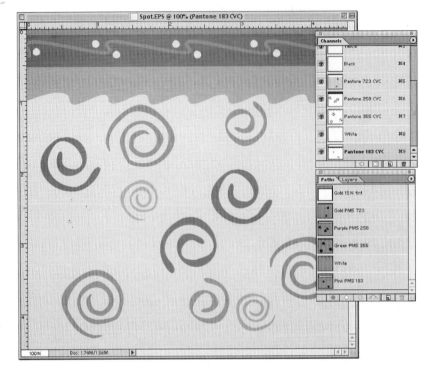

9. We'll add some type to be printed in white over the purple and pink bars. Activate the White channel, and choose the Type Mask tool. Click on the left of the pink image at the crest of the waves. In the Type dialog box, select 36-point ATC Yucatan and type: "Albuquerque, New Mexico". Position the type, press Command-Return or Control-Enter to confirm, and Fill with Foreground color (Option-Delete/Alt-Backspace). Don't deselect.

Type or any element can be on a separate layer as well as appearing on its correct spot channel. Be careful to select the layer, then reselect the spot channel to make certain that the desired pixels are edited.

10. The Pink PMS 183 spot channel is listed below the White in the Channels palette; therefore it blocks us from seeing the white type. Drag the White channel below Pantone 183 in the list.

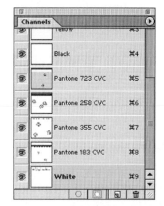

11. Leave the file open for the next exercise. Do not deselect the type.

Shifting the order of spot channels is only for display purposes. Spot channels do not knock out anything, but instead overprint just as the grayscale channel indicates. Manual knockouts and traps must be created. In this case, the type should knock out of the pink and purple where necessary, and slightly spread into the darker colors.

Trap Spot Colors

1. In the open file, use the current selection of the type, and activate the Pantone 183 CVC channel (Pink). Press the Delete/Backspace key to create a pixel-perfect knock-out. Activate the Pantone 258 channel, and press the Delete key again to knock out that part.

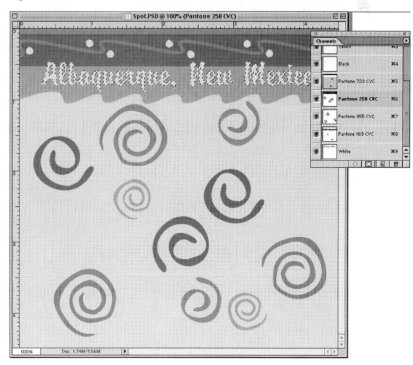

2. Return to the White channel for the spread. To create the overlap, we'll spread the selection. Choose Image>Trap. Select a width of 2 pixels. This automatically spreads light areas into dark ones. (As a rule of thumb, expand 1 pixel for every 100 pixels of resolution.) Notice the overlapping effect. This is a trap. Click OK and deselect.

3. Choose Image>Mode>Multichannel.

4. Recombine the palettes by dragging their tabs into one another, forming the original groups or select Window>Reset Palette Locations.

5. Save the file as "Spot.EPS", to Photoshop DCS 2.0 format, to your **Work in Progress** folder.

Summary

You have learned to perform a number of advanced functions in this chapter. You have added depth to images and created realistic reflections. You have also mixed channels from different images to achieve distinctive effects. In addition, you have learned to create channel libraries, which will make your work flow smoother. You have learned about, and used, special channels for varnish and bumping the value of colors. You have also learned how to create and trap spot colors in a Photoshop image.

ADVANCED SELECTION TECHNIQUES

CHAPTER OBJECTIVE:

To understand the different ways in which selections can be made and used. To study multiple tool selections. To understand the makeup of specific image types in order to choose the best selection process. In Chapter 6, you will:

- Become familiar with the methods for creating selections.

- Learn how selections are made, and experience working with difficult selections.

- Become familiar with the Magic Wand tool, and discover how to adjust the Magic Wand's selection sensitivity with the Tolerance setting.

- Learn how to use density masking.

- Learn how to create custom mezzotints using density masking.

- Become familiar with the Color Range command, and appreciate both its power and its limitations.

- Learn how to use Quick Mask.

- Learn to use the Magic Eraser and the Background Eraser effectively.

- Observe how to and experience extracting delicate elements of images using the Extract command.

PROJECTS TO BE COMPLETED:

- Just Shoot Me (A)
- Baby Shower Invitation (B)
- Retouching the Jones Family Portrait (C)
- The Fix Is In! (D)
- Makeover (E)
- Photomat (F)

Add to a selection by holding the Shift key while drawing a new selection marquee; subtract from an existing selection by holding the Option/Alt key.

Advanced Selection Techniques

Selections can be made in a number of different ways; and the resulting selections can be used in many more ways. Some of the Photoshop tools that can be used for creating selections are the Marquee, Lasso, Magic Wand, and Type Mask selection tools. The Pen, Freeform Pen, and shape tools create paths which can be converted to selections. Selections can be made on the basis of color. They can also be made by painting in Quick Mask mode or painting in a layer mask or alpha channel, or by using Select>All.

Selections can be created with a single tool, or by using a combination of tools to add to and subtract from a selection. During this process, the selection can be saved to an alpha channel or to a Layer mask, which can be updated as the selection is further refined.

When Inverse is selected, a selection is inverted, changing the previously unselected pixels to selected, and the formerly selected pixels to unselected.

Each of these methods, with the exception of Select All, can generate a mask that protects the unselected pixels from change.

Using Selections

Once a selection is made, a localized effect or transformation can be applied without affecting the rest of the image. The hue, or color, of a model's sweater can be changed from blue to red without changing her skin tones. The Dust & Scratches filter can be localized to fix just the damaged portion of the image. The background portion of an image can be deleted to silhouette an object. A selection can be used to define an edge for the application of an airbrushed shadow.

Difficult Selections

In this chapter, we will explore some enhancements to the standard selection methods, based on emphasizing density and color differences to define more clearly a tonal edge for our selection tools.

Rarely will you encounter a natural image that does not require the use of more than a single tool and/or technique to produce a high-quality selection.

At times, simply grabbing the Lasso tool and painfully executing a selection will simply not work. Examples abound in the real world, but two in particular exemplify the problem: hair and foliage. Both are so random in nature and so prone to creating an impossible-to-draw edge that creating silhouettes of such elements is difficult to do well.

We're going to make a selection involving foliage. Hair — or anything else that presents complex edges — would work the same way. But first, let's review the controls for adding to and subtracting from a selection, which we will practice in the following exercise.

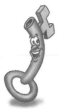

Make Multiple Tool Selections

1. Select New from the File menu, and set the options for an Untitled document window as follows; then click OK.

   Width: 6 in., Height: 4 in., Resolution: 72 pixels/inch, Mode: Grayscale, Contents: White

Notice that each tool now has an options bar that floats at the top of the screen. The functions we are about to discuss are also available in this bar.

2. Press "M" to select the Rectangular Marquee tool. If necessary, rotate through the marquee tools by repeatedly pressing Shift-M until the correct tool is active. Draw two non-overlapping rectangles by holding the Shift key as you draw the second rectangle.

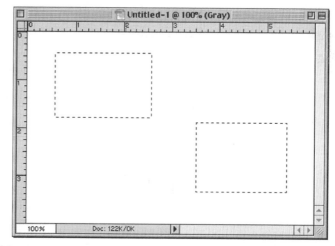

Alternately, you may choose to switch tools by unchecking the Use Shift Key for Tool Switch box under Edit>Preferences> General.

3. Press "L" for the Lasso tool, and if necessary, rotate to it by pressing Shift-L. Hold the Shift key, and draw a small looping selection that intersects a corner of each rectangle.

4. Press "M", then Shift-M to select the Oval Marquee tool. Hold the Option/Alt key or click the Subtract from Selection box in the Options toolbar, and draw a small oval within the first rectangle. This will subtract from the selection.

5. Begin subtracting another oval shape within the second rectangular selection, then add the Shift key. This will subtract a circle. Wait until you've started dragging with the Option/Alt key selected or this will not work.

You may also choose to add to a selection by clicking the Add to Selection box in the Options toolbar.

6. Select Edit>Fill, then fill the selection with the foreground color.

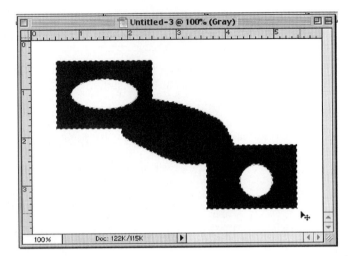

Press Command/Control-Shift-V to access Paste into without using the mouse.

7. Open the file **Market Oranges.TIF** from your **SF-Adv Photoshop** folder. Press Command/Control-A to select all, Command/Control-C to copy the image, and Command/Control-W to close the Oranges image.

8. With the Untitled window open, choose Paste Into from the Edit menu.

9. Close the file without saving.

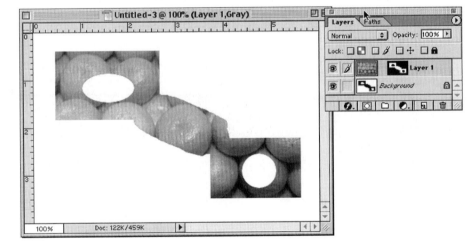

The Magic Wand Tool

You are probably already familiar with the Magic Wand tool. It was discussed in *Adobe Photoshop 6: Introduction to Digital Imaging*. Consider this a refresher. The Magic Wand's selection sensitivity is adjusted with the Tolerance setting in units of tone levels. For example, if the Tolerance setting is 10 levels, the Magic Wand selection will spread from the point of selection to include up to 10 adjacent tone levels, both toward the lighter and darker ends of the scale. The tolerance and various other settings are found in the floating options bar at the top of the screen.

Click on a tool in the Tool palette to access the Options palette for that tool.

The tonal range of an 8-bit grayscale image is comprised of 256 levels. (We'll ignore color for the moment.) The grayscale ramp in the following image shows this tonal range. When the Magic Wand tolerance setting is 3, the selection spreads from the point at which the tool is clicked on the gradient to include tones that are three levels above and below this initially selected level — a total of 6 levels. When the tolerance is set to 10, the selection covers a total of 20 levels around the initial point; a tolerance of 50 generates a 100-level selection; and a tolerance setting of 128 will select the entire image, if the initial point of selection is in the center of the gradient.

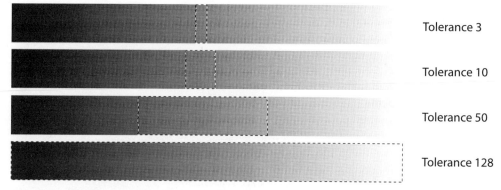

Tolerance 3

Tolerance 10

Tolerance 50

Tolerance 128

Note how the range increases dynamically, progressing through tolerances of 3, 10, 50, and 128.

Use the Magic Wand Selector

1. Open the image **The Tree.TIF** from your **SF-Adv Photoshop** folder. Zoom into the edge of the foliage where it meets the sky. Notice how detailed the edge is between the tree and the sky.

2. Zoom out so that you can see the entire image on your monitor. Select the Magic Wand tool. Move the cursor to the options bar, and set the Tolerance level to 16. Click in the sky anywhere except in the rainbow.

You can add functionality to the Magic Wand tool by choosing whether or not to have the tool select only contiguous pixels or add those of similar color from other areas.

You can supplement the Magic Wand tool with the Select>Similar menu function. This command will extend the selection to include areas of similar tone levels in other parts of the image that are not contiguous with the initial selection.

3. Deselect the area. Set the Tolerance to 64, and click in the blue portion of the sky. When the selection appears, choose Select>Similar; this will select all of the sky, including some small areas totally surrounded by foliage. You may choose to set the options bar to allow the tool to select noncontiguous areas by unchecking the Contiguous box.

With minor cleanup you could probably get away with the selection mask we've created so far; however, there are more accurate ways to make complex selections.

4. Leave the image open for the next exercise.

Use Density Masking

1. In the open image, press Command/Control-D to deselect the current selection.

   Since each channel of an image contains the primary component of the particular color (red, green, and blue, for example), you would think that the most tone in this file is contained in the Green channel. And so it is. Activate the Channels palette, and select and examine the Green channel.

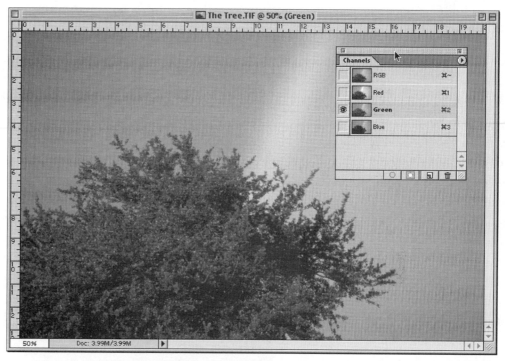

There is a good range of tones in the Green channel, showing a generous amount of detail in the shadows and midtones.

2. Now look at the Blue channel. There's a good amount of contrast but not much detail in the tree.

This is the channel we're going to use, because for masking purposes we don't want a range of tones — we need edges.

When the contiguous box is checked, only pixels within the specified tolerance that touch one another will be included in the selection. If it is unchecked, all pixels in the image that meet the tolerance criteria will be selected.

This is a technique that will yield variable results based on the characteristics of the individual image. At times, as in the case of the tree image, a simple contrast adjustment to one of the color channels will generate a nearly perfect mask. Using the Density Masking approach rather than the Magic Wand tool will save you clicks and time. In other situations, you will have to experiment with Brightness and Contrast — and even the mixing of channels using the Calculate commands.

Duplicate a channel by dragging it to the New Channel icon at the bottom of the Channels palette.

3. Duplicate the Blue channel, and name it "Mask".

4. There are several ways to approach the problem of getting a clean selection, as is often the case when working in Photoshop. The goal is to arrive at a clean white sky and black foliage. Make two copies of the image so that you can compare the results.

   a. Working in the Mask channel of the original image, select Image>Adjust>Levels. Adjust the sliders as shown until the sky is clean white and the foliage is black.

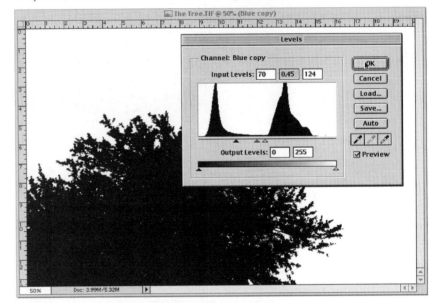

   b. Alternately you may choose to use Brightness/Contrast or Curves to get to this point. Try this using one of the copies you made.

   c. Using the other copy, apply a 1.2 pixel gaussian blur, and then select to Image>Adjust>Threshold. This will close all the small white spots inside the foliage. Notice the jagged edge left by the threshold command. Apply the blur again to smooth the edge of the selection.

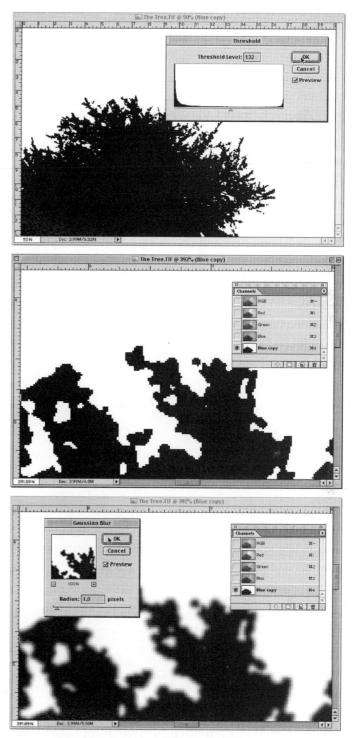

5. Compare the results from the three methods that you used. Pick the result you like best and close the other two images without saving.

6. Return to the Composite channel and load the Mask selection.

7. Save the image as "Masked Tree.TIF" to your **Work in Progress** folder. Leave the file open for the next exercise, where we will apply a mezzotint effect to the sky.

If you drop the Contrast to –100, you'll have a perfectly neutral gray. Then simply increase the brightness until the sky disappears.

Making an Overlay Image

A fun technique to try is to use a density mask as an overlay image on a layer. Since the shape of the mask exactly matches the sky background, you can create some dramatic painting effects in the sky while retaining the image qualities of the tree.

Create Custom Mezzotints with Density Masking

1. In the open file, activate the Layers palette, and drag the Background layer onto the New Layer icon to create a copy of the layer.

2. The Background Copy layer should be active with the Mask selection loaded. Select Image>Adjust>Brightness/Contrast. Adjust both sliders until you've overexposed the sky and removed most of its color. Click OK

3. Set the Blending mode of the layer to Dissolve, and set the layer Opacity to 40%.

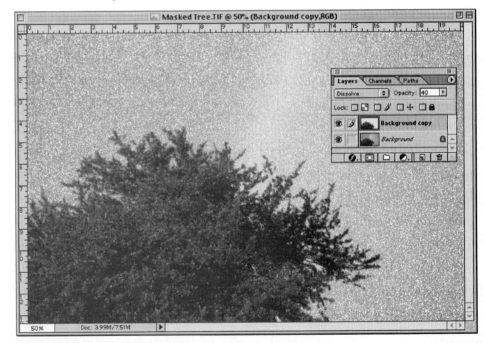

   This produces a mezzotinted sky and rainbow, with the tree untouched by the effect.

4. Deselect the Mask selection. The Mezzotint now includes the tree, although it's a little hard to see.

5. Choose Image>Adjust>Threshold. Move the slider toward the right to create a darker mezzotint, to the left to create a lighter mezzotint. Experiment with it. A lighter effect will give the impression that there is snow on the tree. Click OK when you are happy with the result.

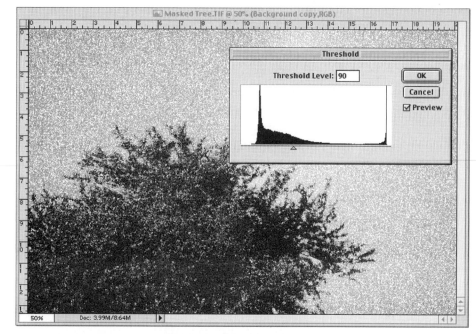

6. Save the image to your **Work in Progress** folder as "Masked Tree.PSD", then press Command/Control-E to flatten the image.

    The mezzotint may appear to change, depending on the zoom factor currently active for your image. This is simply a screen artifact — the data is unchanged.

7. Choose Filter>Blur>Blur, then choose Filter>Sharpen>Sharpen. This will eliminate any moiré patterns created by overlaying the dissolved Threshold layer on the Background image. Look closely at the image.

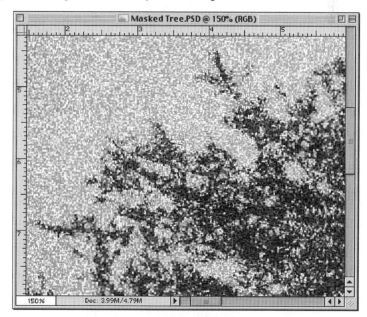

Using variations on this theme, you could create many types of textures, resulting in some excellent mezzotint and patterned effects. While you may see an undesirable patterning in the image you have created, the exercise is useful to demonstrate how you approach this process.

8. Now apply Revert to the file, then change the blending mode of the Background Copy layer back to Normal. Leave Opacity at 40%. Select Filter>Pixelate>Mezzotint; use the Fine Dots option. That should make your image more appealing.

9. Close the file without saving.

Using the Color Range Command

The Color Range command is similar to the Magic Wand tool, but it's considerably more powerful. This brief exercise will help familiarize you with how it works.

Create Masks Based on Color Range

1. Open the image **Shell.TIF** from your **SF-Adv Photoshop** folder.

2. Click the Eyedropper tool in the Toolbox. In the Options toolbar, set the Sample Size to Point Sample in order to narrowly select the colors that we want to affect.

3. We want to make a selection that includes mostly the beach. Choose Select>Color Range. Set the following options in the dialog box:

Select: Sampled Colors
Fuzziness: 46
Click the Selection radio button
Selection Preview: None

Often, threshold adjustments can isolate the edges of images whose contrast has been increased. Try this to generate line art from black-and-white photographs, especially product shots or other images containing lots of lines and curves.

4. Select the middle Eyedropper. Click on the sand to the left of the shell. Notice that the preview box has changed to black-and-white, and a high-contrast mask is beginning to take shape. Click OK.

A moiré is an undesirable artifact generated by pairs of dot or line patterns that fall in a regular, repeating, reinforcing sequence, thus resulting in the appearance of a series of parallel and/or crossed lines.

5. Select Layer>New Adjustment Layer>Levels, and click OK to accept the default name of Levels 1. Move the middle slider to 0.38 and click OK.

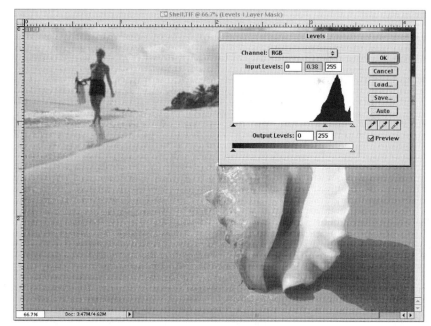

In general, you will have to clean up your selections. In certain situations, a simple click may grab everything you want. Experiment with the Fuzziness control. This increases the tolerance of the Eyedroppers, and it extends what is already selected to match the new tolerance. The pop-up menu at the top of the dialog box provides for selection of specific color channels (red, green, blue) and tonal ranges (highlight, midtone, shadow).

6. Choose a large soft brush with black as the foreground color. Paint in the adjustment layer mask to bring the highlights in the sky and shell back to their original brilliance. If you paint outside the area that you wish to brighten, switch to white, and use a smaller brush for touch-up.

7. Adjust the Opacity slider of the adjustment layer to about 77% or until the sand is darker than it was before we applied the adjustment layer, without being too dark.

8. Turn off the adjustment layer, and highlight the background layer. Using the Type Mask tool, type the words "Shell Game" in ATC Yucatan, 36 pt.

9. Copy and paste (Command/Control>C, Command/Control>V) the resulting selection to place the type on a new layer. Move the new layer above the Levels adjustment layer.

10. Double-click the new layer and check Drop Shadow.

   Set the Structure as follows:
   Blend Mode: Multiply, Opacity: 75%, Angle: 130°, Distance: 5 pixels, Spread: 0%, Size: 5 pixels. Do not click OK.

11. Check Bevel and Emboss.

Set the Structure as follows:
Style: Inner Bevel, Technique: Smooth, Depth: 100%, Direction: Up, Size: 5 pixels, Soften: 0 pixel.

Do not click OK. Continue to set the emboss settings:

Set the Shading as follows:
Angle: 130°, Altitude: 30°, Highlight Mode: Screen, Opacity: 75%, Shadow Mode: Multiply, Opacity: 75%. Click OK and deselect.

12. Save the file to your **Work in Progress** folder as "Shell by Range.PSD".

Select by Color Range is a tool that allows the digital artist to apply what is known as the 90-10 workflow. This means doing 90% of the work in 10% of the time, leaving 90% of the allotted time to refine the final 10% of the job. Since it is these subtle tweaks that separate the pros from the amateurs, the ability to select a complex subject quickly and then refine the selection using any of the painting tools is very powerful.

Creative Techniques

If you modify the suggested steps above, your composition could look quite different from what is pictured here. Techniques covered elsewhere in this course, especially the chapters on Layers (Chapters 7 and 11) and Special Effects (Chapter 13), will give you more ideas for your personal creative expression. Experiment with the Selection and Blending effects to see where they can take you.

As is the case when creating realistic drop shadows under type or generating highlight and shadow masks, these are techniques that you should try to practiced and keep well honed. Learning to create complex selections takes time — it is not a skill that just comes to you when you see it for the first time. Whenever you have to make a complex selection, consider using the masking techniques covered here.

Using Quick Mask Mode

Quick Mask mode allows you to create or edit selections with Photoshop's standard painting tools. This can be extremely useful when creating complex selections.

Paint Selections in Quick Mask

1. With the Shell.TIF image in which you created a Color Range selection still open, delete Layer 1.

2. Under the Foreground/Background color selectors in the Toolbox are two dotted Circle icons. The second (a small, filled, dotted circle) changes the mode of Photoshop from Normal to Quick Mask. Load the selection from the Levels Adjustment Layer. Click the Quick Mask icon once, or press "Q", and see what happens.

The masked areas (outside the selection) have been covered with the digital equivalent of Rubylith, showing you exactly where you have to fix the selection. The Quick Mask feature provides you with the ability to display your selection clearly as you are refining it. The paradigm of painting and erasing the selection is conceptually more comfortable for many users. In addition this method allows for unlimited editing. You can work the file without fear until it is just the way you want it.

3. Select a small, hard, preferably angled brush. Press "D" to set the default colors. With black as the foreground color, begin to paint over areas that should have been left out of the selection. As you paint, the Rubylith grows to cover the painted regions.

4. Press "X" to switch from foreground to background, and paint areas you wish to remove from the selection. This is often necessary when you use Color Range, since a small amount of a tone within a portion of the image can be inadvertently selected because it falls within the selected range.

5. Complete the selection using Quick Mask mode. Click the Normal mode button (the left button) to exit Quick Mask mode and turn the mask into a selection.

Rubylith (and its companion, Amberlith) is opaqueing film used to mask areas of film negatives.

6. When you're done, save the selection into its own alpha channel, then save the image as "Shell Mask.PSD" to your **Work in Progress** folder. Close the file.

Selections and Paths

As you know, paths can be used to generate vector-based selections. They are similar to the paths used in Adobe Illustrator and Macromedia Freehand. For very complex selections, channels are the way to go. When creating simpler selections, however, compared to alpha channel selections, paths keep the file size smaller. In addition, paths offer the distinct advantage of being able to create long, smooth curves.

Paths can be exported with an image and used as a clipping path. When an EPS file with a clipping path is placed into a page-layout program such as QuarkXPress or Adobe InDesign, the area outside of the path is clipped to transparent.

Paths may be converted to or from selections. In some cases, they result in much smoother selections than may be achieved using conventional selection tools.

Use Paths as Selections

1. Open the image **White Vanda.TIF** from your **SF-Advanced Photoshop** folder.

2. Choose the Pen tool (Press "P"). Choose the Create New Work Path option from the Options toolbar.

3. Enlarge the image to the point that individual pixels begin to show (about 400%). Click on the edge of the flower to place the first anchor point. Move a short distance along the edge of the flower and click again. This time hold and drag to curve the path segment to follow the curve of the edge. Note that you can only curve the line in one direction at a time, so choose each segment with that in mind.

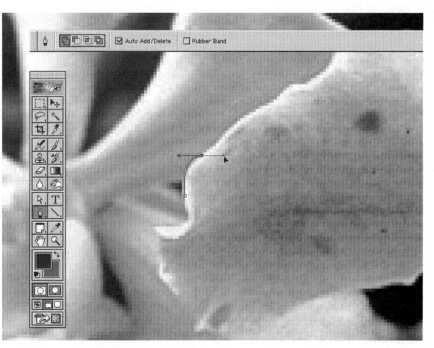

4. Proceed around the flower until the path is complete. The last segment closes the path when it is attached to the first anchor point. A small circle shows next to the cursor when the last point is reached.

5. Double-click the name Work Path in the Paths palette, and rename the path "One Flower".

Using the Pen tool to create paths in Photoshop is identical to using the Pen tool in drawing programs such as Adobe Illustrator and Macromedia FreeHand. The process was discussed in some detail in Adobe Photoshop: Introduction to Digital Images.

6. If needed, zoom in on the path and use the Direct Selection tool (the white pointer) to select and adjust points for a more accurate selection. (Click and hold the Path Component Selection tool to activate the pop-up menu if the Direct Selection tool is hidden.) Careful attention when drawing the path will minimize the need for adjustment.

Examine the Pen tool fly-out palette in the Tool palette.

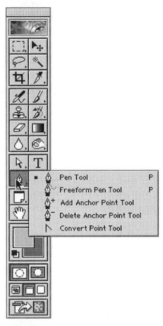

To add points, use the Add Point tool (the Pen tool with the plus sign). To subtract points, use the Remove Point tool (the Pen tool with the minus sign). To change a curve point into a sharp corner, click on the point with the tool on the far right of the palette (the Convert Point tool). To adjust the position of path segments and anchor points, use the Arrow tool. The Freeform tool allows freehand drawing.

7. When you are satisfied that the path is as close as you can get it, click the third button at the bottom of the Paths palette (the make selection icon).

8. Save the selection to a new channel. Press Command/Control-D to deselect.

9. Choose Save As, and check the As a Copy box to save the file as "White Vanda Path.PSD" to your **Work in Progress** folder. Leave the file open for the next exercise.

Use the Pen or Lasso?

The decision whether to use the Pen tool or the Lasso tool — actually, any non-pen selection tool or technique — unfortunately often comes down to "How can I avoid using the Pen tool?" Too many of us have never mastered the drawing techniques that make using the Pen tool enjoyable and effective.

If you need to create an EPS silhouette of an image or wish to create a smooth, flowing selection, the Pen should be the tool of choice. A clipping path is not limited to selection borders and can cut across pixels. As you develop a path, you can save it in the Paths palette, along with other paths that you have created.

You can also save multiple selections in an image file as alpha channels; and these can be used to generate complex masks for a number of special effects. When selecting a tool, try to select the best tool for the job, not simply the one that is easiest for you to use.

Selections with the Magnetic Lasso

The Magnetic Lasso tool incorporates a level of programmed intelligence that can identify an edge (difference) between an object and background. Of course, the intensity and contrast will vary in different images, and there are several option settings that allow you to tune the Magnetic Lasso tool to suit the conditions.

Option Settings

Selecting the Magnetic Lasso tool will display the Tool Options bar and several setting options:

- **Width**. This setting, from 1 to 40 pixels, determines the width of the area in which the tool looks for an edge that it can follow. You can follow a well-defined edge by using a quick tracing movement with a higher width value; for a softer edge, you can use a smaller width value with a precise tracing technique.

- **Edge Contrast**. This setting, from 1% to 100%, specifies the sensitivity to the edge you are following. Raising this value will cause lower-contrast edges to be ignored. Lowering this setting will allow the Magnetic Lasso tool to follow edges lacking in sharpness.

- **Frequency**. This setting determines the rate at which anchor points will be set. Increasing the value, between 0 and 100, increases the precision of the Path/Selection border. To follow detail more precisely, use a higher frequency.

General Magnetic Techniques

Follow these basics when using the Magnetic Lasso, and you'll maximize its benefits as a selection tool. After clicking a starting point on the edge, you can release the mouse button as you trace the edge of the object with the cursor. If your Selection border begins to go astray, you can back up and press the Delete key as many times as necessary to remove the wayward anchor point(s). To assure accuracy, click anchor points as necessary as you move the cursor around the edge of the image.

If the image has a sharp edge with good contrast, use a higher width value and more Edge Contrast and trace the edge rapidly. If the edge is less distinct, use a lower width value, less Edge Contrast, and follow the edge more carefully.

You can close the Selection border by one of the following procedures:

- Move the cursor over the first anchor point and click when you see the Close Selection Border icon — the tool icon with a small circle to the lower right.

- Double-click or press Return/Enter to close the selection with a freehand magnetic segment.

- Hold Option/Alt and double-click to close the selection with a straight-line segment.

Once the selection or path is created, you can use the standard techniques to modify its shape. We will now use the Magnetic Lasso tool to silhouette the single foreground orchid blossom.

Draw with the Magnetic Lasso

1. With the **White Vanda Mask.TIF** image still open, click on the Magnetic Lasso tool and reset the tool options from the Options bar.

2. Click on the edge of the flower to start creating the Selection border. A corner may be a good place to start, but it is not required. Release the mouse button, and follow the edge of the flower with your cursor.

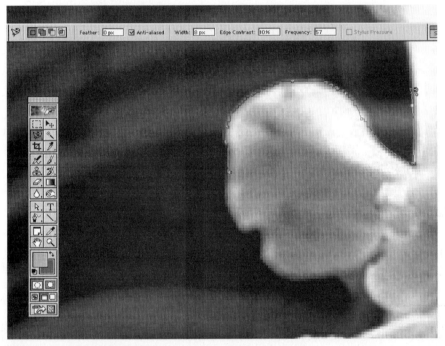

3. When you return to your starting point, look for the small circle beside the cursor, indicating that you can close the selection with a click.

4. From the Paths Palette menu, select Make Selection, Anti-aliased, with a Feather Radius of 2 pixels.

5. Press "L" to select the Lasso tool, and touch up any part of the edge that did not form accurately. (Check the bottom of the blossom where it is cropped at the lower edge.)

6. With the Lasso tool still selected, Control/Right-Click and choose Layer Via Copy from the contextual menu. This will place a copy of the blossom in a new layer with a transparent background.

7. In the Layers palette, turn off the display of the Background layer by clicking off the visibility icon. You can now see the blossom on a transparent background.

8. Option/Alt-double-click on the layer to rename it "One Flower".

9. Switch to the Move tool. Command/Control-click on the One Flower layer to select all non-transparent pixels in the layer.

10. To clean up the edge of the blossom, choose Select>Modify>Border. Set the width to 2 pixels.

11. To perform a visual check on the effect of deleting a 2-pixel border around the blossom, press Command/Control-H to hide the edges — the marching ants — of the selection. The selection is still active, so when you press the Delete key, 2 pixels are trimmed off the blossom edge. If that is too much to suit your taste, apply Undo (or go back in the History palette) and reset the border selection to 1 pixel.

12. At this point the image is ready to be used as an element in a composite or on its own as a silhouette. Save the document as "White Vanda Mask.PSD" to your **Work in Progress** folder, and close the file.

Image Extraction

Photoshop users have tools specifically designed for removing or altering background elements and isolating foreground elements for numerous creative and production tasks. It should be noted, however, that these tools do not actually create a mask but delete pixel information. For this reason, working on a copy of your paint layer is prudent. After you have isolated the image from its background, it can be selected quickly and a layer mask generated. This allows for editing as well as preserving pixel information.

Once background pixels are deleted, the remaining image can be placed in a collage with other Photoshop images, or a clipping path can be created so that the silhouetted image can be placed in a page-layout document. Other uses include GIF files for Web use, preserving the transparency of the background pixels.

In previous versions of Photoshop, masking could only be accomplished by selecting and deleting pixels considered to be background elements, such as an area of sky behind a subject. If the background area was uniform, the process was easier. Complex backgrounds typically took longer to select and delete.

The Eraser Tools

The Magic Eraser and the Background Eraser — both grouped with the standard Eraser tool in the Toolbox — are two of the tools available for deleting background pixels. The standard Eraser tool performs one of two separate functions. If the document is flattened, the Eraser simply applies the background color to the image. If it is layered, it deletes the pixels on the current layer, making that area transparent. Even with precise brush shapes and a steady hand, however, the Eraser is generally not an efficient means of deleting background pixels.

The Magic Eraser functions in a similar manner to the Magic Wand and Paint Bucket tools. Instead of selecting or applying the foreground color, however, this tool deletes the pixels on which you click. If the tolerance is set high, more pixels are deleted than if it is set low. Also, like the Magic Wand and Paint Bucket tools, the Magic Eraser is not limited to contiguous pixels.

The Magic Eraser works well with backgrounds that are relatively uniform. For more complex backgrounds, the Background Eraser is more appropriate. It deletes pixels based on a sampling taken at the first mouse click, and can be configured to protect (not delete) the foreground color.

Use the Magic Eraser

1. Open **Pokey.TIF** from your **SF-Adv Photoshop** folder. (If offered the option, do not convert color when opening.) Make sure the Layers palette is visible.

2. Double-click Background in the Layers palette to convert it into a normal layer. Leave the Opacity setting at 100% and the Mode as Normal. Duplicate the layer and turn off the visibility icon (eyeball) of the original.

3. Select the Magic Eraser tool. Its options display automatically in the Options bar. Set its Tolerance to 32, its Opacity to 100%, and leave Anti-aliasing on. Be sure to check the Contiguous option. Use All Layers should be unchecked.

4. Click on an area of sky in the photograph. If you are not happy with the results, select Undo and experiment with different Tolerance settings. Toggle the visibility icon of the original layer on and off to see how well the Magic Eraser did its job.

5. Open **Clouds.TIF** from your **SF-Adv Photoshop** folder. (Do not convert color when opening.) Choose Edit>Select All, then Copy, and close the file without saving.

6. In the open **Pokey.TIF** file, select Edit>Paste. Move the layer in the Layers palette so that the clouds are behind the mountain, as shown.

7. Save the file to your **Work in Progress** folder, naming it as "Pokey New.PSD". Close the document.

Use the Background Eraser

1. Open **Poolside 2.TIF** from your **SF-Adv Photoshop** folder. (If offered the option, do not convert color when opening.) Notice that palm leaves divide the sky. If we use the Magic Eraser to delete these noncontiguous pixels, however, we will also delete an area of water, swimsuits, and other areas that should not be affected. Before proceeding, duplicate the background layer. Turn off the background layer by clicking its visibility icon. (Doing this every time saves the original for later use or further retouching.)

2. Select the Background Eraser, and go to the options bar. Select Discontiguous, a Tolerance of 32%, Sampling Once, and check the Protect Foreground Color option.

3. Use the Eyedropper tool (Sample Size: 5 by 5 Average) to change the foreground color to that of the palm leaves. These are the pixels that will be protected during background erasing.

4. Using the Background Eraser tool with a soft-edged, 65-pixel brush, click and drag from the sky into the palm leaves. Notice that the sky pixels enclosed by leaves are deleted, but the leaves themselves are not.

Dragging the Background Eraser from the area to be deleted into its complex surroundings deletes similar pixels in the surroundings, while protecting areas of interest.

5. Spend some time using the Background Eraser to delete the sky, changing the protected foreground color by using the Eyedropper tool in different areas adjoining the sky.

6. Open **Clouds.TIF** from your **SF-Adv Photoshop** folder. (Do not convert color when opening.) Choose Edit>Select All, then Copy, and close the file without saving.

7. Paste the clouds data into the Poolside2.TIF image, move the new layer behind the original one, and use the Move tool to position the clouds.

8. Save the file to your **Work in Progress** folder as "Poolside New.PSD". Close the file.

Extracting Images

In addition to the eraser tools, Photoshop has an Extract command for isolating a foreground object from its background. This procedure uses sophisticated edge detection to determine the shape of the foreground object, even if the edge is wispy or intricate. The trick to using the Extraction command is to ensure that the highlighted area includes both foreground information (that will be extracted) and background information (that will be left behind).

Use the Extract Command

1. Open **Watermelon.TIF** from your **SF-Adv Photoshop** folder. (If offered the option, do not convert color when opening.) Make sure the Layers palette is visible. Note the problematic areas where the subject's fine hair is surrounded by a light green background. Duplicate the background layer. The new layer will be named Layer 0. Turn off the background layer, and highlight the copy (Layer 0).

2. Select Image>Extract to display the Extract window. Choose the Edge Highlighter tool, and set its brush size to 54. Use the tool to outline the subject's hair. If you make a mistake, hold down the Option/Alt key to toggle between the Edge Highlighter and the Eraser.

3. After highlighting the hair, set the Edge Highlighter tool's brush size to 5, and outline the remainder of the subject. Zoom in closely, and use the Grabber Hand tool (hold down the Spacebar) to change your view to more accurately highlight the subject.

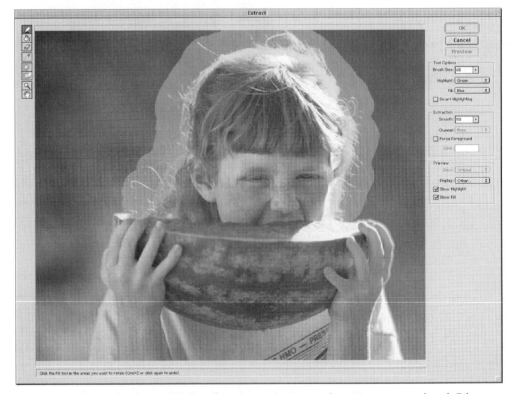

Use a wide brush Edge Highlighter for wispy or intricate edges. Use a narrow brush Edge Highlighter for sharper edges. Check Smart Highlighting to help follow sharp edges.

4. Once you have completely enclosed the subject, select the Paint Bucket tool in the Extract window, and click on the area you want to preserve (the girl).

5. Click the Preview button to see the results. If you are not satisfied, you may edit the highlight with the Edge Highlighter tool and Eraser tools, then refill and preview until you are satisfied.

6. Click OK to extract the image.

7. Create a new layer (Layer 1), and select Layer>Arrange>Send to Back, so that Layer 0 is in front.

8. Create a new foreground color (C: 80, M: 20, Y: 20, K: 40) and a new background color (C: 40, M: 10, Y: 10, K: 20). Use the Gradient tool to draw a foreground-to-background linear gradient from the top to the bottom of Layer 1.

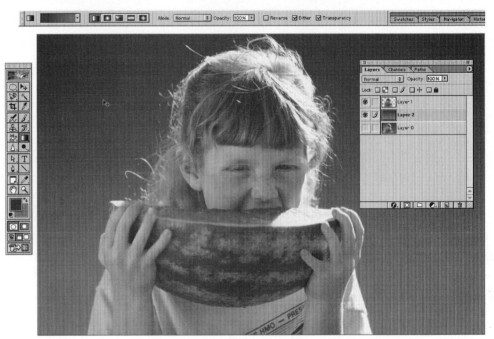

9. If you wish, you may experiment with different backgrounds, or with pasting different images behind the subject. Notice that the subject's hair is accurately silhouetted against the new background. Save the file as "Watermelon Extracted.PSD" to your **Work in Progress** folder, and close it.

Summary

In this chapter, you have reviewed some methods of making selections and learned some new ones. What has been especially important is learning to analyze images to determine the best selection technique to employ. You learned to select elements with advanced selection tools, and also to combine tools and processes, such as in density masking. In addition, you learned to combine different backgrounds with the selections you made in order to create composite images.

CHAPTER 7

ADVANCED LAYERS

CHAPTER OBJECTIVE:

To understand the power and flexibility that layers brings to the design and modification of images. To learn the inherent strategies for using layers. In Chapter 7, you will:

- Learn when it is to your best advantage to use layers in your images.

- Become familiar with how to make changes to images containing layers.

- Learn how to blend layers.

- Learn about layer masks, and how to use them to create composites.

- Discover the use of clipping groups, and learn how to use them to link multiple layers.

PROJECTS TO BE COMPLETED:

- Just Shoot Me (A)

- **Baby Shower Invitation (B)**

- Retouching the Jones Family Portrait (C)

- The Fix Is In! (D)

- Makeover (E)

- Photomat (F)

Advanced Layers

Layering is a powerful technique that allows flexibility in the design and modification of an image. Layers can use up system resources very quickly; therefore, you should plan your documents carefully before working on them.

Some considerations in planning a composite or photo manipulation involving layers are discussed below. The answers to the following questions will determine how many layers you will use, how many layers you will maintain at one time, and how many layers you will keep. To avoid costly delays at the end of a project, it is important to answer as many of these questions as possible before you begin your work.

Strategies for Using Layers

- **What is your largest final use for this image?**
  Before you begin, you should be certain that all of your source images are suitable for the final size of the piece on which you are working, and all images that will be composited are of compatible resolution. Otherwise, you may end up degrading image quality by enlarging or stretching them too much. This strategy helps to avoid creating an entire composite, only to discover that it's too small to print correctly.

- **Will you keep the individual parts of a composite or layer group available in a separate file for later changes?**
  Once you have worked on a composite, you could flatten the image to save space; this is common with an image that is going to be used only once. You may want to save the original image in Photoshop format, however, and save a copy in a print-able, flattened format. This gives you the ability to make later modifications, and to use the image in a variety of printed or on-line pieces. This is especially true in Photoshop 6, which allows you to edit text in a special text layer, include vector information generated by the drawing tools, or to edit layer effects, such as drop shadows. You may even want to maintain several different files. You might want one with all the layers you generated to allow for alterations, one simplified PSD or EPS to allow printing to Postscript-savvy printers, and one flattened file, for printing to non-Postscript devices or for placement in a page-layout application

- **How much scratch disk space and memory do you have available?**
  The more RAM and free disk space you have, the more layers you will be able to use. Photoshop will sometimes request as much as five times the size of the file in scratch disk space, regardless of how much RAM is available. Many users even have an entire hard drive set aside as Photoshop's scratch disk. Many high-end Photoshop users are not satisfied unless they are at the cutting edge in both RAM and hard drive technology as well as system speed. The money spent on these systems is soon made up in time saved or the ability to work in a "job efficient" if not "system efficient" manner. Photoshop 6 allows you to specify up to four separate drives as scratch disk space. Be aware, however, that some filters run entirely in RAM. If enough actual RAM is not available, the filter simply won't run.

- **Can the image be flattened as you work?**
  You can conserve resources by merging certain layers together once they require no more changes. Using this technique, you might find that you use 10 layers to create a final document, but only 2 or 3 layers were active in the document at any given time. Editable text and effect layers cannot be flattened and retain their editability.

Layers consume RAM. Plan your documents carefully, and combine layers as needed to conserve system resources.

Many page-layout programs cannot import images that have not been flattened.

- **How much long-term storage space do you have available?**
  Sometimes you'll find that even though you have enough immediate resources — RAM and scratch disk space — you don't have enough storage space to archive all of your files. In this situation, you may choose to flatten the image once it is finished, simply to conserve hard drive space. If it is imperative that you keep all layers intact, you can separate the layers into individual flattened documents with the layer transparency and masks saved as channels, and save the documents as JPEG or compressed TIFF files. When you need them, simply reassemble them into the original file. Be aware that JPEG can cause a loss of image quality. Also, to do this with editable text and effects layers, you must first render or transform them to a non-editable state. With the proliferation of relatively inexpensive CD burners, this is a problem that is easier than ever to solve.

- **How much time do you have available?**
  The less time that you have available, the more important it is to pick the fastest way to create an image. Working in layers is not always the fastest way to accomplish an immediate, simple project.

Why Use Layers?

Consider the following example:

Suppose we want to put type in the center of the beach scene. The layout calls for a *ghosted box*, or lightened area, on which the image where the type will be set. In this case, both the type and the ghosted box were created in Photoshop.

Doing this with a traditional flat image would require us only to select the area to ghost, fill it with white at 80%, and resave the image. Unfortunately, if any changes in the intensity of the ghosting were necessary, or any other modifications were required, the entire file would need to be recreated. Instead, you can create a layered file to accomplish the same goal, and more.

Create a Layered Document

1. Open the image **Sandy Beach.TIF** from your **SF-Adv Photoshop** folder.

2. Click the New Layer icon — the small page at the bottom of the Layers palette.

3. Using the Rectangular Marquee tool, select an area on the center of the image covering parts of the sand, water, and sky. Choose Edit>Fill. Fill the square with 100% white; leave the Blending mode at Normal.

4. Reduce the Opacity of the layer to 80%.

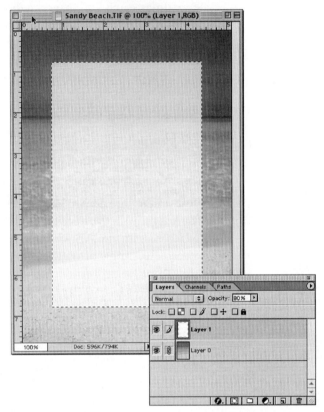

5. Deselect. Save as "Layer Practice.PSD" to your **Work in Progress** folder. Leave the image open for the next exercise.

Making Changes to a Layered Image

It took a few more steps to produce this effect than it would have taken in a document without layers. Let's assume, however, that your client has decided he would like a headline filled with the original, unaltered image inside of the ghosted box. He would also like to see a little more of the image detail in the ghosted area.

If you had created this file in a traditional manner, you'd have to start over again with a fresh copy of the scan. Not so with layers.

Modify Layers

1. In the open image, Layer Practice.PSD, make certain that Layer 1 is active.

2. Select the Type Mask tool.

Click the tool at the top of the ghost box. Using 45-pt. ATC MaiTai Bold, type "RELAX!". Click the checkmark to commit the type, or press Command-Return/Control-Enter.

3. Adjust the type so that it is centered at the top of the box. Use one of the selection tools, to adjust the placement of the type. Choose Select>Save Selection to save your selection as a new channel. Name the channel "Relax".

4. Press the Delete/Backspace key, and deselect. The words are now punched out of the lightened area of the image, allowing the original image to show through.

5. In the Layers palette, adjust the Opacity of Layer 1 to 50% to allow more of the image to show through.

   Unlike a similar flat image, this image is now available for quick changes and revisions. The Opacity of a layer is just one of the many options that you can adjust.

6. Before we leave this image, try one more modification just for fun. Select layer 1, and run a gaussian blur of 15 pixels. Observe how the edge softens. As you can see, the typesetting would have to be done after the blur was applied (as shown in the example below), but the effect is interesting. Undo the change. Save the image before closing.

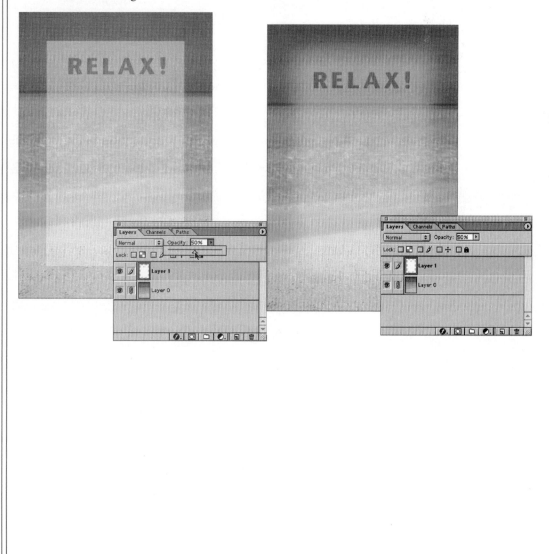

Layer Options/Styles/Properties

Double-clicking a layer brings up the Layer Style box. A wide variety of controls are available here. Spend some time exploring the available options.

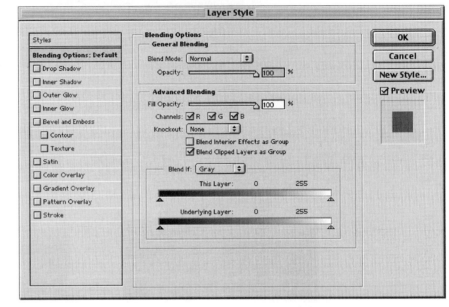

As you can see, the Layer Style dialog box can be very powerful. Keep notes as you explore and save interesting effects for later recall and use. Double-clicking on a style brings up a control box to modify the style. Chapter 11 deals more thoroughly with layer styles.

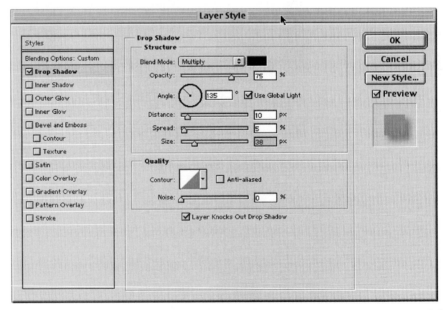

If you are familiar with earlier versions of the program, you will see this as a powerful compilation of tools into one easy to access location. If this version of Photoshop is your first exposure to the program, using the styles should quickly become second nature.

To change the name of a layer, Option/Alt>double-click the layer. You can also assign a color to the layer to make it easier to keep track of what you are doing.

Blending Layers

Photoshop can blend two layers in a document based on the brightness values of pixels in each layer, measured either in gray or in one of the color channels. The Blend section of the Layer Style dialog box defines which pixels within the layer are affected by the Blending Mode and Opacity that is selected. The following example highlights areas in the Layer Style dialog box that control Blending Options.

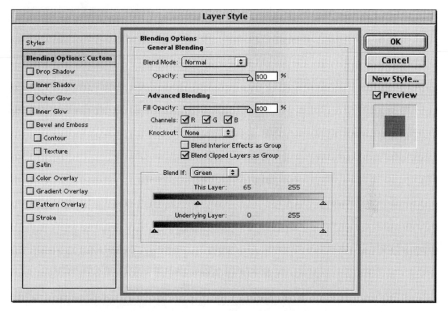

There are two control bars to define the way in which one layer is blended into another. One controls the layer itself; the other controls the layer underneath.

For each layer, the bar represents the full color range, from dark to light, of the channel selected in the Blend If drag-down menu. The sliders control the range of color that will be included in the blend for a particular layer. Option/Alt-clicking the triangles causes them to split apart, allowing soft fades in all areas of transition. To reunite the triangle's halves, simply slide one half back to the other; the triangle will reattach.

Advanced blending options allow you to blend a single channel with another, a group of channels with another, or even a group of channels with another channel group. Experiment and take notice of the color shifts that are possible when using these settings.

Use Layer Option Blending

1. Create a new RGB document called "Layer Options Test"; the document should be 2 in. square and 72 ppi. Set the Contents to White.

2. Make certain that your Background color is set to White. Click on the Foreground color swatch and change the Foreground color to 255 Blue. Green and Red should be set at 0. Click the Linear Gradient tool. On the Gradient Options bar, set the Gradient to Foreground to Background; make sure Opacity is set to 100%. Hold down the Shift key while creating a gradient from right to left.

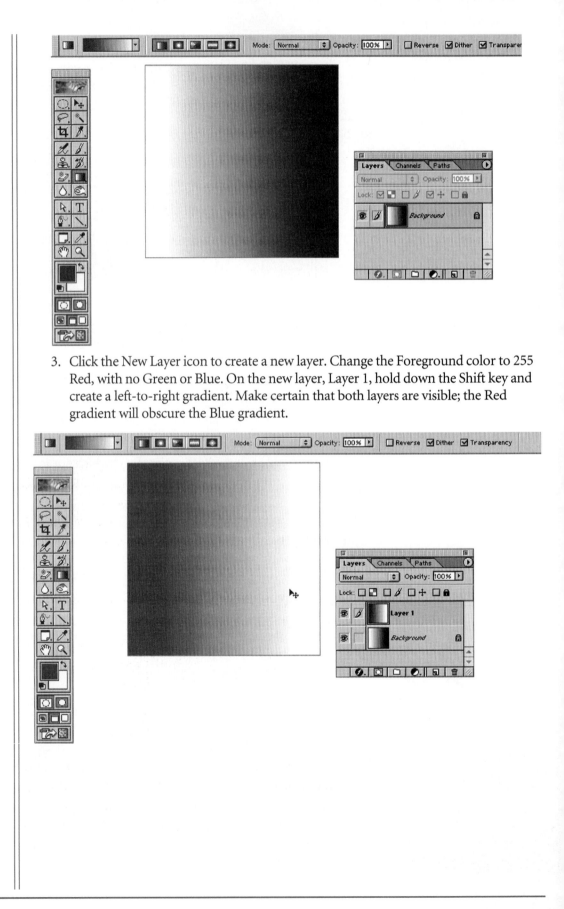

3. Click the New Layer icon to create a new layer. Change the Foreground color to 255 Red, with no Green or Blue. On the new layer, Layer 1, hold down the Shift key and create a left-to-right gradient. Make certain that both layers are visible; the Red gradient will obscure the Blue gradient.

4. Option/Alt-double-click Layer 1 to activate Layer Properties. Change the name of the layer to "Red", and color the layer red for reference. Make certain that the Preview box is checked, and click OK. Double-click the Background layer, name it "Blue", and color it blue for reference.

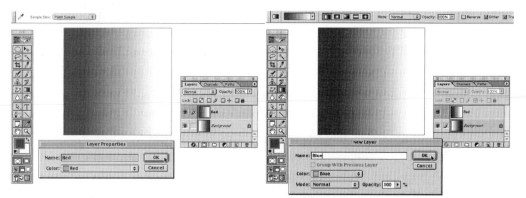

5. Double-click the Red layer to activate the Layer Style dialog box. Change Blend Mode to Multiply and Opacity to 50%. Notice that the bottom layer is partially visible, blended with the new Opacity of the top layer. Move the dialog box to view the image, if necessary. Select Cancel. The Mode remains Normal, the Opacity 100%. Layer Options allows you to test various Opacity and blending mode settings, without affecting the current settings.

6. Activate Layer Styles for the Red layer again. Select Green from the Blend If drag-down list.

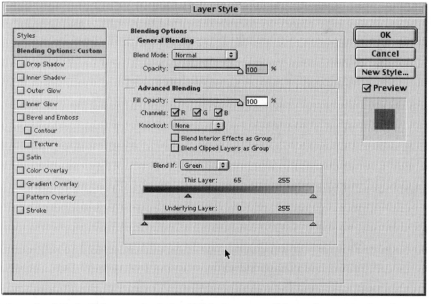

Move the black slider on the left of This Layer until it reads 65. Notice that some Blue gradient is showing through on the left side of the image.

7. Make certain that the Info palette is visible. Drag the cursor over the red area in the image, just before the red cuts off. Notice that the value of green measures 66 or above.

8. Now try adjusting the highlights. Move the white, right slider on This Layer until it reads around 150. Now the Blue gradient is visible again, this time on the right side of the image.

9. Right now the edge where the blend begins is abrupt, but a smooth transition is as easy as it is desirable. Option/Alt-drag the right side of the left triangle of the This Layer bar to 115. The triangle splits apart and a second number appears above the control bar. Adjust the slider until the blend is smooth. Repeat with the white slider to smooth further. Click OK.

10. Save the file as "Blend Options.PSD" to your **Work in Progress** folder for later use, then close it.

Practical Usage of Layer Options

The previous example, though not likely to occur as such in nature, highlights a few important properties of blending layers using Layer Options. With experimentation, you'll discover many uses for Blend Options. For example, in a photo such as a product shot with a white background, you can isolate the image against another background without using selection tools or masks. Scanned logos are another example of the use of the blend tools allowing nearly effortless composition. Blend Options are also great for creating textural backgrounds and special effects.

The basic rules for the Blend Options sliders are:

- In the channel selected for blending, any pixel with a brightness value below the target number on the black This Layer slider on the left does not participate in the blend. It simply disappears from the composite.

- Any pixel with a value above the target number on the white This Layer slider on the right isn't included in the blend either; it also disappears from the composite.

- If you move the sliders on the Underlying Layer bar, the effect is the opposite of moving the sliders on the This Layer bar. The Underlying slider protects the values outside the triangles on the layer below from the effects of the blend. In our example, the blue on the underlying layer would show through because it would not be included in the blend defined on the red layer.

- In both instances, the values between the triangles are the ones that blend.

- Blended edges are smoothed by Option/Alt-dragging the sliders. The space between the split sliders indicates the range of brightness values that will be smoothly blended.

Layer Masks

Layer masking is a faster and more flexible way to make complex composites. Layer masks combine the advantages of Photoshop's layers with the power of masking. Like selection masks, it is possible to edit a layer mask with Photoshop's painting tools. Since layer masks are Grayscale channels, you can use both partial masking and feather masking techniques.

Usually you will manually add a mask to a Photoshop layer. When you use the Edit>Paste Into command, however, a new layer is created with the pasted data, and a mask is added to the layer in the shape of the selection.

With layer masks you can create very complicated blends between many photos quickly and easily. The effects of a layer mask are temporary until you decide to merge the mask permanently with the layer. Because you can edit a mask independent of the layer itself, it is easy to change a composite and see the results before committing to the change.

The following exercise will show you how to combine two separate images, using a layer mask to form an interesting composite result.

Create a Layer Mask

1. Open the files **CD Photo.TIF** and **Couple Lunch.TIF** from your **SF-Adv Photoshop** folder. We are going to position the image of the CD in the upper-left corner of the composite.

2. Make certain that CD Photo.TIF is the active document. Select Image>Image Size, and enter Pixel Dimensions of Width: 232 pixels, Height: 346 pixels. Click OK.

```
                        Image Size
  ┌─ Pixel Dimensions: 236K (was 363K) ─┐      ┌──────────┐
  │                                      │      │    OK    │
  │   Width:  [232]    [pixels    ▲▼]┐   │      └──────────┘
  │                                  ├⊗  │      ┌──────────┐
  │   Height: [346]    [pixels    ▲▼]┘   │      │  Cancel  │
  └──────────────────────────────────────┘      └──────────┘
  ┌─ Document Size: ─────────────────────┐      ┌──────────┐
  │                                      │      │  Auto... │
  │   Width:  [3.219]  [inches    ▲▼]┐   │      └──────────┘
  │                                  ├⊗  │
  │   Height: [4.806]  [inches    ▲▼]┘   │
  │                                      │
  │   Resolution: [72] [pixels/inch ▲▼]  │
  └──────────────────────────────────────┘
    ☑ Constrain Proportions
    ☑ Resample Image: [Bicubic        ▲▼]
```

3. Make certain that both images are completely visible. With the Move tool, click and drag the CD image Background Layer onto the image of the couple. (Without the Move tool, you must drag the actual name of the CD layer to the image of the couple.) When you release your mouse button, a new layer, Layer 1, will be created. Close CD Photo.TIF without saving.

4. Make certain that the Layers and Channels palettes are both visible. If they are both in the same palette window, drag the tab of the Channels palette out, and drop it on the desktop.

5. With Layer 1 selected, click the Add Mask button at the bottom of the Layers palette. A preview of the mask will appear beside the layer's preview. The Layer Mask channel will also appear in the Channels palette. Each layer may use only one mask.

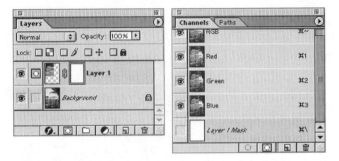

6. Click to the left of the Mask preview on the Channels palette to make the layer mask appear as an alpha channel, just as if you were turning on a channel. You can change the color and opacity of the mask by choosing Layer Mask Options from the Channels palette when the masked layer is active in the Layers palette. Activate the Channels drag-down triangle, and select Layer Mask Options. Leave the Opacity setting at 50%. Click on the Red color swatch to change the mask color to blue, so that you will remember that you are editing a layer mask, not a regular channel. Click OK.

7. Click again on the layer mask visibility icon in the Channels palette to turn the layer mask off.

8. In the Layers palette, click on the layer image preview to continue editing the layer normally. Notice that there is an icon between the eye and the thumbnail previews that indicates whether painting is on the image layer or the mask.

9. Move the CD-ROM image into the upper-left corner of the document.

10. To edit the layer mask, click on the mask thumbnail. The Layer Mask Painting icon appears, indicating that the layer mask is active. To see the results of your changes to the layer mask in the next step, in the 50% blue "Overlay Color," hold down the Option/Alt and Shift keys, while clicking on the mask thumbnail.

11. Make an elliptical selection around the CD-ROM. Make certain that your colors are default black and white. Rotate the elliptical marquee so it is positioned properly over the CD by choosing Select>Transform Selection and dragging to the appropriate position. Confirm, then choose Select>Inverse, Feather the selection by 18 pixels, and fill the selection using Black as the Foreground color.

Loose selection of CD made in pasted-in image (left). Masked image (right).

12. To view the file without the effects of the mask, select Layer>Disable Layer Mask (or hold down the Shift key while clicking the mask thumbnail). With the layer mask enabled, change the Opacity of the layer to 44%.

File without effects of mask (left). Masked image with Opacity change to 44% (right).

13. If you wish, you may also use various soft-edged paint brushes to modify the shape of the mask. By default, painting with black hides (or masks) the layer, allowing areas of the underlying image to show through; painting with white allows areas of the layer to show. As you paint, you will be able to see the effects of the mask.

14. Another way to view the mask over the layer is to turn on the visibility (eye) icon for the mask in the Channels palette, or to turn off the visibility icon for the RGB channels, and edit the mask as a channel by itself.

15. If you are satisfied with your mask, save the image as "Masked Layers.PSD" to your **Work in Progress** folder.

16. A mask can be either discarded or applied permanently to its layer. Select Layer>Remove Layer Mask (or drag the layer mask icon into the trash can at the bottom of the palette). Select Apply (or, if you have dragged the mask to the trash, click Apply). At this point, you could create another layer mask to isolate other portions of the image.

17. Drag the Channels palette over the top of the Layers palette to recombine the palettes.

18. Close the file without saving.

Complex Composites Using Layers

It's time to explore the real advantage of layer masking. Using layer masks, we are going to create several versions of a composite, while keeping an original Photoshop file available for later editing.

Use Layers in Composites

1. Open the files **Sandy Beach.TIF** and **Lovers In A Pool.TIF** from the **SF-Adv Photoshop** folder. With the Move tool, drag the image of the lovers onto the beach image. Make certain that the couple covers the whole image area; adjust it with the Move tool if necessary. Option/Alt-click Layer 1, and rename it "Lovers". Close the Lovers In A Pool.TIF image.

2. Click the second icon in the Layers palette to add a layer mask to the Lovers layer. The brick is pretty unattractive for a romantic beach image. We want the happy couple as far away from that nasty brick background as we can get them. Let's experiment with a few different settings.

3. Activate the Paths palette. Use the Pen tool to select the brick background, making a tight path. Leave a bit of room around the couple's hair. If the Pointer or one of the other path tools is visible in the Toolbox, click and hold the tool to make the Pen tool available for selection, or press "P" until the Pen appears on the Tool palette. Double-click the path, and rename it "Couple Path".

   Adjust the path until you're satisfied with it, then drag it to the third button at the bottom of the Paths palette to create a new selection. Activate the Lovers Mask channel, and fill the selection with black.

4. Use painting tools and complex selection methods to edit the mask around the hair until it looks as natural as you can make it, and until the beach image replaces all of the brick background. If you forgot to draw the path inside the couple (as is the case here), edit the mask with the painting tools as shown in the couple with the oranges background. Deselect.

5. Open the file **Oranges.TIF** from the **SF-Adv Photoshop** folder. Drag the oranges Background layer into the beach image. Make certain that the oranges cover from the top of the image to below the couple in the pool. Rename the layer "Oranges". Close the Oranges.TIF image.

6. In the Layers palette, position the Oranges layer so that it is between the beach and the lovers, and the oranges are blocking out the beach.

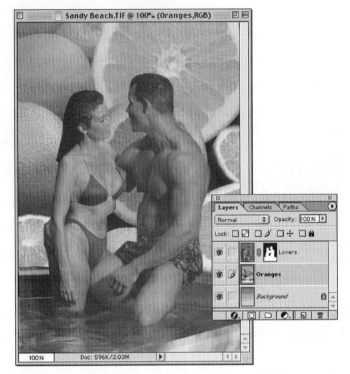

7. What if we want to see the oranges and the beach? Add a layer mask to the Oranges layer. Activate the Gradient tool, and create a gradient from black to white, bottom to top, that allows the oranges to fade in just below the horizon on the beach.

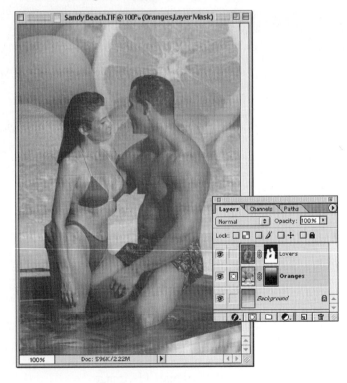

Experiment by beginning and ending the gradient in different areas of the image; hold down the Shift key to constrain the gradient to a vertical axis while you draw. When you are satisfied, save the file to your **Work in Progress** folder as "Beach Ad.PSD".

8. Select File>Save As, then check the As a Copy box. Save a copy of this image as a TIFF file, and name it "Beach Ad.TIF", with the Layers box unchecked. The TIFF will be flattened, and ready for printing, but our layered image is unaffected. Only visible layers will be included in the new TIFF.

9. Open the image **Masked Layers.PSD** that you created in the last exercise. Copy the Background layer (the couple having lunch) onto the beach image. Name the layer "Lunch Couple", and position it above the Lovers layer. Close Masked Layers.PSD. This will allow you to fade the new layer into the Lovers without changing the Lovers mask.

10. Add a layer mask to Lunch Couple to fade them into the right side of the image. Allow the umbrella to show through the lovers for an interesting effect. Experiment until you find an effect you want.

11. Save the image as "On the Beach.PSD" to your **Work In Progress** folder.

12. Experiment with turning layers on and off, adjusting the Opacity and Mode of each layer. Try adjusting the order of the layers to understand how they're interacting.

13. Close the file without saving.

Clipping Groups

A *clipping group* is a collection of Photoshop layers that work together as a team. The bottom layer in a clipping group, known as the "base layer," masks the images on all of the layers above it included within the clipping group. You can have as many clipping groups in one document as you like. Clipping groups are unique because the base layer uses its transparency as a mask for the other layers in the group, rather than adding the same mask to each layer.

You can use blending modes with each layer in a clipping group, but after the grouped layers are blended, the entire group takes on the blending mode of the base layer.

Use Clipping Groups

1. Open **Layer Practice.PSD** from your **Work in Progress** folder.

2. Click the New Layer icon in the Layers palette to create a new layer; the name will default to Layer 2. Choose Select>Load Selection, and load Relax, which you saved when creating a type mask.

3. Using the arrow keys, move the Relax! selection. Position it slightly above and to the left of the knocked-out text. Fill the text with 100% black. Deselect.

4. Activate the Background layer. Use the Rectangular Marquee tool to select an area of water at least as large as the headline. Press Command/Control-C to copy your selection to the clipboard.

5. Paste your selection, thus creating Layer 3. Make it the top layer, and position the selection so that it completely obscures the headline.

6. With Layer 3 selected, choose Layer>Group with Previous. The water will take on the shape of the text on Layer 2.

7. Using the Move tool, change the position of the water. Notice that moving the water doesn't affect any of the other layers, but it does change the way the water shows through the text.

8. You've just created your first clipping group. A clipping group is indicated in the Layers palette by a dotted line between the grouped layers. The base layer for a clipping group is designated by an underlined layer name.

9. Save the image and leave it open for the next exercise.

Properties of a Clipping Group

Clipping groups allow you to link multiple layers. The base layer acts like a mask to all of the layers in the group. Wherever there is image data on the base layer, it interacts with the other layers in the group. Wherever the base layer is transparent, the other layers in the group are masked out. This makes it possible to edit many elements of a picture independently, without disturbing the whole image.

Manipulate Clipping Groups

1. In the open file, Layer Practice.PSD, activate Layer 2, and press Command/Control-G to activate the group with the Previous Layer command. This makes Layer 1 the base layer of the group. Notice how the composite has changed. Layer 1 becomes the mask for all the layers in the group, and Layer 2 no longer masks Layer 3.

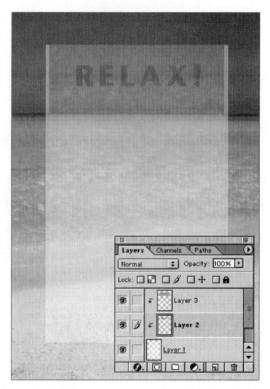

2. With Layer 2 selected, choose Layer>Ungroup, which will also ungroup Layer 3. Then select Layer 3, and choose the Layer>Group with Previous option. This returns the composite to its correct form.

3. Activate Layer 1. Open the image Orange Slice.TIF from the **SF-Adv Photoshop** folder. Activate the Paths palette, and drag the existing path down to the dotted circle button on the palette to create a selection. Copy the image of the orange. Close Orange Slice.TIF without saving.

4. In the Layers Practice file, paste the orange to create Layer 4.

5. If necessary, drag Layer 4 to the position just above Layer 1. Press Command/ Control-G to make Layer 1 and Layer 4 a clipping group. Position the orange so that it gives the composite a special tropical flavor. Notice that Layer 4 is using the Opacity setting of the base layer, Layer 1.

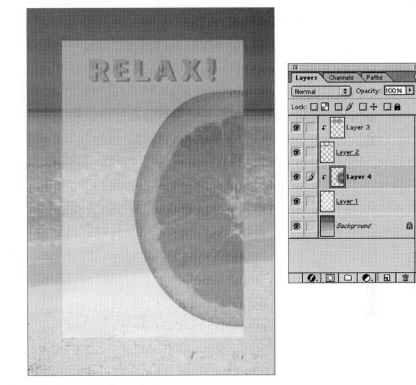

6. Save the image before closing.

Layer Style

Before the introduction of Photoshop 5, special effects such as drop shadows could be created by the creative use of standard layers. For example, a drop shadow could be created by Command/Control-clicking a layer (which selects the layer's contents) then creating a new layer, feathering, and filling the shape with black, and positioning the results appropriately. Photoshop 5 automated the process. Now Photoshop 6 takes it a step further along the evolutionary path. There is so much that is new and exciting that it deserves a whole chapter. Chapter 11 is dedicated to the new Layer Style commands and their uses.

Layer Alignment

Another aspect of Photoshop layers is that they can be aligned or distributed, once they have been linked together. This allows you, for example, to align the top edges of the contents of two or more layers, as shown below.

Align Layers

1. Create a New Photoshop file, approximately 3.5 in. × 3.5 in., at 72 ppi, in RGB color. Name it "Layer Align".

2. Create three new layers, and create a different colored object on each one. Link the layers together by clicking on the space to the right of the visibility icon. Notice that linked layers can be moved simultaneously.

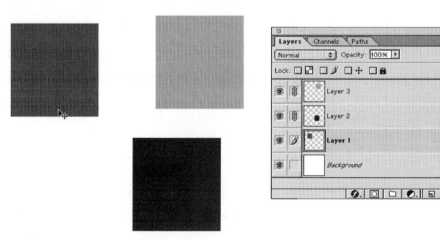

3. Select Layer>Align Linked>Top Edges. Notice the effect on the three objects. Select Undo, and experiment with the other alignment and distribution commands.

4. Close the file without saving.

Summary

In this chapter, you have learned to work with layers, not only to isolate specific image elements, but also to manage alterations you are making to the image so that those alterations will be editable should your client's ideas not mesh with yours. You have seen how creating layers can make your work, over the long run, more worry-free, and far more productive.

Complete Project B: Baby Shower Invitation

RETOUCHING

CHAPTER OBJECTIVE:

To study the many methods of how to retouch an image. To learn how to rebuild, repair, or remove elements in an image. In Chapter 8, you will:

- Practice and master the techniques of the Clone Stamp tool functions.

- Learn to analyze an image and implement the proper method to retouch it.

- Learn how to approach image repairs in a structured manner.

- Become familiar with the tools and brushes used for retouching and repairing an image.

- Learn how and when to use filters for retouching.

PROJECTS TO BE COMPLETED:

- Just Shoot Me (A)

- Baby Shower Invitation (B)

- **Retouching the Jones Family Portrait (C)**

- **The Fix Is In! (D)**

- Makeover (E)

- Photomat (F)

Retouching

The word "retouching" has more than one meaning. It can mean simply removing dust spots, scratches, or other impurities that have been picked up in the scanning process. Retouching can also mean extensive work restoring old photos or compositing images into new and unique visuals.

Professional photographers need the skill of an expert retouch artist to enhance even their best work. Retouching has been performed almost as long as photography itself. Retouching certainly predates the use of the computer. Almost anything we can accomplish digitally has also been done the old fashioned way — by hand. Sometimes, retouching means repairing. Sometimes it means altering an image during the post-production process because the image could not be repaired when it was initially captured. Almost all original images need some repairs if you want perfect reproduction.

The image "mi Casa West," seen later in this chapter, is a classic example of a post-production problem that could not be dealt with at the time the photograph was taken. Knowing that the problem could be addressed in post-production, the photographer was able to make his shot, confident that the client would be satisfied with the ultimate result.

There are several ways to approach retouching an image. Most are manual efforts using portions of the image itself as the "paint" to cover up problem areas. Another approach is to use special filters for the job. The best method for retouching a particular image can only be determined after careful analysis of the scanned image, and the final size and resolution that is required

The Clone Stamp Tool

The photos that you will use in your designs are often imperfect. Elements to remove from an image might include wiring, scaffolding, part of the studio floor that the photographer could not avoid including in the shot, or a competitor's logo on an athlete's jersey. In all of these instances, retouching to change part of the content captured during the original shot is essential.

The Clone Stamp tool excels in reconstructing details within an image. It allows you to recreates photographic details and color already in the image that are impossible to create otherwise. The first click of the tool (holding Option/Alt) designates which pixels the tool is to sample. The second click paints on the image with those pixels. The Clone Stamp tool functions easily, but since it duplicates everything, mastering the techniques requires practice. The examples in this chapter will provide some practice and tips.

Paint with Portions of an Image to Repair Flaws

1. Click on the Brush tool to activate the Brushes Options bar, and create a hard, flat, horizontal brush by selecting New Brush from the Brushes Options menu. Enter Diameter: 25 pixels, Hardness: 75%, Spacing: checked and 25%, Angle: 0°, Roundness: 20%. Click OK.

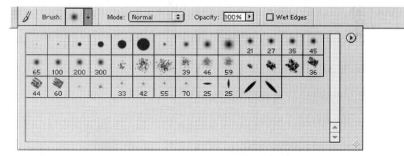

2. Select New Brush from the Brushes menu to create three more brushes: a vertical brush (90° Angle) and two diagonal brushes (one at 45° and one at -45° Angles) with the values left the same as what you set in step 1. You should now have four new brushes that are particularly useful for retouching tasks in addition to the round brushes and others developed for specific jobs.

3. Select Edit>Preferences>Display and Cursors, and set Brush Size for painting tools and Precise for others.

4. Open the image **mi Casa West.PSD** from the **SF-Adv Photoshop** folder. This image was shot for a real estate company. The client wants a photograph of their new sales center for use in a brochure. The best angle, one that shows both the building and the sign, also includes an unsightly pole. After some practice with the various retouching tools, you will remove the pole from the image.

5. Click the Clone Stamp tool in the Toolbox to activate the Options bar for this tool. Like other paint tools, it offers blend Mode and Opacity settings. It is frequently helpful to adjust Opacity in order to avoid noticeable patterns of cloning and to finely blend repairs into the image to appear more natural. For now, leave the Opacity set at 100%.

When working on a layered image, check "Use All Layers" if the sample point includes pixels and effects from other layers to complete the effect (visible layers only). Leave the box unchecked to sample from only one layer (the active layer). Check the Use All Layers box now.

To align or not to align, that is the question. If the objective is to repeatedly clone the same part of the image, uncheck the Aligned option. If you find that maintaining the sample point's relative position to the area being painted is more useful, check it. Check the Aligned box now.

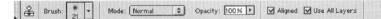

6. Select a medium-sized soft brush (65 pixels), move it over the 30 MPH sign, and Option/Alt-click the Background layer.

    The location of the first Option/Alt-click is the source or sample point for the Clone Stamp tool; the place painted is the destination or target area.

7. Release the mouse button. Move the brush to the sky area. Click the Clone Stamp tool again and start painting. A new sign appears floating in the sky. Do not reselect a different Sample point. Now move the brush down and to the left just a little (just to the left of the top of the orange roof), and continue painting.

    The crosshair (pixels being sampled) followed the cursor. The brush (target area being retouched) paints whatever image is under the crosshair. When Aligned is checked, the sample point tags along, maintaining the same distance and relationship established by the first two clicks.

8. Uncheck Aligned in the Clone Stamp tool's Options palette. Option/Alt-click on the sign, and paint another one in the sky.

9. Release the mouse button. Paint somewhere else in the sky. Release the mouse button again, and paint another sign somewhere else on the image. Do it a third time. Checking the Non-Aligned option anchors the source or sample spot so that it doesn't tag along. With each new mouse click to paint, it uses as its source the exact point originally sampled, not a relative position. If this is your intent, carefully watch the crosshair to capture just the areas of the sample that you desire.

10. After experimenting with the image, choose the first Clone Stamp state from the History palette, and select Delete from the drop-down menu. Keep the file open for the next exercise.

Approaching Repairs in a Structured Manner

In this section, take the opportunity to retouch an image using the skills that we've covered. Don't hesitate to experiment and develop some experience in the use of the Clone Stamp and custom brushes to fix flawed areas in an image. Keep these tips in mind:

- Examine the entire image with a 1:1 aspect ratio. It's easy to become too critical and waste time when you're using high magnifications; it may, in fact, do more harm than good. Keep a reasonable perspective.

- Start working in the upper left and work horizontally across the image when analyzing where retouching is necessary. At the corner, travel back to the left, carefully repeating the analysis and repairs. The technique of randomly searching for flaws rarely ensures catching every mark; attack the image with an organized strategy.

- Consider the file's resolution when choosing a brush size and the distance between sample point and target area. High-resolution files require larger brushes than low-resolution images. Adjust your brush sizes to fit the project. Change the brush shape and size frequently to suit the image and blend changes. If the brush is too big and the distance between sample and target area too close, pixels repeat themselves in an obvious pattern sometimes called "railroad tracks."

- Use a soft-edged brush to create a gradual transition between repairs and the background. If the brush is set to 100% hardness, there will be no transition, often making the repair stand out. If the brush is too big and soft, it will look as though your repair area is smudged or not sharpened correctly.

- Experiment with the Clone Stamp tool's opacity and blend modes. In tight spots where there isn't much from which to sample, vary the opacity to mix the tone values applied for retouching and re-retouching.

- Match tones carefully. If a shadow, tone, or pattern falls in the area to be repaired, align the sample and target to continue the shadow, pattern, or tone.

- When repairing an edge or other line such as a table edge or roofline, the sample and target points should be aligned in exactly the same relation to the pixels that create the edge. For example, sample on the top pixel of the "good" edge, then start painting on the top edge of the line to be repaired. Look for details that can enhance the illusion created by your retouching. The image below shows deleting a post and air conditioning unit while recreating the roofline behind it. Often, exact architectural accuracy is less important than, as in this case, removing an unwanted object. When retouching is done with skill and patience, no one will ever notice the original flaws. Repeating details such as the window and the balcony can help to fine-tune the image and erase any indication that a retoucher was at work

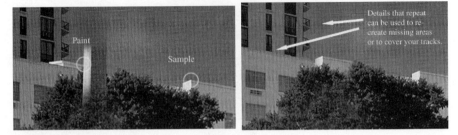

- When attempting to remove a major flaw, work from the outside in, all the way around. Working from only one side is actually more difficult because there are fewer varied pixels to sample. The result is usually railroad tracks and a tendency to clone the image that's being removed. Continue to work on the post until it is completely hidden.

Now it's time to apply your skills. There is no right or wrong way to remove an element such as this pole. Work from many angles and clone from many sources. Experiment. Be critical. Don't settle for good enough — continue retouching until you are satisfied. The trickiest spots are the edge of the roofline and the foreground grass. As we pointed out earlier, it is not necessary to reproduce an architecturally accurate building in the background. Liberties may be taken with anything except the mi Casa West building itself — that, after all, is the only thing that interests the client. It is important to first analyze an image and determine the best way to go about making your repairs. For this reason, the instructions for this exercise are general.

Repair mi Casa West

1. In the open mi Casa West photo, repair the roofline and remove the pole and speed limit sign. Follow the tips above to remind you of the key steps.

2. Use the tree trunk with a layer mask to finish the image. There is a tree trunk in the layer stack to use after the post is gone.

3. Save the file to your **Work in Progress** folder and close it.

Other Retouching Tools

Both the Brush and Clone Stamp tools have two special variations — the History brush and Pattern Stamp tool. Each tool provides some unique possibilities for artistic and practical retouching.

The History brush works like a regular brush, except that it paints with an historical version of the file. During experimentation or intense retouching, a particular area may have looked perfect (about 10 steps ago). By selecting that state (step) in the History palette (by clicking to the left of the state's name, not on the name), the tool will recreate how the image appeared at that point in the image's history wherever the History brush is dragged.

In the Mount Rushmore image, for example, after applying several artistic and brush stroke effects, we painted only the faces with the History brush. We chose a less distorted version of the image by selecting its appearance several states back as the source. Choosing the brush size and degree of softness is as important here as when using the Clone Stamp tool. In this case, the surrounding image appears hand painted while the faces are taken more directly from the photograph. Adding a duplicate layer before using the History brush provides a blended effect, allowing any degree of change from 100% to none at all.

The Pattern Stamp is another specialty tool, since its primary function is to paint with tiles of a Defined Pattern taken from a selection in the image. The first step is to marquee an area (rectangular selection), then choose Edit>Define Pattern. After defining the pattern, you simply switch to the Pattern Stamp tool, which is hidden under the Clone Stamp tool. You then choose a brush tip, and paint. The tiles will align perfectly.

Repair the Flower

1. Open the **White Uanda.TIF** image from the **SF-Adv Photoshop** folder. Notice that the petals are spotted from a fungus.

2. Carefully analyze the photograph. Repair the flower petals using the tools and techniques previously discussed. There are more flaws in this image than you may notice at a casual glance. Imagine that this is your brochure and your flower, and make your image corrections accordingly.

3. Save the image to your **Work in Progress** folder as "[Your Name) White Vanda.PSD" and close the image.

Using Filters for Retouching

The conditions under which a transparency or print is stored, handled, and scanned can have a dramatic effect on its quality.

In this short exercise, we're going to explore a specialized blur filter designed to remove dust and scratches from an image — just the type of flaw that's found in images that have been improperly stored, or that have been scanned without being cleaned first.

Run the Dust & Scratches Filter

1. Open **Trident.TIF** from the **SF-Adv Photoshop** folder. Look at the sky behind the wake. We need to remove some fairly large dust particles that were scanned into the image as small splotches.

2. Select one of the defects, making certain that your Lasso tool has a Feather setting of 1 to 2 pixels. As with many of the settings we use in the practice exercises, this setting would be proportionally higher for a higher-resolution image. The purpose of making this selection first is to limit the application of the filter and to blend its effects into the surrounding pixels of the image.

3. Press Command/Control-H to hide the selection border so that we can compare the selection and background pixels more easily. Remember that the marquee indicates the 50% position of any feathered selection; a few more pixels outside will be slightly affected.

4. With one of the defects selected, choose Filter>Noise>Dust & Scratches.

5. Adjust the magnification of the thumbnail selection inside the Dust & Scratches dialog box by clicking the plus (+) and minus (–) buttons in the dialog box. We find that it is helpful to have the thumbnail selection set to a higher magnification than the file image. (Use the thumbnail selection to keep a perspective on the effects.)

Move the cursor outside the Dust & Scratches dialog box, and click on the image. It will turn into a little square that corresponds to the Preview window. Position the square over the dust marks in the sky to shift the preview over the area being affected. Set Radius to 1 and Threshold to 0.

6. Make certain that the Preview box is checked. Adjust the Radius slider until the dirt disappears.

7. Increase the Threshold from 0, until the defect reappears, then back off a little. When satisfied, click OK.

8. Drag another selection around a spot, and use the filter again, testing the appropriate settings for this patch. Do this for each blotch; it will provide an opportunity to optimize the control settings for a variety of defect and background pixels.

9. Low-resolution files, such as this one, lose significant sharpness when employing the Dust & Scratches filter. To demonstrate this, make a selection around the sailors on the bridge. Apply the Dust & Scratches filter with the Radius set to 2, increase the Threshold to 10, then click OK.

This Radius slider setting determines how far the filter searches for differing pixel values.

The Threshold slider determines how different in tone the pixels must be to be affected. The higher the Threshold, the greater the tonal difference must be to effect a change. A setting of 0 will affect all isolated pixels or pixel groups as specified in the Radius setting.

10. Now apply the Unsharp Mask filter to recover some of that lost detail. Sharpening will slightly reverse the negative effects of the Dust & Scratches filter. It usually doesn't reintroduce the artifacts obliterated by the filter, but practice this process so that you become familiar with how drastically Dust & Scratches can be used before Unsharp Masking is unable to return the image to adequate sharpness.

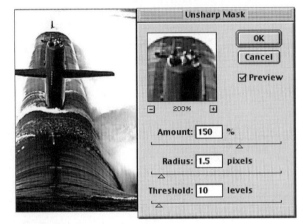

Higher Radius settings combined with lower Threshold settings increase the possibility of blurring the selection too much.

11. Save the file to your **Work in Progress** folder and close the document.

Summary

Retouching photographs requires patience, practice, and a structured style of working. More importantly, it requires a careful analysis of the needs of the image being repaired. The technical skills required are as equally important as the artistic skills, as you discovered when retouching the mi Casa West image. As you gain experience, you will be able to quickly analyze the needs of the image, and choose the most appropriate tools for the task.

Complete Project C: Retouching the Jones Family Portrait

Complete Project D: The Fix Is In!

PROJECT ASSIGNMENT #1

Assignment

You've landed a job that can make your career, as you help models make it to the top. A modeling agency wants to produce a kaleidoscope effect, showing several models' faces on the same page, or better still, one sheet apiece for each model who uses their agency.

Individual pages are 8 ″ × 11″, and must include the models' name(s), and the name, address, and phone number of the agency. Use both sides of the sheet.

Your assignment is to design the pages that will show off the model(s). The agency wants to show several views of each model, rotating around a single central image. Use your imagination.

If you want, you can secure appropriate photographs from any source, but be sure to credit the source. Alternately, you can use the photos supplied in the SF-Adv Photoshop folder. Be sure to adjust the resolution appropriately.

Applying Your Skills

To design the model sheets, you will need to use the following functions, methods, and features:

- Create your design using an 8 ″ × 11″-page size. If you create an image that runs off the page, allow for a ″ bleed.

- Consider using special channel and layer techniques to enhance the photos.

- Revolve your photos around a center point, or use any number of other transformation techniques.

- While you may wish to show your models on location, extract them from their backgrounds to highlight their features.

- Think about using silhouettes to highlight or reveal only specific portions of the image.

Specifications

Execute the design in the center of a 9″ × 12″ page.

The printed page size is 8 ″ × 11″, with the front of the sheet containing larger images and the back selling the details of the model(s).

The resolution of the final image should be 300 ppi.

Use RGB as the color mode.

Included Files

Feel free to use any of the baby pictures, Beach Boy.TIF, Caricature.TIF, Clown.TIF, Couple Dining.TIF (Cranachie Vineyards folder), Exerciser.TIF, Grandpa Joe.TIF, Makeover.TIF, The Mountaineer.TIF (Gallery folder), any images in the Presentation folder, or Woman at Computer. You may also use any other image to enhance the background of your presentation. Using images of your own, however, if you have them, is a better solution.

Publisher's Comments

For this assignment, it's imperative that you review ads in consumer publications and the looks that appear in television advertising to see what works and what doesn't. Don't be afraid to experiment! Remember, however, that even though you have some wild and exotic portions of the presentation, people will want to see the model in his/ her normal state as well.

While you are building an image, you will nonetheless want to keep the design clean, because the real goal is to book assignments.

REVIEW #1

CHAPTERS 1 THROUGH 8:

In Chapters 1 through 8, we learned the value of calibrating the system as a basis for achieving a consistent visual representation of the image. We learned ways to adjust and color-correct images. We transformed images using a variety of commands, and learned to use Photoshop's grids and guides effectively. We made special use of channel operations, gaining proficiency in managing and combining them. Selecting portions of images became easier as we learned to make complex selections with Photoshop's advanced selection tools. We were able to apply special effects to portions of the image, when working with layers, and learned the value of applying layer masks and adjustment layers. Finally, we learned how to retouch images using cloning techniques and filters. Through this series of discussions and projects, you should:

- Know that managed color, a technical aspect of the graphic arts, is achievable, provided that you have a well controlled working environment and a calibrated monitor.

- Understand the relationship between brightness, contrast, and gamma; know which adjustment tools are appropriate to making necessary adjustments; and be able to adjust a variety of images.

- Be familiar with the basic theory of additive and subtractive color, and be able to use the color wheel as an aid to adding and subtracting color to achieve the desired effect.

- Be able to use the transform tools to manipulate images, and to use grids and guides as an aid to positioning elements in an image.

- Be comfortable creating the illusion of depth in images using channels, and mixing channels from different images to achieve specific results. You have also learned to use channels to create special effects, such as spot color.

- Be able to analyze images to determine the best selection techniques, and choose the best tool for the task, based on the type of image with which you are working, to isolate elements of an image and to combine different backgrounds and foreground.

- Understand layers, and be able to use them to make editable alterations to images, utilizing layer masks and clipping groups. You have also learned to use adjustment layers to affect an entire image or a selected portion of an image.

- Know how to approach repairing an image in a structured manner, selecting appropriate tools and brushes to make the retouched work appear seamless, and understand that often a minimum of repair is more effective than making major alterations to an image.

CHAPTER 9

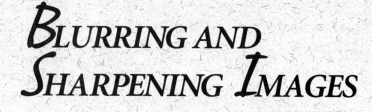

BLURRING AND SHARPENING IMAGES

CHAPTER OBJECTIVE:

To learn to use the Blur and Sharpen filter sets to save bad scans or damaged photographs. To become familiar with and use the focus adjustment blur filters, which allow you to blur similar colors while maintaining images. In Chapter 9, you will:

- Discover how to use the Gaussian and Smart Blur filters, the most important blur filters in the tool set.

- Learn about the special effects blur filters — Motion Blur and Radial Blur.

- Become familiar with how to use the sharpen filters, paying close attention to Unsharp Mask (USM), the most powerful of the sharpen filters.

- Learn how to sharpen an image using luminosity only.

PROJECTS TO BE COMPLETED:

- Just Shoot Me (A)

- Baby Shower Invitation (B)

- Retouching the Jones Family Portrait (C)

- The Fix Is In! (D)

- **Makeover (E)**

- Photomat (F)

Blurring and Sharpening Images

The Blur and Sharpen filter sets provided in Photoshop are true workhorses for anyone faced with the challenge of saving bad scans or damaged photographs. Blur can help reduce *moiré patterns*, which are interference patterns created when scanning printed material that contains a halftone screen. Sharpen can save those old fuzzy photos of your first birthday. Don't overlook the creative uses of these filters, however.

In a professional prepress environment where digital images have become the norm, it is vital for you to understand the need for sharpening images.

The Blur Filters

Experiment with the Smart Blur filter. It will definitely come in handy.

All of Photoshop's Blur filters work essentially the same way: they average the brightness values of contiguous pixels to soften the image.

The Blur filters could be categorized either as focus adjustment blur filters (filters which simulate the effect of an unfocused camera lens), or special effects blur filters, which blur pixels in more unusual ways.

Focus Adjustment Blur Filters

The first two filters in the Blur submenu are Blur and Blur More; they work well, but offer no control over the amount of blurring. The champions of this group of Blur filters are Gaussian Blur, which you may have used already, and Smart Blur, which allows you to blur similar colors while maintaining edges.

Gaussian Blur allows you to define the amount of blurring to be applied to the image. The strength of the blur is specified in pixels in the Radius field. Photoshop uses this value to average the brightness of a pixel with that of the surrounding pixels. A setting of 1 or below can soften an image. (Blur and Blur More are roughly equivalent to 0.3 and 0.7 Radius values, respectively.) Greater values can add atmosphere to an image, or make the contents difficult to recognize. Remember that the higher the resolution of the image, the higher the Radius value must be to achieve the same effect.

Smart Blur filter, which works in Grayscale, RGB, and Multichannel modes, allows you to blur tones closely related in value without affecting the edge quality of an image. You can set a Radius for blurring, just as you can with the Gaussian Blur filter. The Smart Blur Threshold setting, however, allows you to determine how closely pixels must be related in tone before being blurred. Settings can range from 0.01 to 100; the higher the value, the more the image is blurred. Setting a fairly low Radius with a high Threshold produces smooth, broad areas of color with distinct transitions between tones.

You can specify a Quality setting, or change the Mode setting so that the filter isolates only the edges according to the current settings. You can also set the Mode to Overlay Edges. With this option, the image is blurred, and the edges are outlined in white.

Use Gaussian Blur

1. Open **Couple Lunch.TIF** from your **SF-Adv Photoshop** folder.

2. To give the image a soft, romantic feel, use the Elliptical Marquee tool to create an oval selection surrounding our guests.

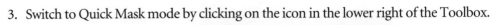

3. Switch to Quick Mask mode by clicking on the icon in the lower right of the Toolbox.

Switching to the Quick Mask mode is only necessary to visualize the softening of the selection edge in this exercise.

4. Select Filter>Blur>Gaussian Blur. Set the Radius to 32 pixels to soften the edge of the selection. Click OK.

The Gaussian Blur has practical, in addition to artistic, uses. When a blend must cover a long distance relative to the change in percentage of color, a Gaussian Blur can prevent or minimize banding. Many production specialists introduce a Gaussian Blur in this situation.

5. Click the icon in the lower left of the Toolbox to return to Normal mode, and turn the Quick Mask mode back into a selection. We want to blur the background, not the couple, so choose Select>Inverse to turn the selection inside out.

6. Select Filter>Blur>Gaussian Blur again and set Radius to 8 pixels. Notice that the work we did in the Quick Mask mode has softened the edge between the blurred and unaffected part of the image. The result should be a soft vignette around the couple for an otherworldly effect. Click OK.

7. Save the file as a Photoshop file named "Couple Lunch Blur.PSD" to your **Work in Progress** folder. Close the file.

Special Effects Blur Filters

The other two options on the Blur menu are Motion Blur and Radial Blur. These filters are generally used only for special effects.

Motion Blur has a wheel for changing the blur angle, and a Distance value for specifying the number of pixels to blur. Motion Blur can create a convincing sense of motion by duplicating an image in the Layers palette, blurring the bottom layer, and using the Eraser tool to remove parts of the top image. This allows the portions that indicate motion to show through, such as the rear bumper of a moving car.

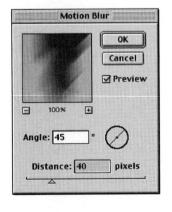

Radial Blur either Spins the pixel around the center point of the image, or Zooms, which blurs in a spoked fashion in the amount specified. The further the pixel is from the adjustable center point, the more it will be blurred. Draft, Good, and Best Quality options are available to improve filter performance. To enhance performance, test the filter in Draft or Good mode; when you find a setting you like, apply Undo, then reapply the filter in Best Quality mode.

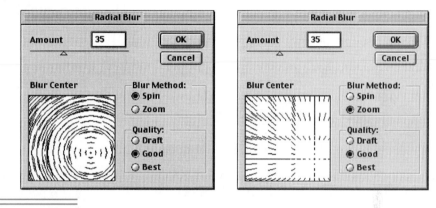

Use Motion Blur

1. Open **Pineapple.TIF** from your **SF-Adv Photoshop** folder.

2. With the Lasso tool, select a portion of the image to blur. Choose Filter>Blur>Motion Blur.

3. Set the Angle of motion by click-holding on the turn wheel and dragging it to 30°, or enter the angle manually in the adjacent box. Set Distance to 60 pixels. Click OK.

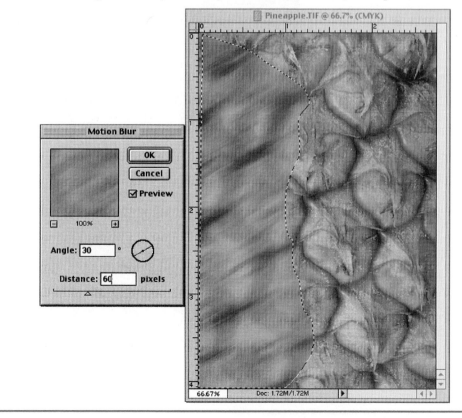

4. Undo the Blur with Command/Control-Z, and select the filter again. This time, try a smaller Distance, such as 10. The image retains a lot more texture.

5. Select the original Snapshot in the History palette to restore the image to its original state. Leave the file open for the next exercise.

Use Radial Blur

1. With the **Pineapple.TIF** image still open, select Filter>Blur>Radial Blur.

2. Click the mouse pointer in the Blur Center box in the Radial Blur dialog box to set the relative center of the blur. This will be the point from which it radiates or the center point of the spin, depending on whether you choose the Spin or Zoom methods.

3. Select an Amount of 35, Zoom Method, and Good Quality. Click OK. If you use Best Quality, rendering may take a few minutes, depending upon the speed of your computer.

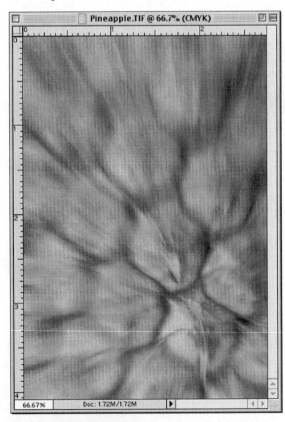

4. Close the file without saving.

The Sharpen Filters

Photoshop offers three preset Sharpening filters: Sharpen, Sharpen More, and Sharpen Edges. The first two operate about as well as their counterparts in the Blur submenu. Although you can apply a filter as many times as you like to produce the desired effect, this can be particularly time-consuming, and generally not as effective as using the other Sharpen filters.

Sharpen Edges operates only on areas of high contrast. It uses the brightness value of a pixel to determine where the edges are, then sharpens only those areas.

Unsharp Mask

The most powerful and useful Sharpen filter is Unsharp Mask (USM) — a special topic that deserves much more than casual interest. This filter, named for a conventional color trade shop scanner method of sharpening, allows you to control the magnitude of sharpening, the width of the sharpened edge, and determines which pixels are sharpened.

All scanned images share a common defect — softening of detail that exists in the original object or image. The manufacturers of conventional color trade shop drum scanners recognized the need for sharpening transparencies scanned on their equipment, and incorporated unsharp masking into the process of generating color separations.

Sharpening is achieved by first identifying which edges will be sharpened (the Threshold). The Amount setting determines the magnitude of the contrast, and the Radius setting specifies the width of contrast enhancement. A Threshold setting of 10 means that any two neighboring pixels must have a brightness value difference of at least 10 levels in order for the filter to apply to those pixels.

To set the Threshold value, push the Amount up high and increase the Threshold gradually until sharpening of grain or dust is eliminated. Next, you set the Radius for a halo width that will not be obtrusive. Finally, you reduce the Amount to the maximum acceptable setting.

The Amount setting is calibrated as a percent from 0 to 500; there is no advantage to using 100%. We want to push the Amount as high as possible while avoiding the artifacts discussed below. An appropriate amount of sharpening will depend upon the individual image.

Unsharp Masking does not actually restore focus to an image; that would be an impossible task. Instead, it artificially creates the impression of increased focus by finding the border

It is not always possible to eliminate unwanted sharpening of grain or dust without losing the ability to sharpen soft edges in an image. Other strategies apply sharpening only to channels that do not contain the grain, select localized areas for USM, or use the Sharpen tool on specific areas.

Localized sharpening can be applied with careful use of the Sharpen tool.

between two pixels that meet the threshold amount, then, within the specified radius, darkening the darker pixel and lightening the lighter one.

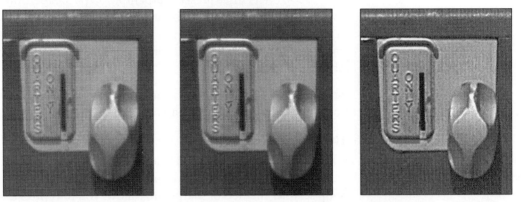

In this example, the image, from left to right, is unsharpened, properly sharpened, and oversharpened.

The key to using the USM filter is to apply as much sharpening as possible without creating another problem. The typical problems that result from misuse of the USM filter are:

- Obvious halos that are clearly visible and recognizable as not being a component of the image. The illustration above is an example of obvious halos.
- Distracting color shifts in the sharpened areas.
- Sharpening of unwanted detail such as scratches, even though the detail may actually be part of the image.
- Intensification of noise or grain.

Work with Unsharp Mask

1. Open **Shell.TIF** from your **SF-Adv Photoshop** folder.

2. Select Filter>Sharpen>Unsharp Mask.

As a rule of thumb, the following parameters may be followed for print images:
Threshold: 2 to 10
Radius: 0.5% of resolution (ppi)
Amount: enough to enhance the edges without a noticeable halo.

3. Check the Preview option. Enter an Amount of 300%, a Radius of 5, and a Threshold of 0. The woman is sharper, but the excessive white halo makes her appear positively saintly. Click on the clouds with the mouse, and notice how grainy they are in the Preview window. (A setting of 5 is actually too strong for an image of this resolution, but it will help you see the effects.)

Change the Threshold gradually, observing the unwanted graininess of the clouds and the desired graininess of the beach sand in the foreground.

4. Change the Threshold setting to 20 levels. Since the pixels in the clouds are similar in brightness, they aren't sharpened. Reduce the Radius to 2 pixels, and the Amount to 250%. This is still fairly extreme USM, but it demonstrates the use of the filter. Click OK.

5. Press Command/Control-Z a few times to compare the image before and after.

Image before sharpening.

In most images you will seek a compromise in the USM settings, attempting to increase sharpness in the detail while minimizing unwanted effects.

Image after USM. Note the woman, palm trees, and sand.

6. Close the image without saving.

Sharpening with Luminosity Only

Sometimes the application of the Unsharp Masking filter to the entire image will produce a color shift along the sharpened edge. This can be minimized by applying USM to the Lightness channel of a L*a*b image, or by following the USM filter with the Fade command (Edit>Fade), set to 100% Opacity.

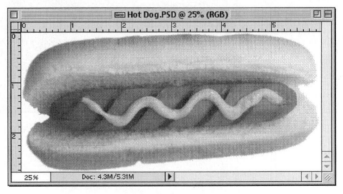

Image before USM.

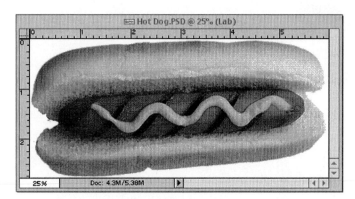

Color shift generated by USM. Note the added graininess.

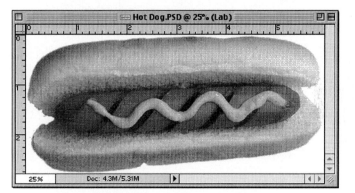

Reduction of color shift by applying USM to Lightness channel in L*a*b image.

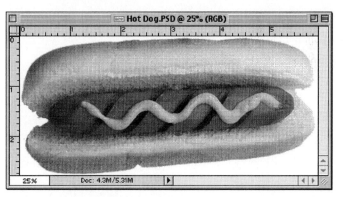

Reduction of color shift by applying Fade filter with 100% Luminosity.

Summary

You have learned to use blurring and sharpening filters to enhance images and to create moods by introducing vignettes. In addition, you have used special effects blurs to create the impression of motion. When you experimented with sharpening filters, you discovered that experimentation with the filters, and using multiple filters, allows you to achieve highly controlled improvements of images.

Complete Project E: Makeover

Notes:

CHAPTER 10

THE REMAPPING COMMANDS

CHAPTER OBJECTIVE:

To learn how Photoshop's remapping commands map or recolor pixels. To learn how this group of commands is dynamically editable through adjustment layers. In Chapter 10, you will:

- Learn how the Invert command creates the photographic negative of an image.

- Become familiar with the Equalize command. You will learn how it reads the brightness level of all pixels in every channel in order to remap and calculate every pixel in an image to redistribute the brightness values along a curve.

- Discover how the Threshold command converts images to black and white pixels giving you control over how much detail is retained.

- Become familiar with the Posterize command, which is similar to the Threshold command, except that it maps color images.

PROJECTS TO BE COMPLETED:

- Just Shoot Me (A)

- Baby Shower Invitation (B)

- Retouching the Jones Family Portrait (C)

- The Fix Is In! (D)

- Makeover (E)

- Photomat (F)

The Remapping Commands

Photoshop's remapping commands *map* or recolor pixels according to the rules (formula) associated with each command. All the commands under the Adjust menu (Image>Adjust) are remapping commands. This chapter focuses on the group that includes: Invert, Equalize, Threshold, and Posterize, as well as the Gradient Map. Most of these are dynamically editable commands available through the adjustment layers by selecting Layer>New> Adjustment Layer.

*Press Command/Control-I
to invert a file.*

Invert

The Invert command (Image>Adjust>Invert) creates the appearance of a photographic negative of an image. In Bitmap, Grayscale, RGB, and L*a*b* modes, you get a very realistic negative. If you use this command in CMYK mode, however, the result may not be what you expect, because the inverted black channel will overpower everything else.

Original RGB Image

Inverted RGB image. The black channel overpowers all three channels when a CMYK image is inverted.

Equalize

The Equalize command (Image>Adjust>Equalize) reads the brightness level of each pixel in each channel. It remaps the pixels with the brightest value to white, and the pixels with the darkest value to black; it then recalculates every pixel in the image and redistributes the brightness values along a curve. The Equalize command is not available as an adjustment layer.

The Equalize command should be used only in special circumstances. By its very nature, it changes the effect that may be built into an image by remapping to a full spectrum, rather than the range that may have been intended by the creator of the image.

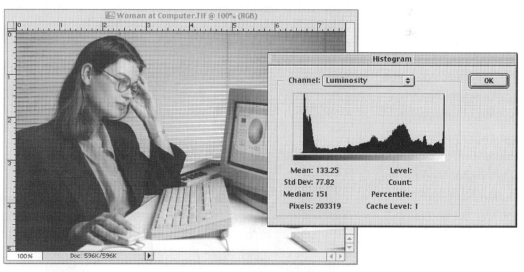

Original image with Histogram.

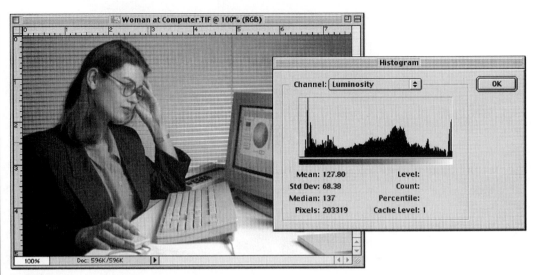

Image and Histogram after the Equalize command.

The result is an increase in contrast and saturation of the color. If you use only a selected portion of an image when equalizing, Photoshop provides an option to map only the selection, or to map the entire image based on the brightness values included in the selection.

Threshold

By selecting Image>Adjust>Threshold or Layer>New Adjustment Layer>Threshold, you have a means of converting the image to black and white pixels only (no grays), while maintaining control over how much detail is retained. The Threshold command offers a single slider below a histogram of the image. Moving the slider to the right causes increasingly dark pixels in the image to become black. Moving it to the left causes increasingly light pixels to become white. Using this adjustment layer option allows the threshold value to be edited at any time based on the original image data.

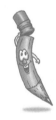

The Threshold command is a quick way to preview the location of the brightest and darkest pixels in a file. This can help guide you to set the highlight and shadow areas in a file to optimize tone and color.

Pixel distributions before and after applying the Threshold command.

The slider determines the brightness value that will be used as the mapping point for the entire image. Pixels having a value brighter than this point will all be turned white, and pixels having a darker value will change to black.

Using the High Pass filter (Filter>Other>High Pass) with a value of 20 or 30 before running Threshold can dramatically improve the amount of detail retained.

Image after a High Pass filter command

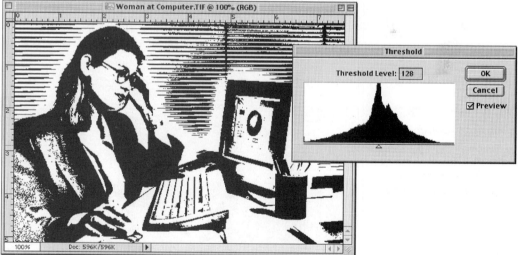

Image after a High Pass filter command followed by the Threshold command.

Posterize

Posterize is similar to the Threshold command, except that it maps colors rather than black and white. When you apply Posterize to an image, Photoshop divides the 256 levels of brightness evenly into the specified number of levels that you enter in the dialog box. This bands the colors, so the smooth transition between colors is replaced by hard-edged blocks of color. The lower the value you enter, the fewer the colors left in the image.

A great way to make images look hand-colored is to duplicate the image in a new layer, desaturate the bottom layer, posterize the top layer, and set the blending mode of the upper layer to Color and adjust the Opacity as desired.

The Posterize command is available as an adjustment layer or by selecting Image>Adjust. The adjustment layer option allows you to edit the Posterize settings at any time in the future based on the original image data.

Running the Dust & Scratches filter after posterizing helps remove single pixels of color, rendering an image suitable for tracing in a program such as Adobe Streamline. If you use the High Pass filter before running Posterize, the edge definition will sometimes be improved, but you will have a definite loss of color. The Posterize command can also assist in imaginative special effects.

If you are using Adobe Streamline to transform a posterized image into vector art and it does not seem accurate enough, try using the Straight Lines Only option. It creates a much more accurate transformation, though with a lot more points than using Streamline's curve.

Posterize command and Posterize command after a High Pass Filter command.

Gradient Map

Gradient Map maps the grayscale range of the image to the colors of a specified gradient fill. If you use a normal black-to-white gradient, the image will appear as a normal grayscale image. If you plan to use a non-standard gradient, however, such as a blue-red-yellow gradient, the darker tones will be mapped to blue gradating to red midtones, and yellow highlights, creating an other-worldly effect.

Original image and image with blue-red-yellow gradient map applied.

Posterize Images

1. Open **Shell.TIF** from the **SF-Adv Photoshop** folder. Press "C" to activate the Cropping tool. Crop the image so that only the shell is showing.

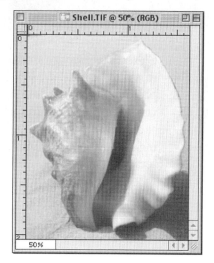

2. Select Layer>New Adjustment Layer. For the Type, select Brightness/Contrast. Accept the default name of Brightness/Contrast 1. Set Brightness to -30 and Contrast to +30. Click OK.

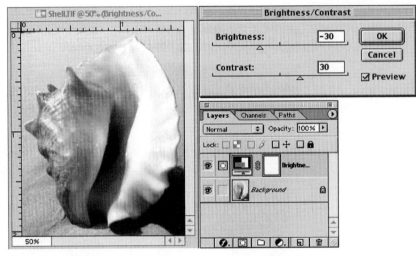

3. Select Layer>New> Adjustment Layer. For the type, select Posterize. Accept the default name of Posterize 1. Set Levels to 4. Click OK.

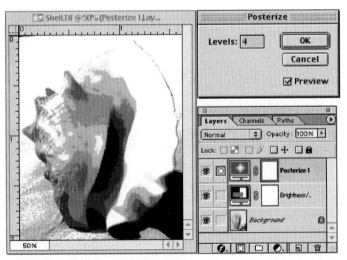

4. Click on the Background layer in the Layers palette to make it the target layer. Then run Filter>Noise>Dust & Scratches, with Radius set to 4 pixels. Click OK. This is a posterized image. The image in this state is well prepared to be transformed into vector art in a program such as Adobe Streamline. We're going to spice up this image as an illustration. Having the remapping commands in the form of adjustment layers means that you can double-click on the layer in the Layers palette and edit the settings at any time.

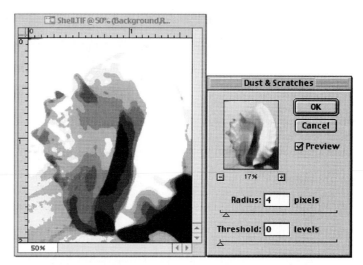

Some filter operations are available in RGB mode only.

5. Select the entire Background layer. Copy the layer as it appears by choosing Edit>Copy Merged. (This will copy the selected area as it is seen rather than as it is in the target layer.)

6. Select Edit>Paste. A new layer (Layer 1) is created. Move Layer 1 to the top of the Layers palette by clicking and holding on the layer and dragging it to the top of the stack.

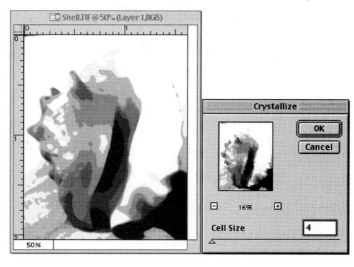

7. On Layer 1, select Filter>Pixelate>Crystalize, set Cell Size to 4 pixels, then click OK.

8. Blur the resulting image using Filter>Blur>Gaussian Blur with a width of 2.0 pixels.

9. Choose Filter>Stylize>Find Edges.

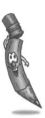

The Desaturate command removes all chromatic values and renders the image as neutral lights and darks.

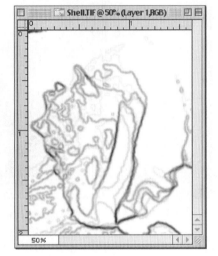

10. Select Image>Adjust>Desaturate.

11. From the Levels dialog box (Image>Adjust>Levels), set the black point slider to 175.

Some filter operations require real RAM to be available; they will not run with scratch disk virtual memory. One workaround is to apply the filter to each of the color channels separately.

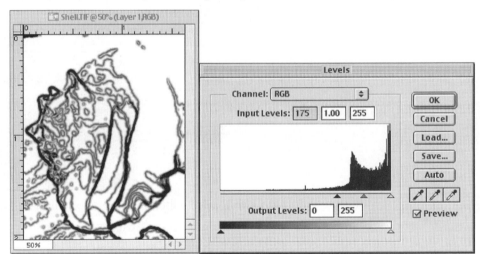

12. Activate Filter>Sharpen>Sharpen More. Press Command/Control-F two times to run the filter repeatedly on the image.

13. Change the Layers blending mode from Normal to Darken.

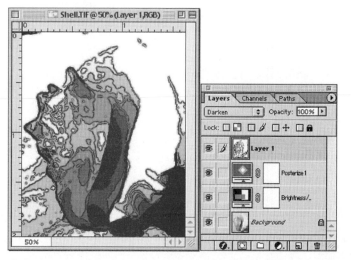

14. Double-click the Zoom tool to view the image at 100% to see the detail. Save the file to your **Work in Progress** folder as "Posterized Shell.TIF". Close the file.

Summary

In this chapter, you learned how to use Photoshop's powerful filters to recolor images. From straightforward inverting of pixels to form a negative image to adjusting thresholds for quick conversion of a grayscale or colored image to stark black-and-white, you've become familiar with these tools. You have also learned what a gradient map can do to an image, and have used the posterization tools to reduce a continuous-tone image to outlines and to a four-level posterized effect. These tools will be useful for creating special effects from real-life images.

Notes:

CHAPTER 11

LAYER STYLES

CHAPTER OBJECTIVE:

To learn how to apply dimension to images and parts of images with Photoshop's Layer Styles feature. To learn to add special effects to layers. In Chapter 11, you will:

- Learn how to apply a drop shadow and inner glow to a type layer.

- Become familiar with and experience creating multimedia buttons.

- Discover how to apply soft embosses and glows.

- Observe how layer styles allow you to easily make dynamic effects.

- Learn how to work with layer styles to easily produce compound layer effects.

PROJECTS TO BE COMPLETED:

- Just Shoot Me (A)

- Baby Shower Invitation (B)

- Retouching the Jones Family Portrait (C)

- The Fix Is In! (D)

- Makeover (E)

- Photomat (F)

Layer Styles

In addition to managing the look of two-dimensional images, Photoshop enables us to give dimension to both full images and parts of images using its powerful Layer Style feature. Layer styles are easy to apply, are editable, and are reversible. As with all other features of Photoshop, the image's resolution and ultimate use must be taken into consideration before applying the effects.

The effects may be applied to images or type, and are not exclusive. Multiple effects may be applied to the same layer. If the same effect is applied over itself, the results may not be as you anticipate — but they can be easily undone.

Drop Shadows

The effect most often used is the drop shadow, which gives substantial depth and realism to an image. Shadows can be combined with other effects to heighten interest or to enhance realism. Be careful to avoid overusing these effects, thus reducing their value to each image.

Apply a Drop Shadow

1. Open **Bull Rider.TIF** from the **SF-Adv Photoshop** folder.

2. Select the Type tool, click the color swatch in the Options bar, and pick a color from the bull's head. Type
"Hang On
COWBOY" in 48 pt. ATC MaiTai Bold. Click the checkmark, or press Command-Return/Control-Enter to commit the type. Position the type below and to the right of the bull. Kern and track, and apply leading to taste.

3. With the Info palette visible and using the Measure tool, measure the angle of the shadow of the bull. Measure toward the bull to find the angle. You'll find it's around 22°.

4. Select the type layer, and apply Layer>Layer Style>Drop Shadow. Set Blend Mode: Multiply, Opacity: 60%, Angle: 22°, Distance: 25 px, Spread: 0, Size: 10 px, and Use Global Light: checked. Click OK.

The Use Global Light checkbox enables you to determine a shadow angle once for the entire image and use it consistently. Check Use Global Light when you set an angle, and it becomes the default for that image.

When creating shadow effects, pay attention to the details of the photograph on which you're working. Shadows created by shadow effects should flow in the same direction and be the same approximate density as shadows in the photograph. When that doesn't happen, the image looks artificial.

Notice that the Type layer has acquired a new symbol, telling you that a layer effect has been applied.

5. Save the file to your **Work in Progress** folder as "Bull Rider.PSD", and leave it open for the next exercise.

Bevel and Emboss Features

Beveled and embossed elements can be used as part of a photograph, very subtly altering the overall effect of the original, or they may be individual elements, constructed for a specific use. More and more people are building Web pages with snazzy buttons, and the Bevel and Emboss features are excellent for these uses.

Add Inner Glow

1. In the open Bull Rider.PSD file, note that the words look stark and out of place. Let's soften them a bit. Select the Type layer, then select Layer Style>Inner Glow. Choose a light tan from the glove on the cowboy's left hand. In the Structure section, set Blend Mode: Dissolve, Opacity: 70%, and Noise: 10%. In the Elements section, set Technique: Softer, Source: Center, Choke: 0%, Size: 0 px. In the Quality section, set Range: 50%, Jitter: 0%.

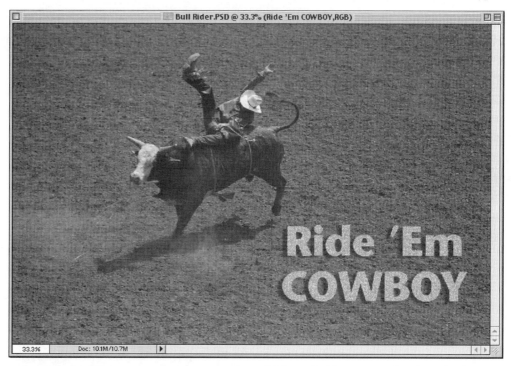

One of the best aspects of Layer Styles is that they are applied to the layer, and not to the object on the layer. Let's see how elegantly this works.

2. Select the Type layer, and highlight the words "Hang On". Replace it with the words "Ride 'Em". All the effects have been added to the new layer data. Commit the type.

3. Save the file to your **Work in Progress** folder as "Ride Em.PSD". Close the file.

Create Multimedia Buttons

1. Create a new RGB file with a width of 72 pixels, a height of 21, at 72 ppi. Make the background transparent. Name the file "Forward".

2. Set the foreground color to red, and fill the layer.

3. Select Layer>Layer Style>Bevel and Emboss. In the Structure section, set Style: Inner Bevel, Technique: Chisel Hard, Depth: 100%, Direction: Up, Size: 4 px, Soften: 2 px. Accept the defaults in the Shading section, and click OK.

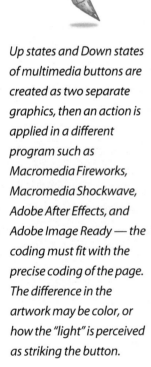

Up states and Down states of multimedia buttons are created as two separate graphics, then an action is applied in a different program such as Macromedia Fireworks, Macromedia Shockwave, Adobe After Effects, and Adobe Image Ready — the coding must fit with the precise coding of the page. The difference in the artwork may be color, or how the "light" is perceived as striking the button.

Note that this is an Up button. Since the highlight comes from above, and as a multimedia element, you can tell that this is the "up" state of the button.

4. Create a New layer. Press "X" to exchange the foreground and background colors, making the foreground color white.

5. Select the Line tool, and set its Weight to 4 pt. Select the End Arrowhead, and set its shape to a Width of 250% and a Length of 300%. Click the checkmark or press return/Enter to commit the action. Draw an arrow in the center of the button. (Press the Shift key to constrain the line to horizontal.)

6. To give the illusion that the arrow is cut into the button, Select Layer Style>Bevel and Emboss. In the Structure section, set Layer Style: Inner Bevel, Technique: Smooth, Depth: 100%, Direction: Down, Size: 3 px, and Soften: 1 px. Leave the Shading section at its defaults. Click OK.

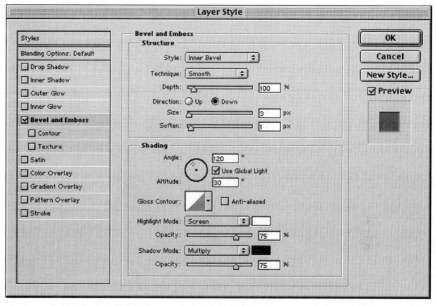

7. Save the file to your **Work in Progress** folder as "Forward Up.PSD".

8. Now let's create the depressed, or down state of this button. Go to Layer 1, and change the Bevel and Emboss effect. Click the Down radio button, and click OK.

9. On the Shape 1 layer, we're going to move the shadow inside the arrow to the bottom. In the Shading area, click on the Gloss Contour icon.

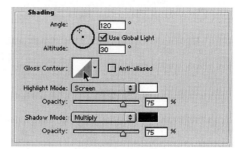

10. In the Contour Editor, reverse the Contour Map by dragging the Input point to 100% and the Output point to 0%. Click OK.

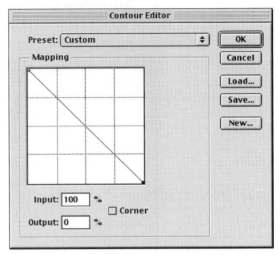

11. Save the button as "Forward Down.PSD" to your **Work in Progress** folder. Close the file.

Forward Up and Forward Down buttons.

Emboss with a Pillow Effect

1. Open **Beach Boy.TIF** from the **SF-Adv Photoshop** folder.

2. Select the Type tool and, using ATC MaiTai Bold, set the Size to 10 pt., and select a blue from the background as the color.

3. Type "JOEY", and center it on the bill of his hat.

4. Select Layer>Layer Style>Bevel and Emboss. In the Structure section, set Style: Pillow Emboss, Technique: Smooth, Depth 100%, Direction: Up, Size: 2 px, Soften: 3 px. In the Shading section, set Highlight Mode: Screen, Opacity: 50%; Shadow Mode: Multiply, Opacity: 50%. Click OK.

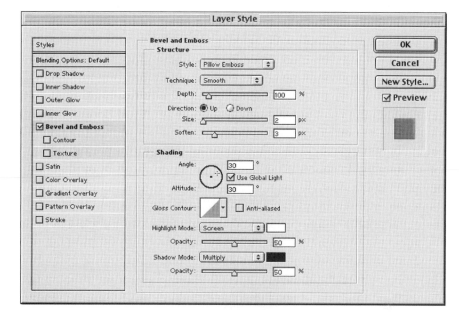

This results in a soft "mashed into the layer behind" look, giving a quilted effect.

5. Save the file to your **Work in Progress** folder as "Joey.PSD". Close the file.

Glowing in the Dark

Sometimes it is useful to create a soft, glow effect, such as might be seen on a sign at night. When the lights are off on the original image, it may be necessary to create the entire effect from scratch. This used to be difficult — now it can be achieved easily using a layer effect.

In the following exercise, we're going to add a neon glow to a sign.

Create a Glow

1. Open **Bakery.TIF** from the **SF-Adv Photoshop** folder.

2. With the Pen tool, create a path outlining all the neon tubing on the word BAKERY. The path will be created in several sections. It should be close, but doesn't need to be perfect.

3. Name the path "Bakery", convert it to a selection, and save the selection as "Bakery". Accept the Rendering and Operation defaults.

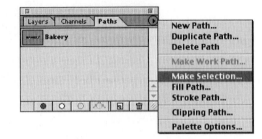

4. Select a red from the BAKERY letters for the foreground color.

5. Create a new layer, and load the selection to that layer. Fill the selection with the foreground color.

6. Select Layer>Layer Style>Outer Glow. In the Structure section, set Blend Mode: Screen, Opacity: 75%, Noise: 0%, Color: red (R: 255, G: 0, B: 0). In the Elements section, set Technique: Precise, Spread: 25%, Size: 40 px. In the Quality section, set Range: 65%, Jitter: 0%.

7. Click the New Style button, name the style "Neon Glow", and click OK. Open the Styles palette, and you will see that the new style has been added to the list. We'll use this style later. Deselect.

8. Select the background layer. From Image>Adjust>Curves, drag the highlight to an Output level of 32.

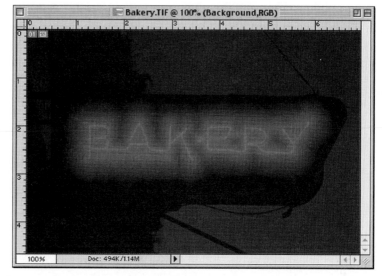

The sign appears to glow in the dark. Save to your **Work in Progress** folder as "Bakery Glows.PSD". Close the file.

Use Created Styles

1. Open the file **Jazzman.PSD** from your **SF-Adv Photoshop** folder.

2. Create a new layer. Allow the name to default to Layer 1.

3. We've already saved a selection for you. With the new layer active, choose Select>Load Selection>Jazz, then click OK.

4. Click on the foreground color icon, and select a hot magenta for the foreground color. (We used R: 255, G: 0, B: 128.) Click OK.

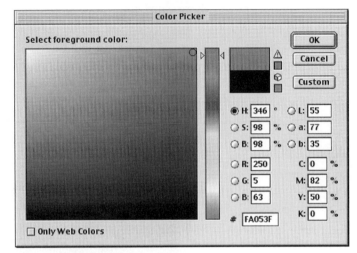

5. Fill the selection with the foreground color.

6. With the selection still active, select the Styles palette, and then click on the Neon style that was added at the end of the list to apply the style that you created in the previous exercise. Deselect.

Since this doesn't look very dramatic, we're going to make some changes to the background layer.

7. Select the background layer, and access the Curves palette (Image>Adjust>Curves).

8. Switch to the Green channel, and pull all the green out of the image by dragging the highlight point to zero.

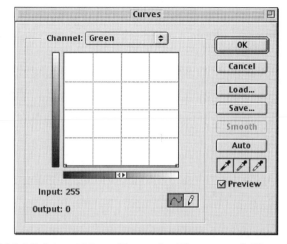

9. Drag the Red highlight to 128, and leave the Blue normal. If you like, experiment with locking the midtones and altering the Red and Blue channels until you have an effect that you like.

10. Save the file to your **Work in Progress** folder as "Hot Jazz.PSD". Close the file.

Summary

The Layer Styles make creating interesting effects relatively easy. When there is sufficient resolution to output these effects, they can add strikingly to the image. Effects should be used to enhance an image, however, not solely for the sake of using the effect. When they are used sparingly, layer styles will make images look more dynamic. If used flagrantly, the images will often assault and offend your audience's sensitivities.

Notes:

CREATING PATTERNS AND TEXTURES

CHAPTER OBJECTIVE:

To learn how to easily create unique, project-specific tiles and textures as backgrounds for brochures, posters, Web pages, or almost anything you want to enhance. In Chapter 12, you will:

- Discover how the method that you use to create tiles depends on the type of tile that you're creating.

- Learn about basic tiling and alternating tiles.

- Become familiar with how to create offset graphic tiles.

- Learn how to create tiles for use with the Clone Stamp tool.

- Discover how to create mirrored tiles.

- Learn how to create textured and generic backgrounds.

PROJECTS TO BE COMPLETED:

- Just Shoot Me (A)

- Baby Shower Invitation (B)

- Retouching the Jones Family Portrait (C)

- The Fix Is In! (D)

- Makeover (E)

- Photomat (F)

Creating Patterns and Textures

Often a designer needs to add a pattern or texture to a project, whether as a background or composited with type or images. While there are many companies offering stock photography suitable for backgrounds, Photoshop enables you to easily create unique, project-specific tiles and textures.

Pattern Definition

Patterns are texturally interesting as backgrounds for brochures, posters, Web pages, and more. Photoshop's patterns tile horizontally and vertically, repeating a square or rectangle. Third-party plug-ins are also available that will allow you to automatically create pattern tiles in hexagonal, triangular, and other shapes. Plug-ins are also available that create random textures and "weld" them together to make tiles.

There are many types of tiles that can be made without special software; the method by which you choose to create a tile depends on what tile you're making. For text, a simple offset tile will usually do; for photographs, more complexity may be required.

Create a Basic Tile

1. Open **Paradise.TIF** from the **SF-Adv Photoshop** folder.

2. Press Command/Control-A to select all, and then choose Edit>Define Pattern. Accept Photoshop's default name for the pattern of "Paradise.TIF".

3. Create a new document named "Tiles.PSD". Make the new image 5 in. × 5 in., RGB mode, 100 ppi, with Contents set to White.

4. Choose Edit>Fill, and select Pattern in the Use drag-down menu. Make certain that the Blending section is set to Mode: Normal and Opacity: 100%. Click on the Custom Pattern drop-down menu and choose the Paradise.TIF pattern. Click OK.

Define Pattern only works when the Rectangular Marquee has been used to isolate the pattern. It will not work with the Elliptical Marquee.

5. This is a simple repeating tile. Save "Tiles.PSD" to your **Work In Progress** folder. Leave it open for the next exercise, in which we'll make this pattern more interesting. Close **Paradise.TIF** without saving.

```
          Tiles.PSD @ 100% (RGB)
     0           1           2           3           4
  0
     Paradise   Paradise   Paradise   Pa
     Paradise   Paradise   Paradise   Pa
  1  Paradise   Paradise   Paradise   Pa
     Paradise   Paradise   Paradise   Pa
  2  Paradise   Paradise   Paradise   Pa
     Paradise   Paradise   Paradise   Pa
  3  Paradise   Paradise   Paradise   Pa
     Paradise   Paradise   Paradise   Pa
  4  Paradise   Paradise   Paradise   Pa
     Paradise   Paradise   Paradise   Pa
  100%        Doc: 733K/733K
```

For easy pattern selection, click the triangle in the upper right portion of the Patterns menu, and select one of the List options instead of a Thumbnail option.

Make Alternating Tiles

1. Create a new document, 150 pixels wide × 150 pixels high, Resolution 100 ppi, with a Background of White. Select Edit>Fill, to fill the document with your Paradise.TIF pattern.

2. Select the middle line of text with the Rectangular Marquee tool. Be certain to select from edge to edge to include the white background of both sides of the type.

3. Choose Filter>Other>Offset, and set the Horizontal Offset Value to 50 pixels. We have three lines of type, and this is one-third of the width of our image. Set the Vertical Offset Value to 0, and click the Wrap Around radio button. Click OK.

If a background tile pattern looks like it will make a boring and repetitive tile, using an alternating tile will spice up the effect with very little additional work.

```
                        Offset
     Horizontal: 50      pixels right    [ OK ]
     Vertical:   0       pixels down     [ Cancel ]
                                         ☑ Preview
     ┌ Undefined Areas ─────────────
     ○ Set to Background
     ○ Repeat Edge Pixels
     ● Wrap Around
```

4. Now select the bottom line of text with the Marquee tool. Choose Filter>Other> Offset. This time, set the Horizontal Offset Value to 100 pixels; leave Vertical at 0. Click OK.

5. You now have three different offset versions of Paradise.TIF. Press Command/ Control-A to select all and choose Edit>Define Pattern. Assign the pattern name of "Paradise 3".

6. Activate Tiles.PSD. Add a new layer, accepting the default name of Layer 1. Choose Edit>Fill, and fill the area with the Paradise 3 pattern.

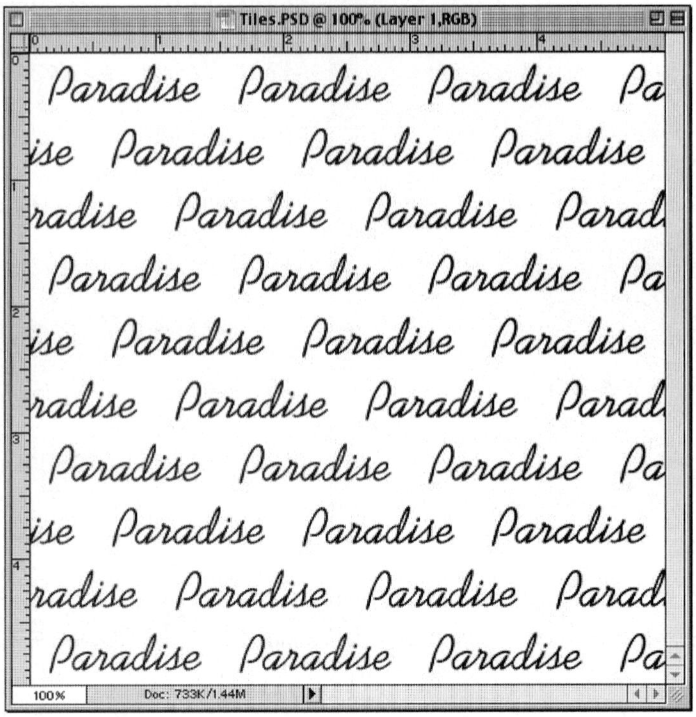

7. Save Tiles.PSD, and leave it open for the next exercise. Close the new pattern document (Untitled 1) without saving.

Create Offset Graphic Tiles

1. Create a new RGB document. Set both Height and Width to 100 pixels; set Contents to White and Resolution to 100 ppi.
2. Select Filter>Noise>Add Noise, and set the Amount to 300%. Make the Noise Gaussian and Monochromatic. Click OK. Apply a Gaussian Blur of 1 pixel to the image.
3. Choose Filter>Distort>Pinch. Set the Amount to 100%, and click OK. Press Command/Control-F 10 times to reapply the filter.

4. Choose Filter>Distort>Twirl. Set Angle to 200°, and click OK.

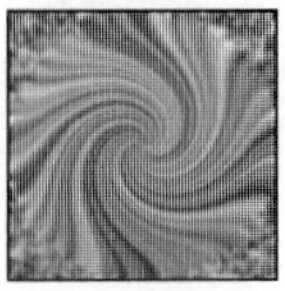

5. Choose Filter>Other>Offset. Change both Horizontal and Vertical to 50; make certain that Wrap Around is selected. Click OK.

6. Choose Filter>Distort>Pinch. Distort the image with the Amount set to 100%. Repeat the filter action by pressing Command/Control-F 10 times.

7. Apply Filter>Distort>Twirl again, only this time set the Angle to -200°. Click OK.

8. Select all and, in the Edit menu, select Define Pattern. Name the pattern "Swirls". Activate the open Tiles.PSD document. Create a new layer, and fill the layer with the tile.

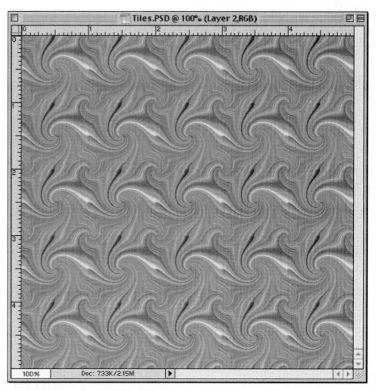

Patterns such as this are especially good for colorizing (Image>Adjust>Hue/Saturation).

9. Save Tiles.PSD to your **Work in Progress** folder. Leave it open for the next exercise. Close the latest pattern document without saving.

Use the Clone Stamp to Enhance Tiles

1. Open **Rock.TIF** from the **SF-Adv Photoshop** folder.

2. Choose Filter>Other>Offset. Set Horizontal to 100 and Vertical to 50; note that this is precisely half of the height and width of the image. Undefined Areas should be set to Wrap Around.

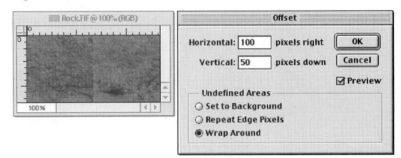

3. Distinct lines will be apparent where the offset occurred. Use the Clone Stamp tool to clean up the edges. Don't get too close to the edge of the image.

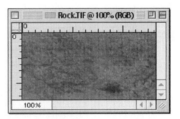

4. Press Command/Control-F to offset the image back into place. Select all, and apply Define Pattern as "Rock".

5. With Tiles.PSD open, create a new layer, and select Edit>Fill to fill with the Rock pattern.

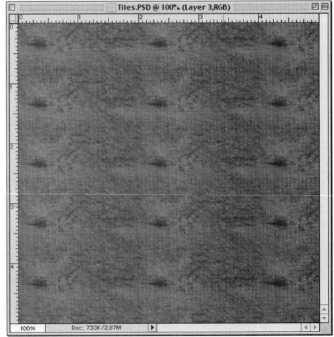

Sometimes it may be advantageous to use a light Gaussian Blur to hide flaws in an image.

6. If the edges don't seem perfect (if you can see them) in the tiled layer, return to the Rock.TIF image, offset it again and do more touchup. If you offset a different amount this time (for example, setting Horizontal to 50 and Vertical to 25), it might make the flaws more apparent.

7. The very light and dark areas spoil the illusion in the Rock.TIF image. Use the Clone Stamp tool to even out the tones. You'll probably want to apply Offset a few times while working, just in case you've messed up the edges. Remove the dark spots completely. Select all, and apply Define Pattern again. Refill the layer in the Tiles document.

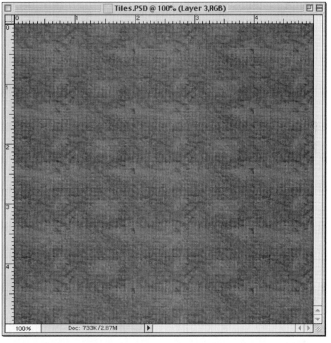

8. Although the pattern is still somewhat apparent, the fill is appropriate for a multimedia background. If you overlay text and graphics, you will enhance the illusion of seamlessness. Virtually any textured background can be treated in this manner. Save Tiles.PSD and leave it open for the next exercise. Close Rock.TIF without saving.

Unique, though sometimes eye-boggling effects can be created by mirroring images, then creating a tile using the mirrored elements. This effect is also useful for hiding unwanted seams.

Create Mirrored Tiles

1. Open **Beach Boy.TIF** from the **SF-Adv Photoshop** folder.

2. Click the Rectangular Marquee tool and, in the Options bar, change the Style to Fixed Size. Set both Width and Height to 50 px. Click the Marquee on the image to select as much of the boy's face as you can within the 50 × 50-pixel area.

3. Copy your selection. Create a new RGB document with a white background. Allow the image size to be the default size of your copied data. Select Command/Control-V to paste the copied data into the new document. Close Beach Boy.TIF without saving.

4. In the new document, press Command/Control-E to merge the layers. Make certain that your background color is white. Select Image>Canvas Size. Click the upper-left corner of the Anchor, and enter 100 pixels for both Height and Width.

```
┌─────────────────────────────────────────────┐
│                  Canvas Size                  │
│  ┌─ Current Size: 8K ──────────┐   ┌──────┐  │
│     Width: 50 pixels               │  OK  │  │
│     Height: 50 pixels              └──────┘  │
│                                    ┌──────┐  │
│  ┌─ New Size: 30K ─────────────┐   │Cancel│  │
│     Width:  [100]  [pixels  ▲]     └──────┘  │
│     Height: [100]  [pixels  ▲]               │
│     Anchor:                                   │
└─────────────────────────────────────────────┘
```

5. Double-click the Background layer to make it a normal layer. Click OK to let the name default to Layer 0.

6. Set the Blending mode of the layer to Darken, and duplicate the layer three times.

7. Click on the top layer. Choose Edit>Transform>Flip Horizontal.

8. Click on the second layer, and choose Edit>Transform>Flip Vertical.

9. Click on the third layer, choose Edit>Transform>Flip Horizontal, then Edit>Transform>Flip Vertical.

10. Select all, and choose Edit>Define Pattern Name the pattern "Mirror Boy". If Tiles.PSD is not already open, open it now; otherwise, activate Tiles.PSD. Create a new layer, and fill it with the pattern.

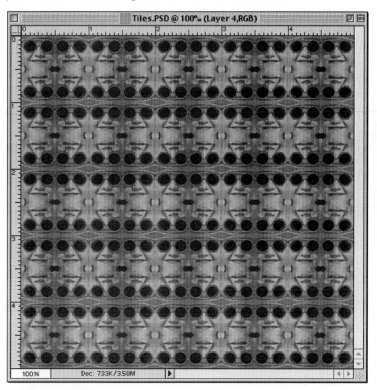

11. Save Tiles.PSD. Close the image containing the tile without saving.

12. Choose Edit>Fill, then access the Custom Patterns. Click the arrow, and select Reset Patterns from the menu. This will remove the custom patterns you created.

13. Close the Tiles.PSD file.

Textured Backgrounds

Pattern tiles are great backgrounds for many purposes. Sometimes, though, you need a more generic background. Photoshop has the ability to create varied backgrounds quickly and easily.

We couldn't possibly begin to show you all the possibilities for backgrounds here. We hope that by showing you a few, you'll get the idea and experiment by creating your own backgrounds.

Noise-based Backgrounds

Many excellent backgrounds begin with the Noise filters. Blur, Sharpen, Emboss, and other filters make the options almost limitless. Here are a few for you to try:

Create Basic Noise Backgrounds

1. Create a new RGB document. Set the dimensions to 5 in. square, 72 ppi, with a white background.

2. Select Filter>Noise>Add Noise. Set the Amount to 300. Make the Noise Gaussian and Monochromatic.

3. Duplicate the Background layer; name the duplicate layer "Basic". Select Filter> Blur>Gaussian Blur, and set the Blur to 2.0 pixels. This is the most basic of textured backgrounds. Adjust Brightness/Contrast, then colorize as you wish by selecting Image>Adjust>Hue/Saturation. We used Hue: 0, Saturation: 60, Lightness: 0 to achieve a rich burgundy color. Experiment and create a color to your taste.

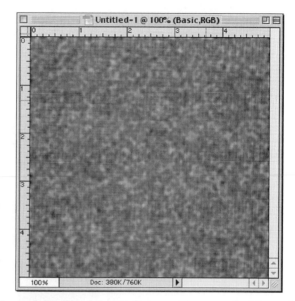

The more you experiment with noise-based textures, the more variety you'll be able to add to your files. When you find one that you particularly like, be certain to save the steps so that you can reuse it. (Saving steps as an Action is described in Chapter 15.)

4. Turn off Basic, and duplicate the Background layer again. Name the layer "Leather". Select Filter>Blur>Gaussian Blur; this time set the Blur to 5.0 pixels. Colorize the image with Hue and Saturation with settings of Hue 30, Saturation 50, and Lightness 20. Select the Add Noise filter again; set Amount to 3%. Be certain to check the Monochromatic box.

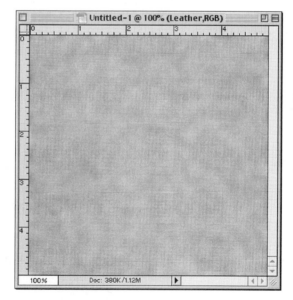

5. Turn off Leather, and duplicate the Background layer. Name this duplicate layer "Stars". Select Filter>Stylize>Diffuse. Activate the Darken Only button, and click OK. Press Command/Control-F three or four times to repeat the filter, until the Background layer resembles a starfield.

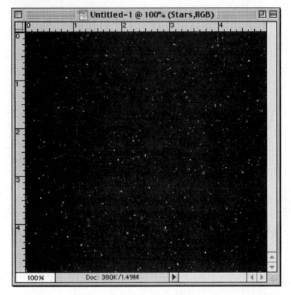

6. Turn off the Stars layer, and again duplicate the Background layer. Name the new layer "Marbled Paper". Apply Filter>Blur>Motion Blur to the image at a 45° Angle, and a Distance of 20 pixels. Choose Filter>Distort>Ripple. Set Amount to -333 and Size to Large. Use Image>Adjust>Brightness/Contrast to bring out the detail. Colorize the image.

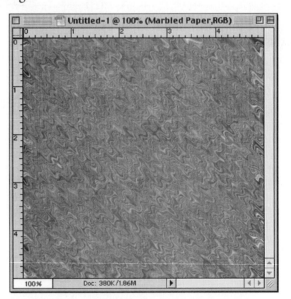

7. Create three unique backgrounds of your own using Noise. Try varying the Blur or Noise amounts, and using the Pixelate and Stylize filters.

8. Save the image as "Textures.PSD" to your **Work in Progress** folder. Leave the document open for the next exercise.

Real-world Backgrounds

By experimenting with Photoshop's tools and filters, you can create textures that imitate patterns and objects in the real world.

Simulate Crumpled Foil

1. In the open Textures.PSD file, create a new layer. Name the layer "Foil". Press "D" to set the default colors, then press Command-Option-Delete/Control-Alt-Backspace to fill the layer with white.

2. Choose Filter>Render>Clouds, then Filter>Render>Difference Clouds. Now, choose Filter>Stylize>Find Edges.

3. Press Command/Control-L to load the Levels dialog box, and click on the Auto button.

4. Run Filter>Sharpen>Unsharp Mask. Set Amount: 200%, Radius: 1 pixel, Threshold: 0.

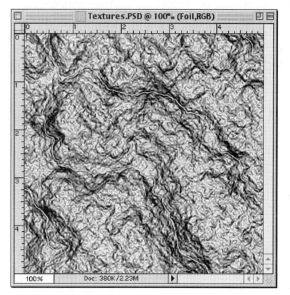

5. For gold foil, colorize with the Hue/Saturation dialog box. Select Image>Adjust>Hue/Saturation. Click Colorize. Set Hue: 40, Saturation: 75, Lightness: -5.

6. Save the file, and leave it open for the next exercise.

This is a nice, easy pattern. You could go wild and create a plaid that would work equally well as a pattern fill. When creating patterns that imitate woven fabrics, remember that a "solid" is the overlap of two 50% layers.

Create Gingham Checks

1. Create a new document in RGB mode. Make it 20 pixels × 20 pixels, with a resolution of 72 ppi, filled with white.

2. Set the foreground color to bright red. Click the Marquee tool. In the Options bar, change the Style to Fixed Size with a Width of 10 px and Height of 20 px. Select the left half of the image with the Marquee, and fill it with red.

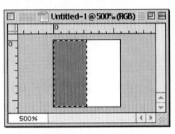

3. Press Command/Control-A to select the entire image, and choose Edit>Define Pattern. Close the document without saving.

4. Return to the Textures.PSD document and create a new layer named "Gingham 1".

5. Select Edit>Fill, and fill with the newly defined pattern.

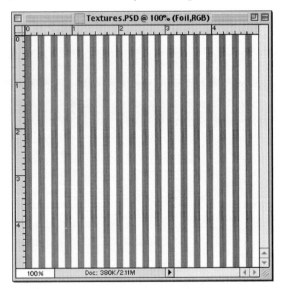

6. Duplicate the layer, naming it "Gingham 2". Select Edit>Transform>Rotate 90° Clockwise.

7. Change the Layer Opacity to 50%.

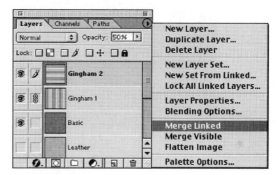

8. Link the two gingham layers, and select Merge Linked from the Layers palette Options menu.

9. Save the file and close it.

Modify Textures to Create New Textures

1. Create a new RGB document. Set the dimensions to 5 in. square, 72 ppi, with a white background.

2. Press "D" to make certain that you're using default colors. Select Filter>Render> Clouds.

3. Select Filter>Distort>Ripple. Change the Amount to 999 and the Size to Large.

4. Duplicate the layer. Rename the original layer "Water". Rename the new layer "Copper Mesh".

5. Activate the Copper Mesh layer, and select Filter>Stylize>Find Edges. Press Command/Control-I to invert the colors in the current layer.

6. Duplicate the Copper Mesh layer. Rename the new layer "Fur".

7. Select Filter>Blur>Motion Blur. Set the Angle to -45° and the Distance to 15 pixels.

8. Select Filter>Sharpen>Unsharp Mask. Set Amount to 100 and Radius to 2 pixels. Leave Threshold at 0.

9. Activate the Water layer, and turn off the other layers. Select Image>Adjust>Hue/Saturation. Click the Colorize check box. Set Hue: 205, Saturation: 50, Lightness: -10. Choose Image>Adjust>Levels, and make the necessary alterations to bring out bright highlights and deep shadows in the image.

10. Activate the Copper Mesh layer. Select Image>Adjust>Hue/Saturation. Make certain that the Colorize checkbox is checked. Set Hue: 35, Saturation: 100, Lightness: 0. Level the layer to bring out detail.

11. Activate the Fur layer. Choose Image>Adjust>Hue/Saturation again. Check the Colorize checkbox. Set Hue: 28, Saturation: 60, Lightness: -35.

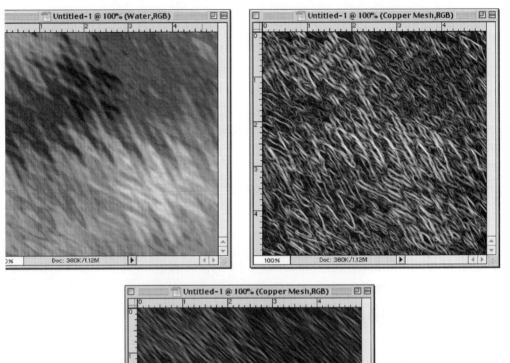

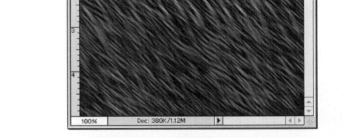

12. Save the file as "Texture Build" to your **Work in Progress** file and close.

Summary

Use the power and versatility of Photoshop to add variety to your images. These patterns and textures can be especially effective when used as backgrounds for other images, or for a combination of images and text, as is found on Web pages. While a few effects have been presented here, creating patterns and textures is limited only by your imagination.

CHAPTER 13

SPECIAL EFFECTS

CHAPTER OBJECTIVE:

To learn how to create Photoshop's nearly infinite variety of special effects. To learn to use special effects that employ type, line art, and images. In Chapter 13, you will

- Discover how to import an EPS illustration.

- Learn how to create jungle type, soft "pillow" type, and type cutouts, as well as how to carve line art out of the background.

- Become familiar with photo edges for creating vignette borders and strokes, rippled borders, wood weathered decoupages, and burn edges.

- Learn to color images as duotones, tritones, and quadtones.

- Discover how to create a "pegboard" image.

- Experiment with the Liquify commands.

PROJECTS TO BE COMPLETED:

- Just Shoot Me (A)

- Baby Shower Invitation (B)

- Retouching the Jones Family Portrait (C)

- The Fix Is In! (D)

- Makeover (E)

- **Photomat (F)**

Special Effects

Photoshop is capable of creating a nearly infinite variety of special effects. Some can be achieved quickly, while others require several intertwined operations. This chapter demonstrates a few building block techniques that can be combined and varied to create hundreds of custom effects for all types of design projects.

Remember that effects are developed through experimentation. With the skills you have learned so far, you have already discovered several effects. Because creativity is serendipitous and hard to duplicate, keep these tips in mind:

- **Write down the steps used to create the effect while you create it.** At least jot down the steps and values when trying something experimental. The History palette can be a reminder, but it has two drawbacks for this purpose. It doesn't display values in dialog boxes and it only goes back so far, depending on memory and how many steps it is set to in History Options. Another possibility is to consider recording frequently used effects (such as borders) as Actions in the Actions palette.

- **Try to recreate an effect at various resolutions.** Some wonderful special effects only work as expected on low- or high-resolution files. Identify when this is the case, and develop a work-around if resolution is a problem before you need to use the effect again.

- **Duplicate layers for experimentation.** They can then be combined with the original layer using blend modes for additional effects. Also, duplicate original Selection channels before modifying them. The raw selection is often useful to combine with the Blurred, Offset, and Filtered channel to create the finished effect. The original selection remains available for trying out other possibilities. Consider duplicating the entire file for a worry-free creative environment.

- **Be sure to use the History palette and History brush,** which add a different dimension to creating effects. They record and allow integration of various stages of the process, including Snapshots. Often, special effects work well on one area but destroy the work performed to perfection on another. These tools give you ample freedom and good documentation to repeat effects and get them to where they work best.

- **Don't be afraid to try techniques that obviously won't work, even those that "just aren't done,"** such as applying Sharpen More or Auto Levels. No one knows just what effect a filter or command will have on a particular image until it's tried.

Special Effects Using Type and Line Art

Although Photoshop is an image-editing program, type and line art are often important elements in the design. Line art from vector programs and Photoshop type can be included, edited, and integrated using special effects throughout the design process. The following exercises will demonstrate how type and line art can be manipulated into the image, using filters and a combination of Photoshop effects.

Plug-ins are available for some of these effects, as well as Layer Style commands to speed the process along. The results from these filters are often good enough, but rarely offer the flexibility and quality (if needed) that performing the steps yourself can accomplish.

Additionally, the plug-ins that may be available on one computer may not be available on all the computers that you will use.

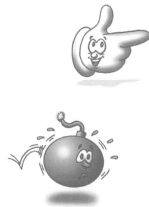

Press Command/Control-U to access the Hue/Saturation dialog box from the keyboard.

About Raster and Vector Images

A fundamental difference between working with raster-based images, such as photographs, and vector-based images is the scaleability of the results. Vector art is abbreviated — even to the extent that a rather elaborate design can be defined by only a few points (and the equations of the curve between them).

Visualize a Photoshop file as a logo printed on a balloon. By adding or subtracting air to the balloon, the logo will enlarge or reduce — usually looking crisper and denser when the balloon is at its proper or smaller size. As the balloon is inflated, the logo loses definition and density. A Photoshop file has the same problem: it won't enlarge or reduce forever without sacrificing quality.

The graphic below illustrates an aliased bitmap . While a vector image can be enlarged infinitely with no deterioration in quality, the bitmap image can only get worse. *Anti-aliasing* — the softening of the bitmap edges — will help, but eventually it, too, will degrade.

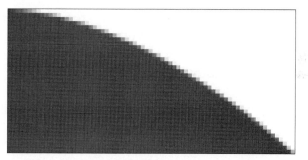

It's not necessary to abandon Photoshop altogether in favor of Adobe Illustrator. The two applications coexist well, as shown when the Tropical Interiors logo was imported in Chapter 5, Advanced Channel Operations.

In addition, as you have experienced, Photoshop's tools can be used, in some instances, to create vector elements such as shapes and type. To retain their vector qualities, though, the file must be saved as Photoshop (PSD), Encapsulated PostScript (EPS), or Portable Document Format (PDF) documents. Of those, EPS is the format of choice for importing into page-layout programs, although PDF is accepted by many programs.

Import an EPS Illustration

1. Open **Tropical Interiors.EPS** from the **SF-Adv Photoshop** folder. Set it to rasterize into an RGB image at 100 ppi, 5 in. wide, with the Anti-aliased and Constrain Proportions boxes checked.

2. Choose Image>Canvas Size to enlarge the canvas to 6 in. × 2.5 in. Anchor the current image in the center.

3. Choose Select>Load Selection, and load Layer 1 Transparency as a selection. Save the selection to a new channel, and name it "Type". Deselect.

4. With the RGB composite active, choose Image>Adjust>Hue/Saturation and turn the logo black by dragging the lightness slider to the far left (−100).

5. Make certain that the background color is white. Select Flatten Image from the Layers palette Options menu. Rename the Background layer "Type Layer".

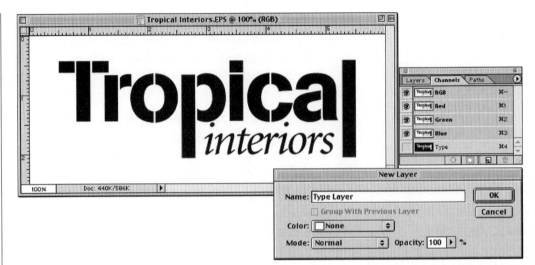

6. Save the image as "Tropical Type.PSD" to your **Work in Progress** folder. Leave the file open for the next exercise.

Create "Filtered" Type

"Distressed" type can be very effective. To invent your own, experiment with Text channels and the Noise and Pixelate filters.

Press Command/Control-F to apply the same filter repeatedly. Press Command-Option/Control Alt-F to repeat the same filter while changing settings in the dialog box.

1. With the Tropical Type.PSD file still open, duplicate the Type layer. On this layer apply the following filters: Filter>Pixelate>Crystalize with a Cell Size of 3, Filter>Blur>Gaussian Blur 2.5 pixels, and Filter>Stylize>Find Edges. Finally, choose Filter>Sharpen>Sharpen More, and press Command/Control-F to repeat the Sharpen More effect nine more times.

2. For a cleaner look, load the Type channel, choose Select>Inverse, and fill with white.

Some blending modes work better than others. Make a note of which work best for specific applications.

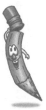

Third-party plug-ins aren't all bad — learning the basics from doing the steps yourself can help you understand how the plug-in works more quickly and enable you to control it. Often, using a combination of manual techniques and plug-ins makes the image better and work-time more efficient.

3. Save the selection as a new channel to create a mask for the background (name it "Background"). Deselect and create a new layer. Create an interesting texture on the new layer, such as one from Chapter 12. Start by filling the layer with white before adding Noise, and then use the blend modes to combine the layers.

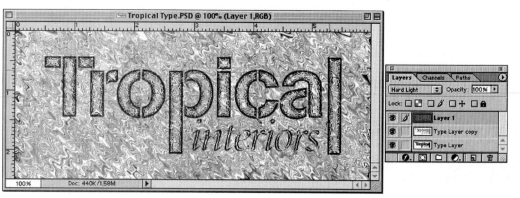

4. Save as "Filtered Type.PSD" to your **Work in Progress** folder and close the file.

Create Soft "Pillow" Type

1. Open **Tropical Type.PSD** from your **Work in Progress** folder.

2. Load the Type channel as a selection. Feather the selection 4 pixels.

3. Save the new selection. Allow Photoshop to assign a name (it will be Alpha 1). Click on the new Alpha 1 channel to make it active.

4. Load the Type channel as a selection. Choose Select>Inverse, and fill the area with white. Deselect.

5. Click on the RGB Composite channel.

6. In the Layers palette, create a new layer and fill it with white.

7. Load the Type channel selection and run the Lighting Effects filter (Filter>Render>Lighting Effects). Make the following settings:

Light Type section, set drag-down menu: Omni, On: checked, Intensity: 15
Properties section, set Gloss: 60, Material: –20, Exposure: 0, Ambience: 15
Texture Channel section, set drag-down menu: Alpha 1, White Is High: Checked, Height: 75. Click OK.

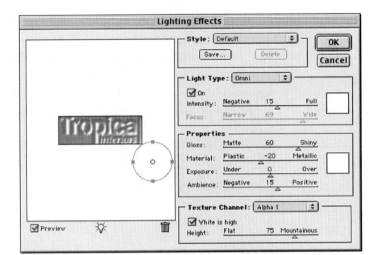

Many of the type effects shown in this book are best when used with heavy typefaces. To use a light typeface, work in a higher resolution. Even then, avoid fine serif lines that get lost in the pixels.

8. Return to the layer, and choose Select>Inverse. Delete the background.

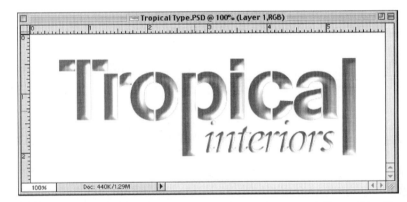

9. Select Inverse, and colorize the type to your taste (Image>Adjust>Hue/Saturation). Deselect.

10. Replace the original background, Type Layer, with a textured background.

11. Add a drop shadow (using Layer Styles) behind the type. The drop shadow should fit the feel of the textured background that you created. Remember — you can change the color of the shadow from its default black.

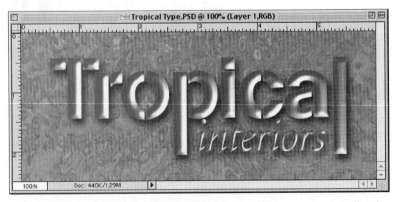

12. Save the file to your **Work in Progress** folder as "Pillow Type.PSD". Close the file.

Create Type Cutouts

1. Open **Sandy Beach.TIF** from the **SF-Adv Photoshop** folder. Double-click the Background layer, and rename it "Beach".

2. Place the **Tropical Interiors.EPS** logo from your **SF-Adv Photoshop** folder into the document, and position it on the horizon. Press the Return/Enter key to finish placing. Load the selection Tropical Interiors.EPS Transparency, and drag the Tropical Interiors.EPS layer to the trash; we just need the selection. The Beach layer should be active. Press the Delete/Backspace key to cut the type out of the image and leave only transparency. Deselect.

3. Add a new layer, and position it below the Beach layer. Name it "Shadow", and fill the layer with black.

4. Command/Control-click on the Beach layer to load the layer transparency as a selection. Choose Select>Inverse. With the Shadow layer active, fill the selection with white. Deselect.

You can use cutouts to great effect by combining two photos instead of just using a photo and text. You cut the top layer out of the selection built from the bottom layer. For example, you can use the shape of a wine-glass or house to mask an image of something else.

5. Choose Filter>Blur>Gaussian Blur 3 pixels. Choose the Move tool, and use the arrow keys to offset the Shadow layer down and right.

Notice that the smaller fine-lined type is lost in this effect.

6. In the History palette, return to the "Delete Layer" step prior to the "Clear" step to create a new version using Layer Groups. This technique will allow the type and shadow to be placed anywhere in the image.

7. Create a new layer named "Shadow", and fill the active selection with black.

8. Create a new layer named "Highlight", and fill the active selection with white.

9. Nudge the selection three pixels right and three pixels down. Apply a Gaussian blur with a radius of 3 pixels.

10. Link the Highlight and Shadow layers by clicking the square next to the Shadow layer, and you will be able to move the headline anywhere in the document.

11. Save the file to your **Work in Progress** folder as "Tropical Shadow.PSD". Close the document.

Carve a Line Art Image Out of the Background

1. Open **Slime.TIF** from the **SF-Adv Photoshop** folder.

2. Create a new channel and fill it with white. With Channel 1 active, choose File>Place to place **Fleur.EPS,** from the **SF-Adv Photoshop** folder.

3. Press the Return/Enter key. Deselect. Choose Image>Adjust>Invert.

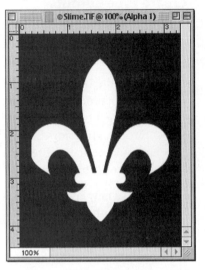

4. Return to the RGB composite, and create a new layer above the Background layer. Name it "Image" and load the Alpha 1 channel as a selection. Choose Select>Feather 1 pixel, and fill it with black. Deselect.

5. Choose Filter>Stylize>Emboss. Set the Angle, Height, and Amount desired. This example uses Angle: –45° angle, Height: 3 pixels, and Amount: 250%.

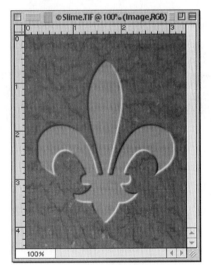

Record each step you take to create a special effect. While it may seem that we stress this point too strongly, we know of a designer who created an engraved text effect which was approved by his client, then spent three weeks trying to recreate the effect for the actual job.

6. Click OK, and set the Blend mode for this layer to Overlay.

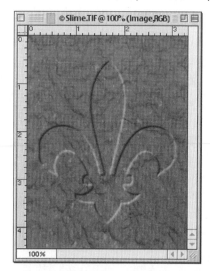

7. Again load the Alpha 1 channel as a selection, and choose Layer>New Adjustment Layer>Levels. Allow the name to default to Levels 1. In the Levels dialog box, drag the shadow and/or midtone slider to the right to darken the inside of the carved area to enhance the effect.

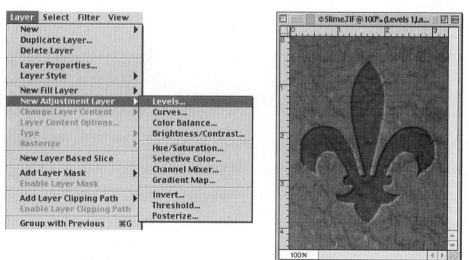

8. Try replacing the background (since it's on an independent layer) to test the effect on different textures. Continue experimenting with this technique by adding a second texture on a new layer for the inside of the black-and-white image using the alpha channel as a mask.

9. Save the file to your **Work in Progress** folder as "Carved Image.PSD". Close the file.

Can you recreate the effects of the Creating Soft "Pillow" Type exercise? If so, you followed the instruction at the beginning of this chapter to write down the steps used to create an effect when it's created. Give yourself a pat on the back.

Photo Edges

Photo edges of various types are quite popular. Though you can buy a selection of photo edges, you can create many of these effects easily in Photoshop.

The first edge that we will create is a mask for a vignette border, which is a soft, graduated edge that was originally created in the photographer's darkroom. You may have seen old photos that used this technique. With minor modifications, a basic vignette border can be used to create a variety of special photo edges.

Remember that all of the techniques used in this section can be applied to a border of any shape, not just a rectangular border. Simply create the initial selection using the Lasso tool instead of the Marquee tool. They can also be created quickly using Quick Mask instead of channels, if no need exists to save the selection effect.

Create a Vignette Border

In a previous exercise we locked the dimensions of the marquee. The style must be returned to Normal.

1. Open **Hammock.TIF** from the **SF-Adv Photoshop** folder.

2. Choose the Rectangular Marquee tool. Draw a rectangle in the middle of the image, as shown below:

3. Choose Select>Feather, and enter a Feather Radius of 5 pixels.

4. Save the selection, naming it "Edge", then save the document as "Borders.PSD" to your **Work in Progress** folder.

5. Choose Select>Inverse. Fill the selection with white. This is a basic vignette border. Deselect, and keep the file open for the next exercise.

Create a Stroked, Rippled Border

1. In the open file, select Revert from the File menu.

2. Duplicate the Edge channel, saved in step 4 of the previous exercise. On this new channel, choose Filter>Distort>Ocean Ripple. Drag the preview until an edge of the border is visible. Set Ripple Size to 5 and Ripple Magnitude to 10. Click OK.

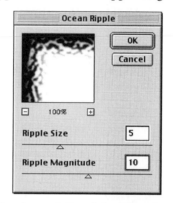

3. Select the RGB composite channel. Load the Edge Copy channel. Choose Select>Inverse. Fill with white. Deselect.

4. For a variation of this, open the History palette. Click to select the step Ocean Ripple, and thus return to the stage of this file just after the Ocean Ripple filter was used. Deselect. While active on the Edge Copy channel, choose Image> Adjust>Levels, and drag both Highlight and Shadow sliders toward the center. Click OK.

5. Choose the RGB composite, and load the Edge Copy channel as a selection. Choose Select>Inverse, and fill the selection with white.

6. Choose Select>Inverse again. Choose a light blue for the foreground color and stroke this selection using Stroke Width: 5-pixel Width, Location: Center.

7. Now we need to select all the border pixels. Choose Select>Modify>Border, and set Width: 5 pixels. With the Magic Wand tool, deselect the "contiguous" box in the Options bar. Click on the blue border. Subtract from the selection any areas of the image that are included.

8. Access Filter>Stylize>Emboss for just the border using Angle: –45°, Height: 2 pixels, Amount: 400%.

9. Choose Image>Adjust>Hue/Saturation to uniformly colorize the embossed border as desired.

10. Make the Background layer transparent by double-clicking on it. Click OK to Save As Layer 0.

11. With the Magic Wand tool, select Contiguous in the Options bar, then click on the white area around the border. Press Delete/Backspace to remove the background.

12. Using Layer Styles, create a drop shadow for Layer 0.

13. Save the document to your **Work in Progress** folder as "Borders 2.PSD". Close the document.

Create a Wood Weathered Decoupage

1. Open **Borders.PSD** from your **Work in Progress** folder.

2. Activate the Edge channel. Drag a marquee inside the area. Feather it 10 pixels. Choose Select>Inverse, and fill with black to contract the transition area. Deselect.

3. Choose Filter>Pixelate>Mezzotint, and select Long Strokes from the pop-up menu. Click OK.

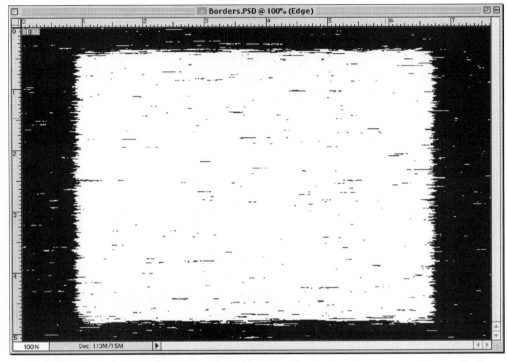

4. Return to the RGB composite, and add a new layer; name it "Texture". Press "D" to return to default colors, and select Filter>Render>Clouds.

5. Choose Filter>Blur>Motion Blur. Set the Angle to 0° and the Distance to 150 pixels.

6. Add texture by choosing Filter>Texture>Craquelure and set Crack Spacing: 15, Crack Depth: 6, Crack Brightness: 9.

7. Choose Image>Adjust>Hue/Saturation. Click Colorize, and set Hue: 36, Saturation: 32, Lightness: −25.

8. While still on the Texture layer, load the Edge channel as a selection, choose Select>Inverse, and click on the Add Layer Mask icon in the Layers palette.

9. For a little extra ambiance, duplicate the Texture layer, and delete its Layer mask. Choose Hard Light for the Blend mode, and decrease the Opacity to about 25%.

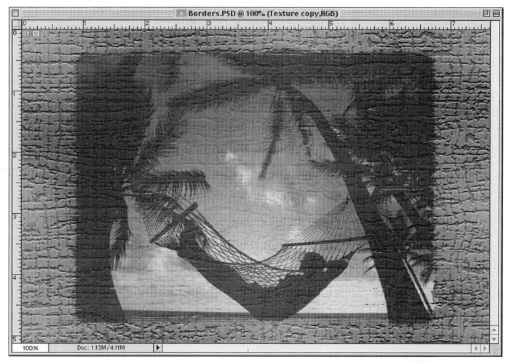

Borders.PSD @ 100% (Texture copy,RGB)

100%   Doc: 1.13M/4.11M

10. Add a drop or carved shadow to the Texture layer to enhance the depth of this effect.

11. Save a copy of the file to your **Work in Progress** folder as "Borders 3.PSD". Leave the file open for the next exercise.

Create Burnt Edges

1. In the open Borders.PSD file, select File>Revert. Activate the Edge channel.

2. Choose Filter>Pixelate>Crystalize. Set Cell Size to 15.

3. Using the Magic Wand tool with the Tolerance set to 4, click on the white area inside, then Shift-click on the solid-black area of the channel. Choose Select>Inverse to get a selection of just the border edge. Choose Filter>Pixelate>Pointillize with a setting of 5.

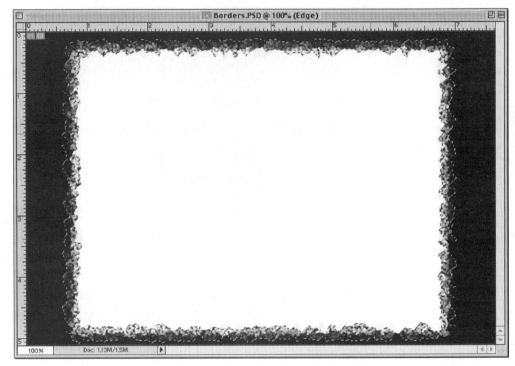

4. Apply a Gaussian Blur of 0.5 pixels to the channel. Deselect.

5. With the RGB composite active, load the Edge channel, and choose Select>Inverse. Press Command/Control-I to invert the colors of the image outside the border.

6. Choose Select>Inverse again. Choose Select>Modify>Contract, by 16 pixels. Feather this selection 12 pixels, and choose Select>Inverse. The outside edge should be selected with most of the border included in the feather.

7. To combine this with the Edge selection, choose Select>Load Selection.

To intersect a channel selection with the current selection, hold Command-Option-Shift/Control-Alt-Shift, and click on the other channel.

8. Choose the Edge channel, and click Intersect with Selection. Choose Select>Modify>Expand by 1 pixel. Fill with black.

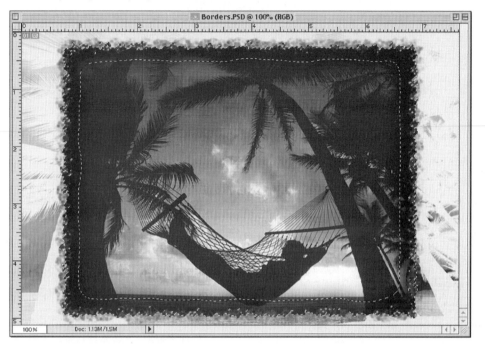

9. Choose Image>Adjust>Hue/Saturation. Click Colorize, then set Hue: 35, Saturation: 100, Lightness: 10. Deselect.

10. Load the Edge channel. Expand 1 pixel. Save this as a new selection.

Depending upon the exact size of your selection, you may end up with an image where no more than 50% of the pixels were selected. If so, don't worry about it.

11. Load the Edge channel again, and access Select>Inverse. Feather 6 pixels. Load the Alpha 1 channel to intersect with this selection. Fill with black.

12. For a variation of this, choose the Crystallize step in the History palette. Apply Threshold to get a hard, jagged edge, then continue from step 4 through step 11.

13. Save the image to your **Work in Progress** folder as "Borders 4.PSD". Close the file.

Special Effects and Images

Images often work well on their own. There are times, however, when your message can be made more effective by applying special effects to images.

Coloring an Image with Duotones, Tritones, and Quadtones

Budgets don't always allow for process color printing. Even when they do, using a duotone, tritone, or quadtone can add richness, quality, and a dramatic mood to the image and the entire piece.

Duotones can be tricky to output. Talk to your service provider before using them in a job to avoid problems.

Duotones are frequently used to reproduce the look of an antique photographic process known as "sepia tone," but any combination of colors that suits the mood is possible. If color tinting is your design objective, choose a color that most effectively communicates the feeling of the message you are trying to convey. For example, red suggests action, danger, or heat, while blue often represents calm, security, or cold. Printing a black-on-black duotone dramatically increases the tonal range of the image; Ansel Adams prints are often reproduced using this method. One grayscale emphasizes the highlight-to-midtone range and the other emphasizes the shadows. Depth and intensity are added without obscuring detail.

Tritones and quadtones can also be used to add color tinting to an image but are most often used to create a full-range grayscale look. This effect is achieved by printing the image with process inks using separations that are generated in perfect gray balance throughout the image. The curves of each grayscale version of the image are manipulated in multichannel mode to capture a specific tonal range and balance for each ink. Using Photoshop's Duotone mode, it's possible to create most of these effects by manipulating the ink coverage curves.

The key to colorizing part of an image using duotones is to isolate the section of the image that you want colored, and restrict its range of grays. For example, if by restricting most of one image to grays in the 0 to 127 range, and designating the grays you want colored as the 128 to 255 range, you can add color to just the areas in the upper range of grays. The only catch to this is that the lower gray range must be inverted to create a smooth duotone curve.

Colorize with Duotones

1. Open **Berries.TIF** from the **SF-Adu Photoshop** folder. Choose Select>Color Range to select the red raspberries within the image.

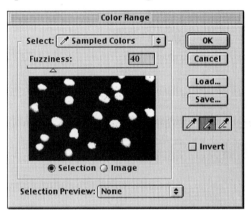

Be certain to select the raspberries completely, or you will end up with hard edges between the colors. Use the Eyedropper and the Add to Sample eyedropper.

2. Save the newly created selection. Deselect. Activate the new channel Alpha 1. Choose Filter>Noise>Dust and Scratches to remove any unwanted areas from the channel. Slide the Radius until it looks clean. Click OK.

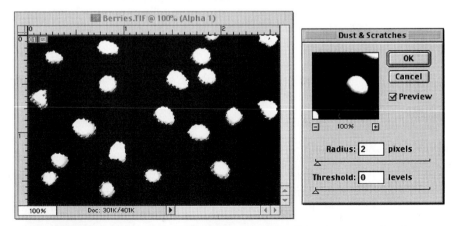

3. Choose Image>Adjust>Threshold. Set the Threshold value to 128 levels.

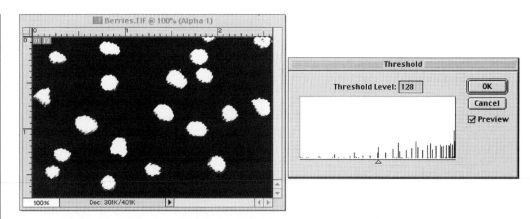

4. Activate the RGB composite channel. Choose Image>Mode>Grayscale. Images intended for Duotone mode must first be converted to Grayscale.

5. Choose Image>Adjust>Levels. Move the white Output Levels slider (be certain to use the Output Levels slider, not the Input Levels slider) to 128.

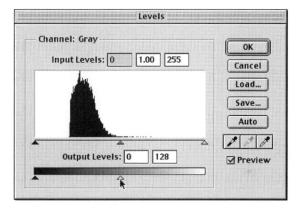

6. Load the Alpha 1 channel as a selection. Press Command/Control-I. This will ensure that the raspberries encompass a different range of grays than the blueberries. In addition, inverting the map makes it easier to set a Duotone curve to cover the entire dynamic range of the raspberries.

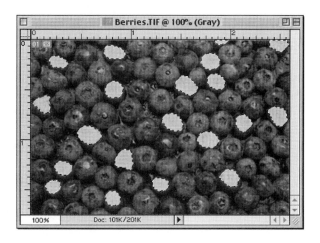

7. Choose Image>Mode>Duotone. Make certain that Type is set to Duotone. Click on the color swatch for Ink 1, and change it to Pantone 2757. Click on the Ink 1 Curve icon, and drag the midpoint (50%) down to 0. The curve should look like the one shown below:

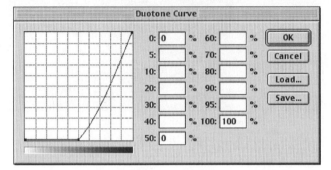

8. Click the Ink 2 color swatch, and change its color to Pantone 202. Click the Ink 2 Curve icon. Drag the midpoint (50%) and shadow (100%) point to 0, and the highlight (0%) to 100. Click OK, then click OK again.

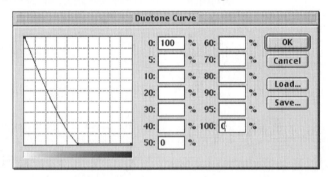

9. Choose Select>Inverse, then select Image>Adjust>Levels to adjust the highlights and shadows of the blueberries. Drag the highlight slider to 215 and midtone slider to 0.67.

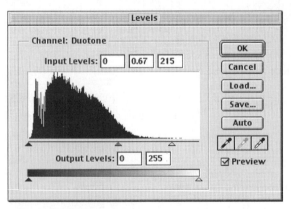

10. Choose Select>Inverse and Image>Adjust>Levels again. Drag the highlight slider slightly in to adjust highlights, increase the range of shadows, and add detail to the image.

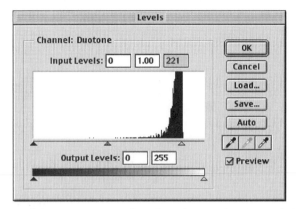

Note: inverting the image requires that the white and gamma slider move to the left to darken the image.

11. Save the file as "Berries Duo.PSD" to your **Work in Progress** folder. Close the file.

Using Layers and Channels for Special Effects

You have already learned to use layers and channels to work on specific elements of an image. You have used them to create masks, create depth, and create additional plates. Now you will combine channels and layers to achieve special effects — some realistic, other surreal. In addition, you will discover how several of Photoshop's filters can be applied to channels and layers to create unique effects.

In the next series of exercises, we will use a patterned fill and several filters to build a wall. We will then apply graffiti and, using special effects, apply a posterization of an image that will make it appear as though the image has been painted directly on a rough brick wall.

Build a Wall

1. Create a new document and set Width: 300 pixels, Height: 300 pixels, Resolution: 100 pixels/inch, Mode: RGB, Contents: Transparent. Press "D" to set the colors to their defaults.

2. Select all. With black as the foreground color, choose Edit>Stroke. Set Width: 6 pixels, Location: Inside. Click OK, then deselect.

3. Change the Canvas Size to 150 pixels wide by 50 pixels high. Anchor the image in the upper-left corner. Click OK. A warning will appear, noting that doing this will crop the image. Click to proceed.

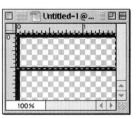

4. Select all of the image, and choose Edit>Define Pattern; name the pattern "Upper Left". Close the file without saving.

5. Create a new document, and set Width: 150 pixels, Height: 100 pixels, Resolution: 100 pixels/inch, Contents: Transparent.

6. Fill the image with the defined pattern. Select the top half of the image, making certain that the marquee goes through the middle horizontal line.

7. Choose Filter>Other>Offset. Set Horizontal Offset: 75 pixels, Vertical Offset: 0, Undefined Areas: Wrap Around.

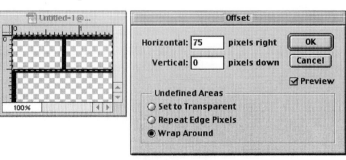

8. Deselect. Choose the Offset filter again. This time use 25 pixels for Horizontal and Vertical.

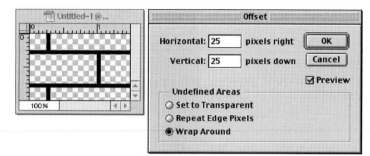

9. Duplicate Layer 1, and name the duplicate "Mortar". Choose Select>Load Selection. Choose Mortar Transparency as the Channel, and check to Invert. Fill this selection with white.

10. Deselect. Choose Filter>Blur>Gaussian Blur 1 pixel.

11. Select Filter>Stylize>Emboss, and set Angle: –40 degree, Height: 2 pixels, Amount: 75. In the Layer palette, change the Blending mode to Hard Light.

12. Create a new layer below the Mortar layer. Name it "Brick". Fill the layer with white. Select Filter>Noise>Add Noise. Choose Monochrome and Gaussian options, and set Amount to 400. Adjust Filter>Stylize>Diffuse using Lighten Only.

13. Choose Filter>Blur>Gaussian Blur, and set Radius: 0.5 pixel. Select Filter> Stylize>Emboss, and set Angle: –40°, Height: 2 pixels, Amount: 25.

14. Choose Image>Adjust>Hue/Saturation. Check "Colorize", and set Hue: 10, Saturation: 60, Lightness: –30.

15. Activate Layer 1. Choose Select>Load Selection. Choose Layer 1 transparency as the channel. Activate the Brick layer, and choose Image>Adjust>Desaturate.

16. Choose Flatten Image from the Layers palette menu. Select all, and define it all as a pattern named "Bricks".

17. Create a new RGB document, 5 in. × 5 in., 100 ppi, with a white background.

18. Fill the new document with the pattern. Close the file in which you defined the pattern without saving.

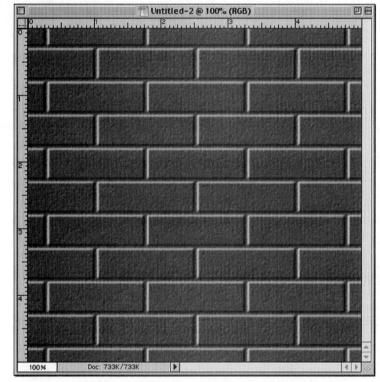

19. Save the file to your **Work in Progress** folder as "Wall.PSD". Leave it open for the next exercise.

Write on the Wall

1. With Wall.PSD still open, select the Type tool and choose the Type Mask option.

2. Click in the lower-left corner. In the Options bar, choose ATC Monsoon, 150 pt., and type "USA". Drag to center the type near the bottom. Apply appropriate kerning and tracking. Press Command-Return/Control-Enter to commit the type.

3. Choose Edit>Transform>Scale, and drag to stretch the type vertically almost to the top. Press Command-Return/Control-Enter to commit the transformation. Save this selection as "USA Image". Press Command/Control-S to save the file to your **Work in Progress** folder.

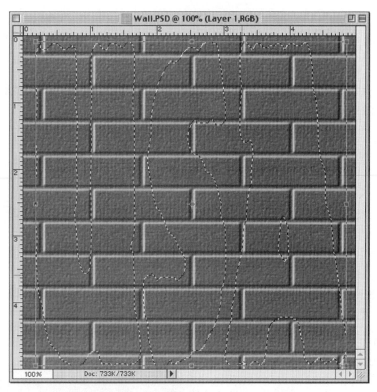

4. Open **Mt. Rush.TIF** from the **SF-Adv Photoshop** folder. Marquee just around Washington's head, as shown, and select Edit>Copy.

5. Close Mt. Rush.TIF without saving. Load the USA image channel. Choose Edit>Paste Into, and position the image so that both eyes clear the mask.

6. While on this layer, choose Filter>Brush Strokes>Spatter (Radius 7, Smoothness 5) and Filter>Artistic>Cutout (# of Levels 4, Edge Simplicity 4, Edge Fidelity 2).

7. Use the Magic Wand tool on the Background layer with a Tolerance of 10. Click on the brick, then choose Select>Grow and Select>Similar. Save this selection.

8. Activate Layer 1. Choose Filter>Render>Lighting Effects. Apply these settings:

In the Style section, set Style: Soft Omni
In the Light Type section, set Light Type: Omni, On: checked, Intensity: 44
In the Properties section, set Gloss: –41, Material: –36, Exposure; –8, Ambience: –44
In the Texture Channel section, set Texture Channel: Alpha 1, White Is High: checked, Height: 42

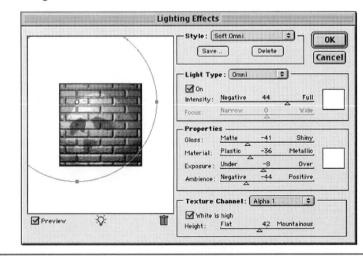

9. Choose Edit>Fade Lighting Effects. Use the Luminosity Mode at 40% Opacity.

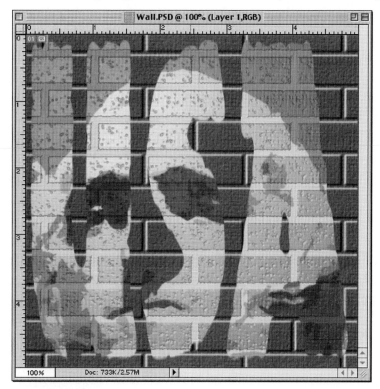

10. Save and close the file.

This exercise gives you the effect of looking through a pegboard at an image, where the central image is a highly pixelated mosaic, and the balance of the holes in the image reflect the original image. In it, you will work with calculations, and then create and use a bump map for an interesting final effect.

Create a "Pegboard" Image

1. Create a new Grayscale document, 20 pixels wide and 20 pixels high, white background, resolution of 150 ppi.

2. Choose the Elliptical Marquee tool, then, in the Options toolbar, change the Style to Fixed Size. Enter Height and Width at 18 px.

3. Hold Option/Alt and click in the center of the image to position the circular selection. Press Command/Control-Shift-I to invert the selected area. Fill with black. Deselect.

4. Choose Select>All. Choose Edit>Define Pattern; name the pattern "Peg". Close the document without saving.

5. Open **Beach Boy.TIF** from the **SF-Adv Photoshop** folder. Double-click on the Background layer, and convert it to a normal layer.

6. Choose Image>Image Size. Change the pixel dimensions to 800 × 800 pixels.

7. Choose Filter>Pixelate>Mosaic. Set Cell Size: 20 square. Save the image as "Pegboard.PSD" to your **Work in Progress** folder.

8. Create a new channel for this image. Select Edit>Fill, and fill with the Peg pattern at 100% Opacity. Rename the channel "Original".

9. Duplicate the Original channel. Name the duplicate "Shadow". Choose Filter>Blur> Gaussian Blur with a setting of 2 pixels.

10. Duplicate the Shadow channel, and rename the copy "Highlight".

11. Press "D" to change the background color to black. Choose the Move tool, and, using the arrow keys, offset the Shadow channel down one pixel and to the right one pixel. Switch to the Highlight channel. Offset it up one pixel and to the left one pixel.

12. Save the image, and leave it open for the next exercise.

Calculate and Apply Channels

1. With Pegboard.PSD still open, choose Image>Calculations. Add the Original channel to the Shadow channel with the following parameters:

Source 1: Pegboard.PSD, Layer: Layer 0, Channel: Original, Invert: unchecked
Source 2: Pegboard.PSD, Layer: Layer 0, Channel: Shadow, Invert: checked
Blending: Add, Opacity: 100%, Offset: 0, Scale: 2, Mask: unchecked
Result: New Channel

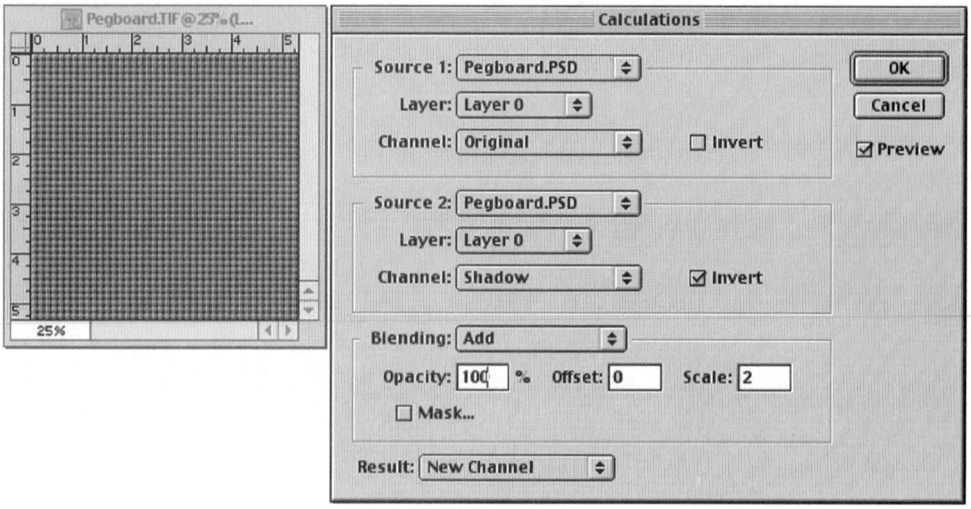

2. Choose Image>Calculations again. This time, add the Shadow Channel to the Highlight channel with the following parameters:

   Source 1: Pegboard.PSD, Layer: Layer 0, Channel: Shadow, Invert: checked
   Source 2: Pegboard.PSD, Layer: Layer 0, Channel: Highlight, Invert: unchecked
   Blending: Add, Opacity: 100%, Offset: 0, Scale: 2, Mask: unchecked
   Result: New Channel

3. Activate the Alpha 2 channel created in step 2. Choose Image>Adjust>Auto Levels to flatten the tones.

4. Choose Image>Calculations. Set the calculations as follows:

   Source 1: Pegboard.PSD, Layer: Layer 0, Channel: Alpha 1, Invert: unchecked
   Source 2: Pegboard.PSD, Layer: Layer 0, Channel: Alpha 2, Invert: unchecked
   Blending: Add, Opacity: 100%, Offset: 0, Scale: 2, Mask: unchecked
   Result: New Channel

   Click OK. Rename the channel "Bump Map".

5. Delete the channels Highlight, Shadow, Alpha 1, and Alpha 2. Original and Bump Map should be the only additional channels remaining.

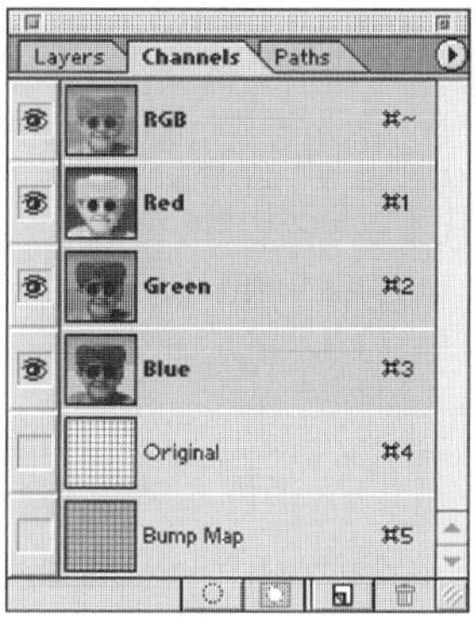

6. Activate the RGB Composite channel. Choose Filter>Render>Lighting Effects. Set the effects as follows:

In the Style section, set Style: Soft Omni

In the Light Type section, set Light Type: Omni, On: checked, Intensity: 35

In the Properties section, set Gloss: 100, Material: 100, Exposure: 0, Ambience: 30

In the Texture Channel section, set Texture Channel: Bump Map, White Is High: checked, Height: 100

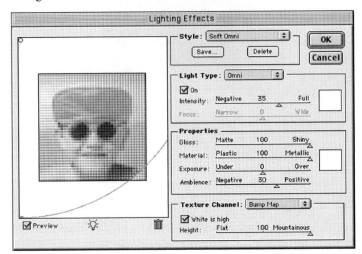

7. Load the Original channel as a selection with the Invert box checked. Fill the selection with black. Deselect.

8. Open the original **Beach Boy.TIF** image from the **SF-Adv Photoshop** folder. Select Image>Image Size. Resize the image to 16 pixels × 16 pixels.

9. Double-click the Background layer of the Beach Boy.TIF image, then click OK to change its name to Layer 0, thus allowing transparency in the layer.

10. Select Image>Canvas Size. Change the size of the image to 20 pixels by 20 pixels, with the image anchored in the center. Select this entire image, and choose Edit>Define Pattern; name it "Beach Boy". Close the Beach Boy image without saving.

11. Create a new layer in the Pegboard.PSD image. Fill the layer with the pattern. Change the Layer Blending mode to Darken and the Layer Opacity to 80%.

12. Choose Image>Adjust>Levels. Drag the white slider down to 175 to lighten the layer.

13. Select Flatten Image from the Layers palette menu. Choose Image>Adjust>Brightness/Contrast. Set both the Brightness and the Contrast to 20.

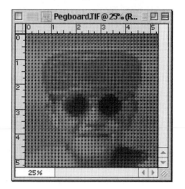

14. Save and close the file.

Achieving 3D Transforms

So far, you have achieved the perception of depth through a number of special effects and Layer Styles, such as drop shadows. The 3D effects allow you to change the aspect of an image by rotating groups of pixels using a special palette of tools. As you will see, you can use the tools delicately, just enough to alter the perception of the viewer, or you can make radical changes to the image.

As you have learned, there are a variety of ways to create effects in Photoshop — none of which are chiseled in stone. The next exercise takes four U.S. presidents who *are* chiseled in stone and allows you to create different perspectives of them.

3D Mt. Rushmore

1. Open **Mt. Rush.TIF** from the **SF-Adv Photoshop** folder.

2. Reset the Elliptical Marquee style to Normal. Using the Elliptical Marquee, select Washington's head. Copy it to the clipboard.

3. Choose File>New. The dimensions are already preset. Click OK. Choose Edit>Paste.

4. Erase areas of the sky that were included, but leave pieces of surrounding rock.

5. Choose Filter>Render>3D Transform. Choose the Spherical tool, and drag a circle around the entire head. Use the Selection and Direct Selection tools to position and mold the wire frame.

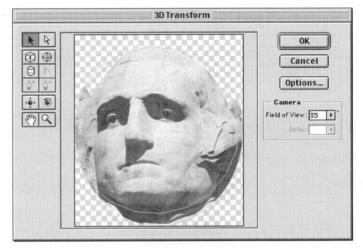

6. With the Track Ball tool, drag up and to the left to achieve this perspective.

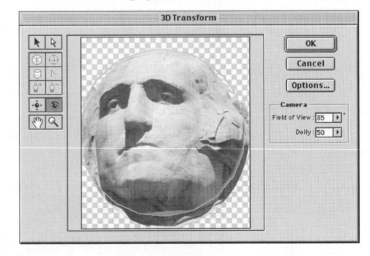

Effective use of the Track Ball tool requires practice, practice, and more practice. Work at it for long enough, and it will start to feel natural.

7. Click OK. In the Image window, perform a little retouching under Washington's chin to blend the rock.

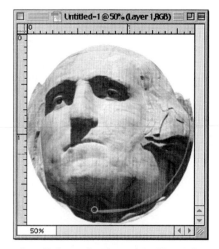

8. Select all, and copy to the clipboard. Close this file without saving.

9. In the original Mt. Rush.TIF image, deselect and paste from the clipboard into the original image. Perform a little retouching to blend the 3-D image into the rock. Check Use All Layers in the Clone Stamp Options palette to access background pixels while painting on this new layer. Rename this layer "Washington".

10. With the Magnetic Lasso tool, select Jefferson's head, avoiding Washington. Be sure you're on the Background layer, then copy to the clipboard and paste to a new file.

11. Choose Filter>Render>3D Transform. Select the Cube tool, and drag to encompass Jefferson's head. Use the Direct Selection tool to move the lowest, front corner point, aligning the front edge of the cube with his nose.

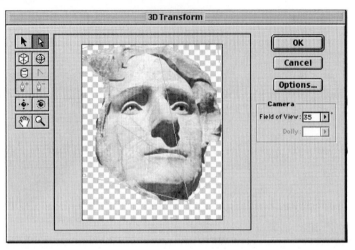

12. With the Track Ball tool, drag up and left to rotate the cube perspective.

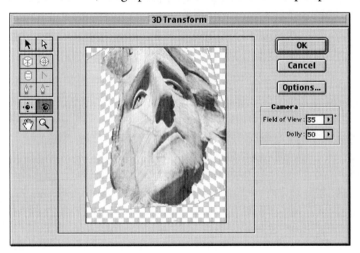

13. Click OK, and retouch the image a little to blend where necessary with the rock. Select all, and copy to the clipboard. Close this file without saving.

14. In the original Mt. Rush.TIF image, choose Edit>Paste Into for the original selection left behind. Deselect, and retouch around the edges using the Eraser and Clone Stamp tools.

15. Select the Lincoln head, including the blocks to the right of his chin, with a combination of Lasso tools. Copy and paste to a new file.

16. Choose Filter>Render>3D Transform. Select the Cylindrical tool, and drag to select most of Lincoln's head.

17. With the Track Ball tool, drag up and right to rotate the cylinder perspective to make it appear as if he's cocking his head. Shift the image with the Pan Camera tool to align it somewhat with the existing hair and beard. Click OK.

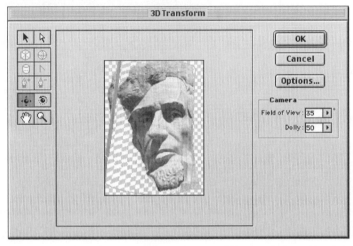

18. Retouch the image slightly. Most retouching will be performed back on the original image. Select all and copy to the clipboard. Close this file without saving.

19. On the original Mt. Rush.TIF image, choose Edit>Paste and position Lincoln to align the rotated image over the original. Use both the Rubber Stamp and Eraser to retouch the hair and beard into the Background layer.

20. Now that the heads of several great presidents have been turned, the image is ready for additional special effects as desired. Save the file to your **Work in Progress** folder as "Heads Turned.PSD" and close.

Applying the Liquify Command

The Liquify command provides special tools to manipulate parts of an image, as if those areas had been melted. Only 8-bit images in RGB, CMYK, Lab, and Grayscale modes may be liquified. Special tools allow you to expand, contract, warp, twirl, shift, and reflect areas of an image. You can see how much distortion you have created by using the optional warp mesh.

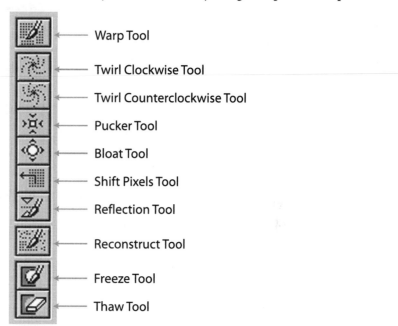

Warp Tool

Twirl Clockwise Tool

Twirl Counterclockwise Tool

Pucker Tool

Bloat Tool

Shift Pixels Tool

Reflection Tool

Reconstruct Tool

Freeze Tool

Thaw Tool

- **Warp tool.** This tool pushes pixels as you drag. It is probably the most liquifying of this tool set.

- **Twirl Clockwise** and **Twirl Counterclockwise tools**. These tools rotate pixels in the prescribed direction as you hold the mouse button or drag.

- **Pucker tool.** This tool moves pixels toward the center of the brush area as you hold the mouse button or drag.

- **Bloat tool.** This tool moves pixels away from the center of the brush area as you hold down the mouse button or drag.

- **Shift Pixels tool.** This tool moves pixels perpendicular to the direction of the movement of the tool. If you drag top to bottom vertically, the pixels will move to the right. If you drag left to right horizontally, the pixels will move up. Hold down the Option/Alt key to cause the pixels to move in the opposite direction.

- **Reflection tool.** This tool copies pixels to the brush area in a mirror image of the area perpendicular to the direction of the stroke. When dragging left to right, the area below the brush is reflected. When dragging top to bottom, the area to the left of the brush is reflected. Hold down the Option/Alt key to reflect the pixels in the opposite direction.

- **Reconstruct tool.** This tool can be used to fully or partially reverse changes made to the image.

- **Freeze** and **Thaw tools**. These tools are used to protect and unprotect areas of the image.

In addition to the tools, a variety of menu commands are available to assist you in liquifying images.

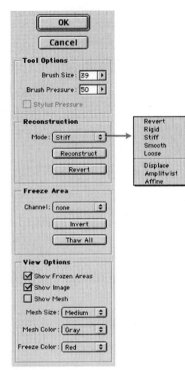

The menu is divided into four primary sections: Tool Options, Reconstruction, Freeze Area, and View Options.

- **Tool Options**. This section includes Brush Size (1 to 150) and Brush Pressure (1 to 100).

- **Reconstruction**. The three primary options in this section — Mode, Reconstruct, and Revert — are used to restore part or all of an image that has been distorted.

  - Mode changes one or more unfrozen areas back to their state when the Liquify dialog box was opened using the Reconstruction tool. The areas over which you place the brush are changed.

    The first five levels of reconstruction: Revert, Rigid, Stiff, Smooth, and Loose suggest how close to the original image the resulting reversion will be, with Revert being a complete reversion to the original and Loose providing the greatest continuity in transition between frozen and unfrozen areas.

    The last three reconstruction methods: Displace, Amplitwist, and Affine are designed to reconstruct areas to match distortions at a starting point.

    Use Displace to move all or part of the preview image to a different location. Use Amplitwist to reconstruct unfrozen areas to match the rotation, overall scaling, and displacement that exist at the starting point. Use Affine to reconstruct unfrozen areas, matching local distortions that exist at the starting point, including rotation, horizontal and vertical scaling, skew and displacement.

  - Select Mode>Revert, then click Reconstruct to change all unfrozen areas back to their state when the Liquify dialog box was opened.

  - Use the Revert button to return the entire image to its state when the Liquify dialog box was opened.

Don't confuse the Revert button, which returns the entire image to its pre-distorted state, with the Revert mode, which changes all areas painted over with the Revert tool to its pre-distorted state.

- **Freeze Areas**. This section designates areas that are protected from distortion. They may be defined as an alpha channel or inverted. They may be removed (thawed) with the Thaw tool or by clicking the Thaw All button.

- **View Options**. This section allows you to show the frozen areas, much like a Quick Mask, to show or hide the image (if the Mesh is visible), and to show the Mesh, which graphically displays the amount of distortion you have made to the image. The Mesh Size, Mesh Color, and Freeze Color can also be defined.

Liquifaction can be used to make a point, to enhance images, or to create unique effects.

Original image (left) is easily manipulated to distort the balloon.

Let's use the Liquify command on a variety of images.

Wave the Flag

1. Open the image **Flag.TIF** from your **SF-Adv Photoshop** folder.

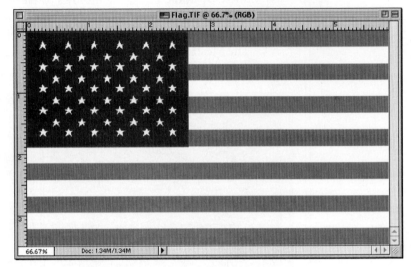

Often, when a flag image is available as clip art, it is in this form — flat and uninteresting. Let's put a little wind into Old Glory.

2. Select Image>Canvas Size. Leaving the Anchor Point in the center, change the Width to 7 in. and the Height to 4.5 in. This will give us some room to make waves.

3. Select Image>Liquify. Set Brush Size: 85, Brush Pressure: 10, with View Options of Show Image and Show Mesh: checked, Mesh Size: Medium.

4. Select the Warp tool, and drag the first wave vertically about 3/4 of the way to the right.

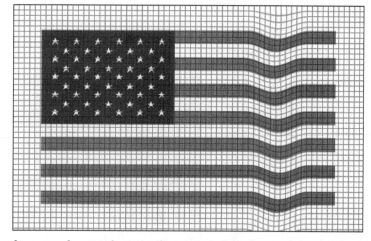

5. Create the second wave about in the center of the flag and the third within the first quarter. If you wish, drag the brush so the center crosses the very end of the stripes. Click OK.

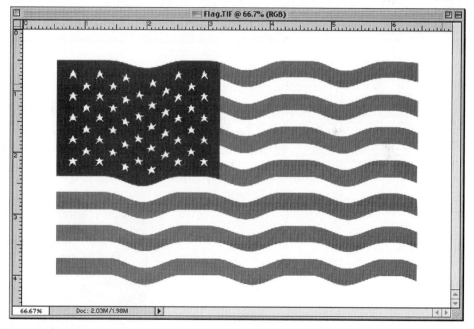

6. Save the image as a copy to your **Work in Progress** folder as "Warp Wave.PSD".

7. Revert the image, and again change the Canvas Size Width to 7 in. and the Height to 4.5 in.

8. Select Image>Liquify. Leave the settings the same as they were before, but increase the Brush Pressure between 25 and 50.

9. Select the Twirl Clockwise tool. This tool increases its effect with the length of time it is on top of a section of the image. The higher your Brush Pressure, the faster you'll want to move the cursor.

10. Drag similar waves to those you produced earlier. If you don't like the way a wave turns out, press Command/Control-Z to undo it.

11. When you're happy with the result, click OK, and then save to your **Work in Progress** folder as "Twirl Wave.PSD". Close the file.

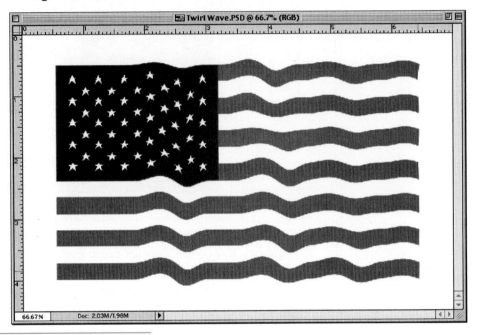

Your Nose is Gonna Grow

1. Open the file **Storytime.TIF** from your **SF-Adv Photoshop** folder.

   Here, Dad is reading a story to his youngster. The story is *Pinocchio*, and you're going to help him act out the part of the little story-telling puppet.

2. Marquee the portion of the image you're going to work on. In this case, include Dad's head, and an area out beyond the lamp.

3. Select Image>Liquify. Choose the Warp tool, and set the Brush Size to 40 and the Brush Pressure to 35. This exercise is a little easier to do if you turn off Show Mesh and turn on Show Frozen Areas.

4. Click on the nose, and drag it out until it almost hits the lamp. This will take more than one dragging.

There's a problem, isn't there? The brush ends up distorting the lamp — and you may even have distorted some of his face. Let's fix that.

5. In the Reconstruction area, click the Revert button.

6. Select the Freeze tool. Choose an appropriate-sized brush, and paint areas that could be affected by the distortion to freeze them.

6. Now switch back to the Warp tool, and drag his nose. When you're satisfied, click OK. Save to your **Work in Progress** folder as "The Nose.PSD" and close the file.

Take a serious subject and make a satire or parody of it. Here, we're going to put a smile on this overly serious face.

Help the Caricature Smile

1. Open the file **Caricature.TIF** from your **SF-Adv Photoshop** folder.

2. Marquee his face, so we have a reasonable close-up with which to work.

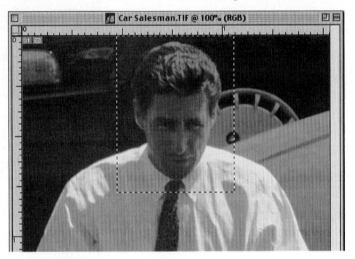

3. Select Image>Liquify, then choose a Brush Size of 20 and a Brush Pressure of 50. Choose the Warp tool.

4. Trace along the upper-lip line, and draw both sides of his mouth into a "smile."

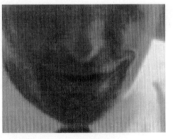

5. As you can see, the edges of the smile are puffy. Select the Freeze tool, and freeze the areas you want to protect.

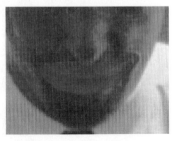

6. Select a Reconstruction Mode of Stiff and click Reconstruct. Click OK. Save to your **Work in Progress** folder as "Smiley.PSD". Close the file.

Experiment with other Liquify features and a variety of images.

Summary

In this chapter you have learned to combine functions to achieve special effects, using layers, channels, filters, and the Liquify commands. More importantly, we hope that you're encouraged to expand your thought process to include "what if?" As you experiment with additional features of Photoshop, keeping in mind principles of solid design, you will discover new and exciting effects to add to your arsenal of tricks. Always remember — the best effect is the one that is repeatable. Be sure to write your technique down in a step-by-step process.

Complete Project F: Photomat

Notes:

CHAPTER 14

WORKING SMARTER

CHAPTER OBJECTIVE:

To learn how to work efficiently when performing color correction and manipulation of large files or batches of files. To learn how to use Photoshop's automation tools. In Chapter 14, you will:

- Discover how the Actions palette allows the recording of a series of commands for playback and application to files and groups of files.

- Learn to use droplets to automate file manipulation and management.

- Learn to use Batch commands to automate the production of entire folders.

- Observe how the History palette gives you the ability to revert up to 100 actions and steps backward to correct an image or task.

- Become familiar with the Art History brush.

- Use Contact Sheet II to create visual references of the contents of folders.

- Learn the Conditional Mode change.

PROJECTS TO BE COMPLETED:

- Just Shoot Me (A)

- Baby Shower Invitation (B)

- Retouching the Jones Family Portrait (C)

- The Fix Is In! (D)

- Makeover (E)

- Photomat (F)

Working Smarter

When performing color correction and other photo-manipulation tasks, your file processing can really bog down the computer. When you consider that an 11 in. ¥ 17 in. poster printed at 150 lpi is approximately 57 MB, it's not surprising.

Here are a few suggestions for making the most of your time when performing color correction and manipulation on large files or batches of files.

The most important thing you can do to improve Photoshop performance is to have RAM, RAM, and more RAM! Some Photoshop filters run entirely in RAM.

- **Do your initial corrections/experimentation on a low-resolution version of the file.** Many dialog boxes, such as Curves and Levels, have options to save settings. When you find settings or corrections that work well for you, those settings can be saved, then loaded and applied to the high-resolution file.

- **For commands whose settings can't be saved,** such as Photoshop's filters, keep a written log of the specific steps that you used to produce the effect. Then apply the steps, in order, to a higher-resolution file.

- **Make certain that the white and black contrast point of the image are adjusted to maximize the overall contrast of the image.** To save time in correcting the contrast of an image, use the Auto Levels command and the Auto buttons in the Levels and Curves dialog boxes. An exercise showing how to set and apply the Auto Levels will be presented later in this chapter.

- **When running a preset list of commands, turn off the Preview option in all dialog boxes before running the commands.** This will save a lot of time on screen redraw.

- **When running complex filter commands or editing colors, work on a single channel at a time.** An RGB channel requires one-third of the memory that working on the composite does. In a CMYK file, a single channel requires only one-fourth the memory. If the command in question is a filter, run it on each channel in the document in succession.

- **Maintain a Photoshop (.PSD) file of all images that you send to a client, output vendor, or a Web site.** If you have to make alterations, you will save time maintaining a copy of the file that has been saved in an editable form. Store the .PSD files in a separate folder, on your computer or a removable disk.

There are graphics accelerator cards designed specifically to speed up Photoshop's performance.

- **Make certain that the scratch drive is defragmented.** In addition, click on the triangle in the lower-left corner of the screen and change it to scratch size. Pay close attention to these numbers. The first number indicates the amount of memory required by all open documents. The second number is available RAM. When the first number becomes larger than the second, the scratch disk is being utilized, and program operation will slow down.

- **To save time when performing close-up work on an image, select View>New View when zooming in and out.** This command produces a second window of the active document. Zoom into one window and use the Hand tool to move around the image. The second window will display all of the changes that you make in the first image, giving you a view of the big picture without excessive zooming.

- **Running in 256-color video mode can speed up screen redraws considerably** (the image data will still contain full-color information). Be forewarned: become familiar with correcting by using the readings from the Info palette before attempting to color correct in 256-color mode.

- **Store extra channels and layers in a separate document.** They're easy to bring back into the old image, provided the resolution and color mode are the same as the original file. Every channel you add to an image increases its file size. For example, a CMYK file with six additional channels would be 2.5 times the size of a regular CMYK document. If the channels aren't being used for the moment, why deal with all of the extra file overhead? Save them into their own document, and load them back into the image when needed.

- **If you plan to exchange your file with others using previous versions of Photoshop, save the file as a TIFF.** Saving the file as a Photoshop 2.0 file will take longer and will waste disk space.

- **Turn off the preview icons in the Layers and Channels palette.** These icons, while convenient, use more Photoshop resources than you might think. Getting into the habit of naming the layers and channels according to the data they contain makes previews unnecessary.

- **On Macintosh systems, quit any running applications or TSRs before loading Photoshop.** (Terminate-and-Stay-Resident programs are utilities which load automatically when you start your system.) Quitting these applications after Photoshop is loaded will prevent the available memory from being used.

- **If you have commands or tasks that are repeatable in several images, use the Actions palette.** The Actions palette can record, and then play back, repeatable tasks on many images with the same needs, such as preparing images for Web-site placement. The Actions palette will be described later in this chapter.

- **Use keyboard commands.** All of Photoshop's tools and many of its menu items are available using keyboard commands. Many of Photoshop's menu items are two or three levels deep, so using the mouse for every command can become cumbersome. The more of these commands that you commit to memory, the more efficient you will be working in Photoshop.

- **Don't wait for screen redraw when working on large files.** For example, when zooming into an image twice, don't wait for Photoshop to redraw the image before clicking the Zoom tool a second time — better still, enter the Zoom percentage in the Zoom Percentage box at the lower left of the window.

- **Use the History palette to allow your image to return to a previous level of correction.** We will explore the History palette later in this chapter. There are instances, however, where the palette's overhead simply gets in the way. If it's not needed, lower the number of History states to 1 in History Options.

Keyboard Commands

Throughout this course, you've learned many keyboard shortcuts for Photoshop's commands and functions. In the manual that comes packaged with your Photoshop software, you will find these keyboard commands and shortcuts, as well as other shortcuts, listed in a useful pullout chart.

Some of the shortcuts listed have always been shown as commands in the form of Menu>Submenu>Command. Why? The way that Photoshop is used varies widely from user to user; it's often easier to remember a less commonly used command via the menus

Don't use a compressed drive or removable disk for a scratch disk; it will degrade Photoshop's performance.

When you realize you've been using a menu command regularly, look at the right side of the menu. There, you'll discover the keyboard shortcut for each menu command for which such a shortcut exists. Soon you'll have memorized those that are important for the way you work.

than as an esoteric keyboard shortcut. When you repeatedly use a particular command however, it's time to learn the shortcut. Don't underestimate the time-savings. It may seem like only a few seconds here or there, but knowledge of shortcuts often makes the difference between someone who merely knows Photoshop well and someone who can complete nearly any job quickly and efficiently.

Adobe supplies a Quick Reference Card for the most popular keyboard commands/shortcuts. Photoshop's on-screen Help is set up to provide effective assistance in finding the proper keyboard commands/shortcuts. Select Help>Keyboard to access a list of on-screen tips. These Help pages can also be printed.

Keep a copy of these commands nearby while you're working in Photoshop. When you find yourself repeatedly using commands, make a concerted effort to memorize the shortcuts.

Using the Auto Levels Command and the Auto Button

The Auto Levels command, located in the Adjust drag-down menu (Image>Adjust), and the Auto button, located in the Levels and Curves dialog boxes, can speed the application of the proper white and black points to an image. Using preset values in the Auto Option window, located in the Levels and Curves dialog boxes, allows you to set values for the white and black points as dictated by the output vendor or application used, and apply these values to many images. The Auto Levels option will redistribute the values of the intermediate pixels proportionally.

Use the Auto Levels Option

1. Open **Work.TIF** from the **SF-Adv Photoshop** folder.

2. Select Image>Adjust>Levels to view the histogram of this image.

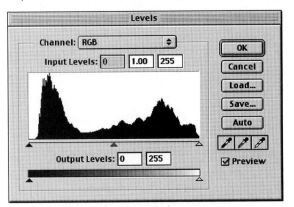

As the histogram shows, the concentration of the pixels is in the highlight and shadow areas, with very little distributed through the midtones on the image.

3. Hold down the Option/Alt key. The Auto button in the Levels dialog box turns into an Options button. Press the Options button to open the Auto Range Options dialog box.

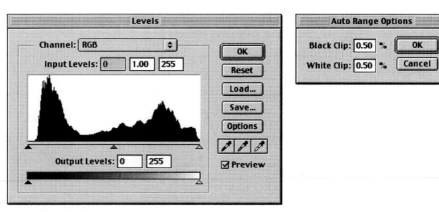

The Auto Range Options dialog box allows you to set the value that the image will have in the white and black point set. Any pixels that have a value greater than these settings will be set to a representative, rather than an extreme, pixel value. The balance of the pixels will be redistributed throughout the image.

4. For this example, maintain the default value of 0.50% for the White and Black Clip point. Click OK.

5. Select the Auto button in the Levels dialog box to apply the Auto Range Options values. The pixels in the image are redistributed in a more pleasing manner, as represented in the Levels histogram.

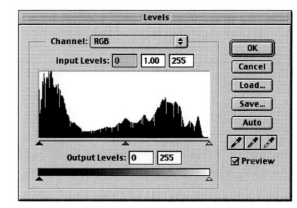

6. Press Command/Control-Z a few times to toggle the image and compare the before and after Auto Levels effect.

7. Close the file without saving.

The Auto Levels command is best used when similar images will be included in the same document. Be careful when images are drastically different, or if they will be used in different processes, such as process color printing and on the Web.

Using the Actions Palette

The Actions palette allows the recording of a series of commands that can be played back and applied to any file, or group of files, as needed. In addition, it provides the ability to add or delete commands from an action, edit existing commands, and insert "stops," which allow the pausing of the action to insert undefinable commands, such as creation of selections.

Using the Actions palette can automate special effects such as three-dimensional type, or the ability to batch-correct a group of files.

The Photoshop CD includes
many useful special effects
Actions.

With the release of
Photoshop 6, Actions which
include a Save As, may not
function correctly unless
you select Edit>
Preferences>Saving Files
and check the Use Lower
Case box. Be sure that this
preference is correctly set.

Use the Actions Palette

1. Open **Button1.PSD** from the **Buttons** folder inside your **SF-Adv Photoshop** folder.

2. Select Window>Show Actions to make certain that the Actions palette is visible.

3. From the Actions palette Options menu on the upper-right corner, select New Set.

4. Name the new set "Web Actions".

5. From the same drag-down menu, and with the Web Actions folder highlighted, select New Action.

6. Name the action "GIF Files", and click Record.

You can swap Actions between platforms, provided you name the action with a PC extension (.ATN) and that you change the items that are specific to a single platform, such as the Windows Window>Tile option.

7. Choose Image>Image Size, and change both Height and Width in Pixel Dimensions to 50 percent. Click OK.

8. Choose Image>Mode>Indexed Color. Merge the layers. Make the following settings:

   In the Palette section, set Palette: Web, Transparency: unchecked
   In the Options section, set Matte: None, Dither: Diffusion, Amount: 75%, Preserve Exact Colors: unchecked. Click OK.

You can edit an individual step of an Action to customize it for your particular task.

9. Save the image in CompuServe GIF format, with a Row Order of Normal, allowing Photoshop to add the ".gif" file extension. Save the file to your **Work in Progress** folder.

10. Close the file. Choose Stop Recording from the Actions Palette drag-down menu, or click on the black square at the bottom of the palette.

Creating Batches and Droplets

Closely related to Actions are two elements that are located by selecting File>Automate: the Batch and Create Droplet commands. These commands further automate the Actions palette. The menu for both is the same. The Batch command however, must be recreated each time you automate an Action. As an alternative, you can create a droplet from an action and drag and drop folders or individual files on top of it; the droplet retains the command set.

Batches and droplets work in the same manner; we will practice the Batch command here and use a droplet in a later exercise.

Create a Batch Process

1. Locate the newly created GIF file (**Button1.GIF**) in your **Work in Progress** folder, and drag it to the Trash/Recycle Bin.

2. Select File>Automate>Batch.

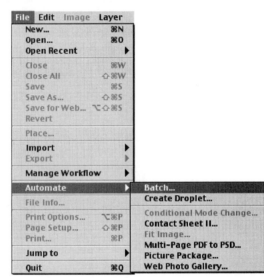

Make certain that Source is set to Folder. Click Choose and specify the **SF-Adv Photoshop**>**Buttons** folder. Change Destination to Folder; click Choose in the Destination box, and select the **Work in Progress** folder (not the Buttons folder). Leave all other settings at their defaults, and click OK. Wait until Photoshop is no longer automatically opening and saving files.

If you set File>Preferences>Saving Files to Always Append File Extension, Photoshop will automatically append the correct extension to your files.

If you click the second box next to the Action name, Photoshop will display dialog boxes for the commands in the Actions.

A program-wide change is a change to palettes, color settings, actions, and preferences. Since these changes do not affect a particular file, they will not be stored in the History palette.

3. Examine the contents of your **Work in Progress** folder; note that there are now four GIF files in the folder which have been created by running the GIF Files Action.

The History Palette

One of the problems that Photoshop users have faced in the past has been the inability to revert further than one step backward to correct an action or a task. The History palette now allows you to set up a "file" of up to 100 actions to apply to a Photoshop image. The default is 20. Be forewarned that the History palette is a RAM hog; add states only if you need them.

The History palette maintains a record of non-program-wide changes to the current working file as long as the file remains open. The Photoshop user can return to a previous change in the file through the History palette items, called "states," to review or change from that point. Once the file is closed and the work session is ended, these states are removed.

When the number of states exceeds the maximum states specified in History options, the older ones will scroll off the palette list. There is a way to maintain a state longer than the maximum levels specified; the Photoshop user can create a snapshot of the state, and keep it throughout the work session, or create a new file from a snapshot.

The history can be linear (the default), or you can select the Non-linear History option in the History palette's Options menu. Choosing Non-linear History enables you to delete specific states, while leaving subsequent states untouched. You should be aware, however, that the results may be somewhat unpredictable.

Use the History Palette

1. Open **CD Photo.TIF** from the **SF-Adv Photoshop** folder. Select Window>Show History and Window>Show Layers.

Make certain that your RAM allocation is sufficient to operate the History palette. Photoshop 6 works best with at least 64 MB of allocated RAM. Without the RAM allocation, the History palette, and Photoshop, will run slowly or possibly crash your computer.

Notice that in the History palette, the image appears as a thumbnail with the History brush appearing to the left of the thumbnail, and Open appears as the first state.

2. Select the regular Type tool, and select a location in the center of the monitor screen. Select ATC RumRunnerScript Regular from the Font drop-down menu. Enter 30 pt. in the size window. Click the color window, and select 255 in the red, blue, and green windows to produce white. Select the Center Type icon. Type the words "New CD Disc". Click the checkmark to commit the type, or press Command-Return/Control-Enter. Notice that a new state, Type Tool, appears in the History palette.

3. Select the Magnetic Lasso tool. Set Feather: 2px, Lasso Width: 5 px, Edge Contrast: 10%, Frequency: 59, Anti-aliased: selected. Follow the edge of the CD in the image, and close the selection. A new state, Magnetic Lasso, appears in the History palette.

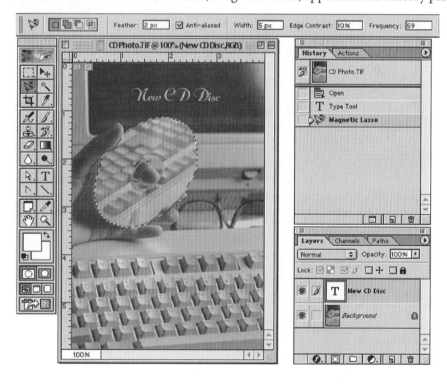

4. Use the Lasso tool to remove the center finger and complete the edge selection of the CD. Notice that every time a new task is finished, a new state appears in the History palette.

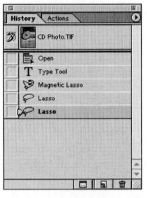

5. Select the Background layer in the Layers palette. Choose Layer>New>Layer Via Copy. Rename the layer "CD Layer". Notice that all of these tasks appear as states in the History palette.

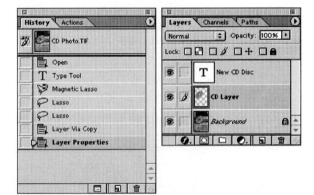

6. Deselect the eye icons in the Background and New CD Disc layer, leaving only the CD Layer visible. Select the Magic Wand tool, select 2 in the Tolerance window of the Magic Wand Options palette, and make certain that Use All Layers is not selected. Select a point near the transparent area around the CD. Choose Select>Inverse, making the CD the selected area. Notice that all of these actions appear again as states in the History palette.

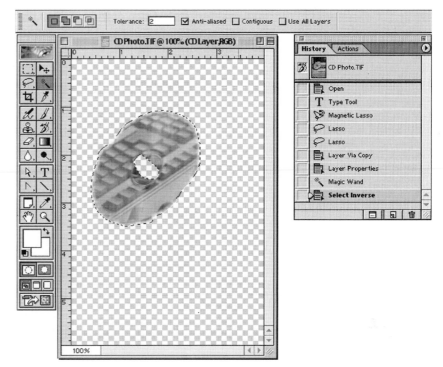

7. Turn on all of the layers in the Layers palette. With the CD Layer selected as the active layer, select Edit>Transform>Flip Horizontal. Select the Move tool, and move the selection to the right, so that it looks like a mirror image of the original CD. Deselect the CD. Additional states appear in the History palette.

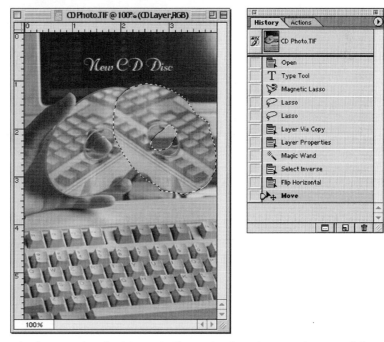

8. Select the box next to the Type Tool state in the History palette, and then click on the Type Tool state itself. Notice that all of the states below the Type tool become gray and their names become italic. The CD Layer disappears from the Layers palette. Select Delete from the History palette drag-down menu. Notice that all states from

the Type Tool state down disappear from the list, leaving only the Open state. Click Command/Control-Z to reinstate all of the deleted states.

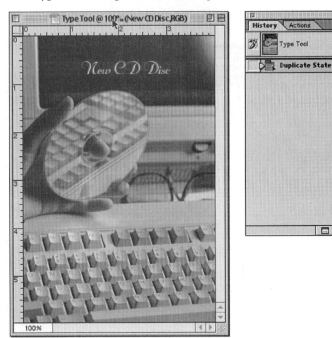

9. With the Type Tool state still highlighted, click the Create New Document from Current State button at the bottom of the History palette.

A new document named Type Tool, holding only the original image and the type, appears on the screen with only Duplicate State appearing in the History palette. Close the Type Tool image without saving.

10. Select the Flip Horizontal state in the History palette, and the History Brush box next to the Flip Horizontal state. Notice that the image returns to the point prior to moving the CD Layer. Select the Delete button (trash can) from the bottom of the History palette.

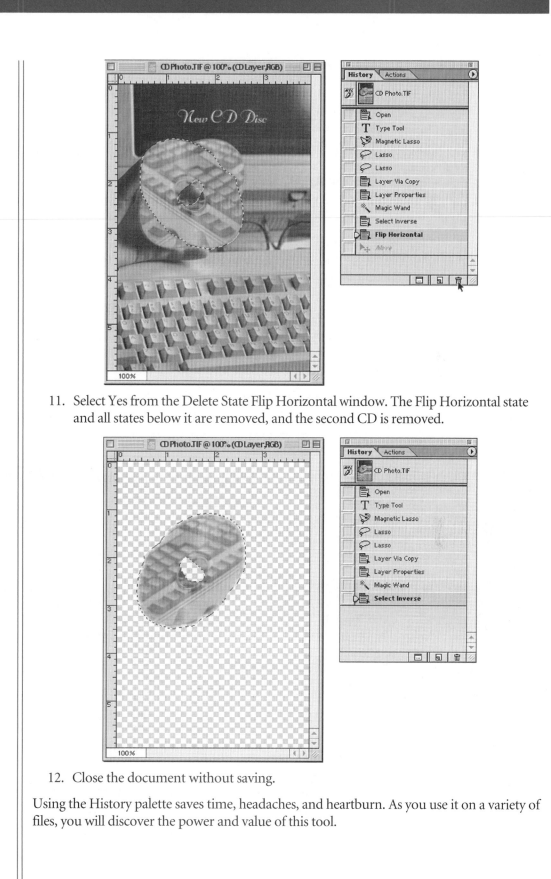

11. Select Yes from the Delete State Flip Horizontal window. The Flip Horizontal state and all states below it are removed, and the second CD is removed.

12. Close the document without saving.

Using the History palette saves time, headaches, and heartburn. As you use it on a variety of files, you will discover the power and value of this tool.

The Art History Brush

The History Brush (see Chapter 8), allows you to select any history state and paint those pixels onto the image. The Art History brush also uses source data from a specified History state — and it allows you to paint with stylized strokes. Creative application of previous History states is not limited to the literal pixels from that state.

Use the Art History Brush

1. Open **CD Photo.TIF** from your **SF-Adv Photoshop** folder.

2. Make sure that the History palette is open, and set History Options to Allow Non-Linear History. This allows you to make changes to a selected history state without deleting the states that come after it.

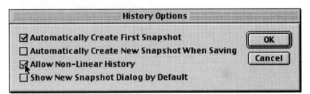

3. Change the foreground color to 65% yellow. Then select Edit>Fill to fill the entire image with the foreground color. Notice the new history state, called "Fill."

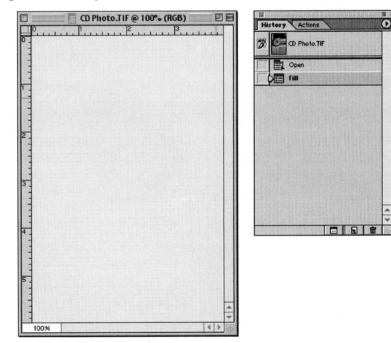

4. In the History palette, click on the Open history state. Notice that the fill state does not dim. Then select Image>Adjust>Invert to create a negative version of the original image. This creates a third history state, called "Invert."

5. To set the context for the Art History brush, again click on the open history state to return to the original view. Then click the square to the left of the fill history state. This sets the source for the Art History brush.

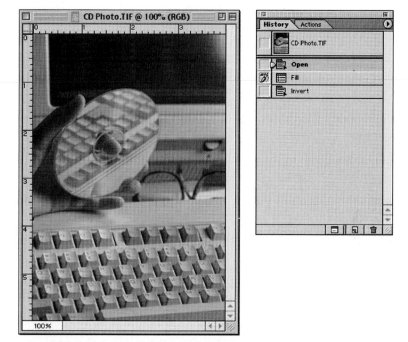

The selected history state (Open) will be affected by pixels from the source history state (Fill).

6. Choose the Art History brush (under the History brush). Select the 17-pixel soft-edged brush, as shown, and adjust the Art History Brush Options to Mode: Normal, Opacity: 40%, Style: Tight Long, Fidelity: 100%, Area: 20 px, Spacing: 0%.

7. Use the Art History brush to paint near the center of the CD. Experiment with different settings and duration of mouse-clicks to vary the "lightning" effect on the photo.

By combining different brush types and options, the Art History brush can have almost unlimited variations.

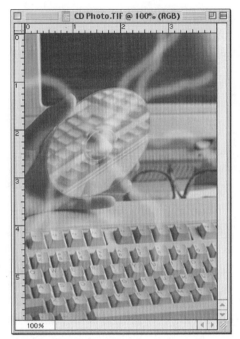
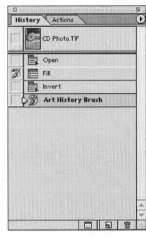

8. Reselect the Open history state, and set the source by clicking the box to the left of the Invert history state. Set the Art History brush options to Mode: Lighten, Area: 50 px, Spacing: 90%. Leave the rest of the settings the same.

9. Paint around the edges of the CD with the Art History brush. Notice that you are using pixels from the inverted state to create stylized color strokes around the image edges.

10. Experiment with different settings and brush styles. Close the file without saving.

Contact Sheet II

Imagine working on a project with many Photoshop and Adobe Illustrator EPS files supplied by a client with a tight deadline. The task is to color correct all these images with no knowledge of what the images look like. In addition, you have been provided no hardcopy proofs of the images for organizing the files.

Contact Sheet II allows the Photoshop user to create one image of all the files in a particular folder. The images can be placed either in a horizontal row or vertical column order. The images can then be viewed like a contact sheet from a photographer.

Use the Contact Sheet

1. Choose File>Automate>Contact Sheet II.

2. In the Contact Sheet dialog box, select the Choose button from the Source Folder area. Choose your **Work in Progress** folder. Keep the defaults in the rest of the window. If you have only a black-and-white printer available, use Grayscale in the Mode drag-down window. Click OK.

Contact Sheet II

Source Folder

[Choose...] Rob:Desktop Folder:Work in Progress:

☑ Include All Subfolders

[OK]
[Cancel]

Document

Width: 8   [inches ▼]

Height: 10   [inches ▼]

Resolution: 144   [pixels/inch ▼]

Mode: [Grayscale ▼]

✓ Grayscale
RGB Color
CMYK Color
Lab Color

Thumbnails

Place: [across first ▼]

Columns: 5   Width: 0.939 inches

Rows: 6   Height: 0.939 inches

☑ Use Filename As Caption

Font: [Helvetica ▼]   Font Size: 12 pt

3. The Contact Sheet tool will adjust the thumbnail image size to fit onto the file by processing the files through a Preset Action set. Click OK.

4. After all the images are placed in one file, select Flatten Image from the Layers palette Options menu to save storage space.

5. Save the file as "WIP Contact.TIF" to your **Work in Progress** folder. Print the file, and view all the images on three sheets. Close the file.

Conditional Mode Change

Sometimes a job will contain several types of files, and each discrete file type may receive different treatment. For example, there may be RGB and grayscale images in a job that will be printed using traditional lithography. The Conditional Mode Change feature allows an "if/then"-type query: if a file is RGB, change it to CMYK; otherwise leave it alone.

Conditional Mode Change

Source Mode

☐ Bitmap   ☑ RGB Color
☐ Grayscale   ☐ CMYK Color
☐ Duotone   ☐ Lab Color
☐ Indexed Color ☐ Multichannel

[All]   [None]

[OK]
[Cancel]

Bitmap
Grayscale
Duotone
Indexed Color
RGB Color
✓ CMYK Color
Lab Color
Multichannel

Target Mode

Mode: [CMYK Color ▼]

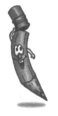

If the majority of your images are light, make certain that your background color in your Tool Bar is set for black, for easier viewing.

In the folder you'll be using, there are a number of image types. Open one or two of the color images and you'll see that at least some of them are RGB. We're going to print a brochure including these images on a traditional lithographic press. The images must be converted to CMYK. There are also grayscale images, however, in the folder. These must remain grayscale — there's no sense making them four times their current size. To make these changes manually would be a time-consuming process. We're going to use Photoshop's Conditional Mode Change.

Create Conditional Mode Changes

1. From your **SF-Adv Photoshop** folder, copy the **Cranachie Vineyards** folder to your **Work in Progress** folder.

2. Open the file **Couple Dining.TIF** from the **Cranachie Vineyards** folder. We're going to create an action using Conditional Mode Change that we can then run against the entire folder.

3. In the Actions palette, create a new Action set named "Custom". Within it, create a new action named "Conditional to CMYK". Click Record.

> **New Action**
>
> Name: Conditional to CMYK   **Record**
> Set: Custom Actions   **Cancel**
> Function Key: None   ☐ Shift ☐ Command
> Color: ☐ None

4. Select File>Automate>Conditional Mode Change.

5. In the Source Mode section, check RGB Color and Lab Color. Select CMYK Color for the Target Mode. Click OK.

> **Conditional Mode Change**
>
> **Source Mode**
> ☐ Bitmap   ☑ RGB Color   **OK**
> ☐ Grayscale   ☐ CMYK Color   **Cancel**
> ☐ Duotone   ☑ Lab Color
> ☐ Indexed Color   ☐ Multichannel
> [All] [None]
>
> **Target Mode**
> Mode: CMYK Color

6. Look at the Title bar of the picture. It now tells you the image is in CMYK mode.

7. Click the Stop Playing/Recording button in the Actions palette.

   Since we will likely want to repeatedly perform this process, we're going to create a droplet.

8. Create a new "CMYK Images" folder within your **Work in Progress**>**Cranachie Vineyards** folder.

9. Select File>Automate>Create Droplet.

10. Click the Choose button to save the Droplet to your **Work in Progress** folder as "Conditional to CMYK.EXE". In the Play sections, assign Set: Custom Actions, and Action: Conditional to CMYK. In the Destination section, set Destination: Folder. Select the **CMYK Images** folder within the **Cranachie Vineyards** folder. In the File Naming section, set it to the default of Document Name + Extension. Under Compatibility, check Windows and Mac OS, and set Errors: Stop for Errors. When you have confirmed your settings, click OK.

Create Droplet

Save Droplet In

[Choose...] Rob:...:Conditional to CMYK.EXE

[OK]
[Cancel]

Play

Set: [Custom Actions ↕]

Action: [Conditional to CMYK ↕]

☐ Override Action "Open" Commands
☐ Include All Subfolders
☐ Suppress Color Profile Warnings

Destination: [Folder ↕]

[Choose...] Rob:...:CMYK Images:

☐ Override Action "Save In" Commands

File Naming

Example: MyFile.gif

[Document Name ↕] + [extension ↕] +
[↕] + [↕] +
[↕] + [↕]

Compatibility: ☑ Windows ☑ Mac OS ☐ Unix

Errors: [Stop For Errors ↕]

[Save As...]

11. Drag the **Cranachie Vineyards** folder on top of the droplet. You will be given the opportunity to convert or cancel the EPS file and the PDF file. Click Cancel, then allow the droplet to continue. If a conversion cannot be performed on a file, you will receive a message. Click OK. Examine the files to see that each has been converted to CMYK.

Multi-page PDF to PSD

Occasionally it may be desirable to convert a PDF document to another format, such as GIF or JPEG for inclusion on a Web page. This automation feature opens each page of the PDF file (or the pages you select) into a separate Photoshop document and saves it to a specified location.

Convert a Multi-page PDF to PSD

1. In Photoshop, select File>Automate>Multi-page PDF to PSD.

2. For the Source PDF, choose **Cranachie Vineyards.PDF**, located in your **SF-Adv Photoshop>Cranachie Vineyards** folder. Set the Page Range to All. Leave the default Resolution: 72 pixels/inch, and Mode: RGB Color, Anti-aliased: checked. Set the Destination as your **Work in Progress** folder. Click OK.

Convert Multi-Page PDF to PSD

Source PDF
Choose...
Cranachie Vinyards.PDF

OK
Cancel

Page Range
◉ All ○ From: 1 To: 1

Output Options
Resolution: 72 pixels/inch ▼
Mode: RGB Color ▼ ☑ Anti-aliased

Destination
Base Name: Cranachie Vinyards
Choose...
Work in Progress

3. Open your **Work in Progress** folder. You will see four new files named Cranakie Vineyards0001.pdf through 0004.pdf.

Fit Image

It may be necessary to fit images to a specific height/width dimension (meaning to the greater of the two dimensions, with no distortion). Such projects could include catalogs or ads with standard image holes, such as an automobiles or real estate catalog. Simply applying this automation can save numerous steps. Fit Image, like Conditional Mode Change, must be run based on an action.

Fit Image

Constrain Within
Width: 288 pixels
Height: 430 pixels

OK
Cancel

The Fit Image process is generally equivalent to resizing the image with Image Sampling turned on. If the target size is larger than the original, unwanted interpolation may result.

Fit Images to a Specific Size

1. Open the file **Banana Split.TIF** from your **SF-Adv Photoshop>Dessert Company** folder. In this folder are a number of images that vary in their height to width ratios. Some are horizontal and others are vertical.

2. In the Actions palette, create a new Custom action. Name it "Fit to 500". Click Record.

3. Select File>Automate>Fit Image.

4. Constrain Within a Width and Height of 500 pixels to accommodate both the horizontal and vertical images.

Fit Image

Constrain Within
Width: 500 pixels
Height: 500 pixels

OK
Cancel

5. Click the Stop Playing/Recording button in the Actions palette. Save and close the Banana Split.TIF file.

6. Either run a Batch or create a Droplet that will run the "Fit to 500" action against the **Dessert Company** folder and will place the results in a destination folder named "Dessert" in your **Work in Progress** folder.

Picture Package

Windows users must create the folder in creating the Batch or Droplet. Macintosh users can create the folder on the fly by clicking the New Folder button.

The Picture Package command enables you to include several sizes of the same image on a single page, which is often useful when creating ad slicks. For example, you could include one 4 × 5-in. photo, two 2.5 × 3.5-in. photos, and four 1.25 × 1.75-in. photos on a single page.

You can select the layout from the drop-down menu, or you can create your own using a text editor and editing or creating a file within the Layouts folder, which is in the Photoshop Presets folder. The existing layouts will probably be appropriate to suit your needs. Specify the resolution for the images and the mode. You can use the active Photoshop document by clicking the Use Frontmost Document box, or by selecting a saved document.

Create a Picture Package

1. Open the image **Diamonds & Rust.TIF** from your **SF-Adv Photoshop** folder.

2. Select File>Automate>Picture Package.

3. For the Source Image, click the Use Frontmost Document box. In the Document section, set Layout: (2) 4 × 5 (2) 2.5 × 3.5 (4) 2 × 2.5, Resolution: 300 pixels/inch, Mode: RGB Color. Click OK.

4. Watch Photoshop build the page of images.

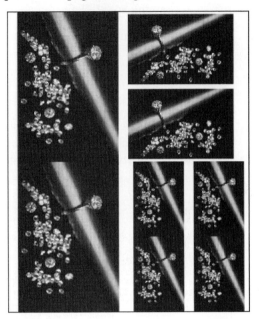

5. Save the file as "Diamonds & Rust Pkg.PSD" to your **Work in Progress** folder. Close the file.

Web Photo Gallery

A Web Photo Gallery is a Web site featuring a home page consisting of thumbnails, and gallery pages with full-sized images. There are several available styles and options, and you can also create your own, if you are an advanced user with knowledge of HTML.

To create a Web photo gallery, select a source folder and destination folder. Photoshop places a home page for your gallery named "index.htm," JPEG images in an "images" subfolder, HTML pages in a "pages" subfolder, and JPEG thumbnails in a "thumbnails" subfolder.

Create a Web Photo Gallery

1. In Photoshop, select File>Automate>Web Photo Gallery.

2. Examine the thumbnail for the four different styles, then select the one you like best.

3. Set Options: Banner as follows — Site Name: [Your Name] Web Photo Gallery, Photographer: Comstock, Date: [Today's Date (automatically generated)], Font: Arial, Font Size: 3.

4. Set Options: Gallery Images at the default — Border Size: 0 pixels, Check Resize Images: Medium, 350 pixels, JPEG Quality: Medium, 5.

5. Set Options: Gallery Thumbnails at the default — Captions: Use Filename, Font: Arial, Font Size: 3, Size: Medium, 75 pixels, Columns: 4, Rows: 3, Border Size: 0 pixels.

6. Leave Custom Colors at their defaults.

7. In the Files section, set the Source to your **SF-Adv Photoshop>Gallery** folder and the Destination to your **Work in Progress** folder. Click OK.

8. Photoshop will make all the conversions and should launch your browser, then open the new page index.html. If it does not, open your browser, and open **index.html** in your **Work in Progress** folder.

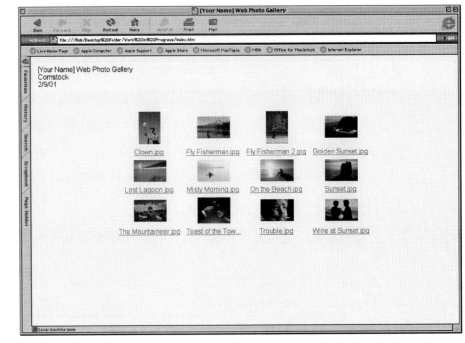

9. Click on the thumbnails and work with the page. Try the other Style options.

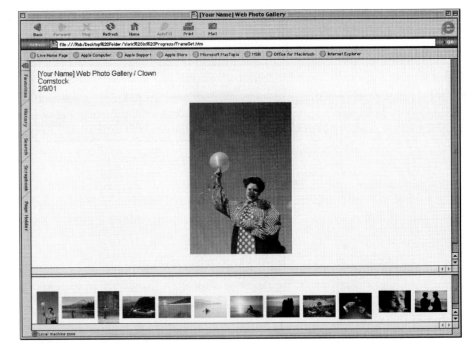

10. Close the file when you are finished.

Summary

Automation enables us to meet nearly impossible deadlines and deal with complex file issues. It provides us more time to experiment and expand our skills. Photoshop's tools must be combined with good planning and the ongoing improvement of your workflow. Taking advantage of the available automation features and shortcuts constitutes the difference between productivity and frustration.

CHAPTER 15

IMPORTING AND EXPORTING

CHAPTER OBJECTIVE:

To discover how to import files from vector drawing programs into a Photoshop document; to become familiar with the file formats used for images on the World Wide Web, and to learn which format to use, depending on the type of image that you're creating. In Chapter 15, you will:

- Discover how to save files in JPEG and GIF formats.

- Learn about filters with a range of color.

- Become familiar with how to save a file with transparency.

- Observe how creating images for the Web is different than creating images for print production.

PROJECTS TO BE COMPLETED:

- Just Shoot Me (A)

- Baby Shower Invitation (B)

- Retouching the Jones Family Portrait (C)

- The Fix Is In! (D)

- Makeover (E)

- Photomat (F)

Importing and Exporting

As you've seen, information comes to Photoshop from many different sources, but Photoshop's own layered images aren't compatible with most other applications. Most desktop-publishing programs, for example, prefer TIFF or EPS files for importing.

Most formats are easily accessible using the Save As and Save a Copy As commands from the File menu. There are certain situations, however, that require actions that are somewhat trickier than simply opening or saving a file.

Importing Files

Throughout this course, we have opened TIFF, EPS, and Photoshop (PSD) files. Through the use of special filters, Photoshop is able to import a number of other graphic formats. These include Anti-aliased PICT, PDF Image, PICT Resource, Annotations, and the special formats of scanners, digital cameras, and other peripheral devices. We will address only the file import options in this chapter. Files are imported by selecting File>Import.

Anti-aliased PICT (Macintosh)

Because PICT files are, by definition, the same resolution as the monitor, they tend to have some rough edges. Selecting Anti-aliased PICT smooths out some of the roughness. The file may be imported as Grayscale or RGB Color, and may be scaled upon import. Even though the image is scaled, the original resolution remains.

PDF Image

The logical assumption is that this option would open PDF files as images. The logical assumption, however, is incorrect. This option actually opens individual images contained in a PDF document. If only one image is contained within the document, it will open that image. If there is more than one image, you will have the opportunity to review all the images, then select which ones to import or to import all. Each image is opened in its own file.

PICT Resource (Macintosh)

This is a file contained in the Macintosh's resource fork. It could be a splash screen, a logo, or the contents of the Scrapbook. As with the PDF image, you have the opportunity to scroll through the images to choose the one you want. If you simply click OK, you will open the first image, similar to choosing File>Open>PICT Resource.

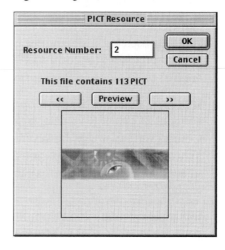

Annotations

Using this import option, you can import annotations that were included in a PDF or FDF page. To open annotations, you would navigate to the document, then click Load. The annotations then appear on screen in the position in which they appear on the page. Only annotations appearing on the first page will display.

Working with Files Containing Vector Data

FDF is Form Data Format, which is used in conjunction with PDF files.

By now you have experience in opening vector-based documents and placing EPS files into existing Photoshop files. In addition to these methods, however, you can import an Adobe Illustrator or Macromedia FreeHand file by copying a graphic from within a drawing program, then pasting the files into a Photoshop document. The advantage of using this method is that you may paste the image as a rasterized image (which is similar to placing an EPS file), or you can specify that the graphic be pasted as a path or as a shape layer (layer clipping path), which will add it to the Paths palette. This is an excellent way to create custom clipping paths for images to be saved as EPS files.

In addition to the Import filter, selecting File>Export>Paths to Illustrator enables you to export paths created in Photoshop for use in vector-drawing programs. This is a great way to accurately wrap type around an irregular shape or create a trap for an image that includes a clipping path.

When files were saved in EPS format, earlier versions of Photoshop preserved clipping paths as vector data, but converted type and objects drawn with the Pen tool to raster elements. Photoshop 6, however, preserves vector elements in EPS and Acrobat (PDF) files, so type — even in smaller sizes — retains its smoothness when imported into page-layout programs. When you have vector elements in your Photoshop document to be imported into another program, be sure to save as Photoshop EPS.

Saving Images for the World Wide Web

Three types of images are commonly used on Web pages — GIF, JPEG, and PNG. These compressed file types offer substantial savings of load time (and disk space) over typical print-oriented formats such as TIFF files. The main drawback to this is that compression algorithms have their limitations.

Which format should you use? It depends on the type of image you're converting. JPEG is generally used for photographic images, but does not support transparency. GIF and PNG files are preferable for computer-generated artwork, especially those containing large, flat areas of color. GIF and PNG formats support transparency.

JPEG images allow the user to specify the level of compression required. The resulting file contains 24 bits of RGB data, yielding high-quality photographic results in most instances. Compressing an image, however, reduces its quality. More compression means lower quality. When saving a JPEG image, you also have the option of saving the paths associated with the image (but not clipping paths), though a JPEG saved with paths may cause some browsers to choke.

The PNG format is not supported by all browsers, and should be avoided when Web images require the broadest visibility.

GIF images contain 256 colors or less, as defined in the Index Color mode. Any colors not contained in the Color palette may be remapped to another color in the palette. For more photographic results, the converted file can be dithered. Under this compression scheme, if a color does not exist in the palette, dots of different colors in the palette are closely placed together to achieve the illusion of the missing color. Dithered GIF files are more photorealistic, but are usually larger than undithered files.

The color palette used in a GIF file may be the standard System palette from Macintosh or Windows-based systems. A 216-color Web palette includes only the colors common to both Macintosh and Windows, so graphics will be viewed cross-platform with relative consistency. The Adaptive palette draws on the most commonly used colors in the existing image to define its color group. Custom Color palettes may be loaded and saved to ensure consistency among graphics on a Web page.

The PNG format is actually two formats in one. PNG-8 supports 8-bit color, with lossless compression, much as the GIF format does. Like the GIF, it also supports background matting and transparency. Some PNG files will achieve 10% to 30% better compression than their GIF counterparts. PNG-24 also uses lossless compression while supporting 24-bit color. Because the compression is lossless, the files will be somewhat larger than corresponding JPEG files. PNG-24 files support up to 256 levels of transparency; the edges of the image will blend smoothly with virtually any background color.

JPEG and GIF files may be saved as *interlaced* (GIF or PNG) or *progressive* (JPEG). This means that if the browser supports it, the image will appear in stages, beginning with a low-resolution image and then filling in the blanks until the image is at full resolution. The purpose of this is to give the viewer a framework of the image early on, instead of waiting for the entire image to paint before it is displayed. An indexed color file may be exported with a certain color or colors designated as background matting, to match the Web page's background, simulating transparency.

Using the Save for Web Feature

Photoshop offers the ability to preview files prior to making decisions about acceptable quality levels. This is especially useful when viewing different compression levels for JPEG files, but it can also be used to good effect when viewing GIF and PNG images. We will use this feature, Save for Web, in the next series of exercises to compare the differences in quality and, of equal importance, speed at which an image loads, using JPEG, PNG, and GIF file formats.

Save a JPEG File

1. Open **Woman at Computer.TIF** from the **SF-Adv Photoshop** folder. This image includes some delicate skin tones and detail in fabric that we don't want to compromise any more than necessary.

2. Select File>Save for Web. This gives us the opportunity to compare the deterioration of the image based on its compression. Note that there are four tabs: Original, Optimized, 2-up, and 4-up. We want to compare the original with the three primary JPEG settings. Select the 4-up tab.

   | Original | Optimized | 2-Up | **4-Up** |

3. Leave the setting in the upper-left window set to "Original." Set the upper-right window to JPEG High, the lower-left to JPEG Medium, and the lower-right to JPEG Low.

Press Command-Option-Shift-S (Macintosh) or Control-Alt-Shift-S (Windows) to access the Save for Web menu.

4. As you can see, there is considerable deterioration between the original (JPEG High) and JPEG Low. Note especially the front of the blouse and the hair. The JPEG Medium, however, has not deteriorated appreciably. The quality level here is 30. Click on the JPEG Medium view to select it, then click OK.

5. Photoshop will automatically assign the ".JPG" file extension. Save to your **Work in Progress** folder in Images Only format. Click OK.

Although a JPEG image can be compressed to a very small size, the compression method is lossy — the more the file is compressed, the more data the compressing mechanism throws away or "loses." Use only as much compression with JPEG images as necessary, or you will begin to see artifacts and a loss of detail within the image.

Not all browsers support PNG format at this time.

6. Leave the file open for the next exercise.

As you work with different types of files, you will discover that, in the case of saving to JPEG, one size does not fit all. After awhile, you will note specific image characteristics that will require higher-quality settings, and characteristics that will allow you to accept lower settings, while not detracting too greatly from the image.

Let's see what differences exist between a JPEG file and a PNG-24 image.

Compare JPEG and PNG Images

1. With **Woman at Computer.TIF** still open, select File>Save for Web.

2. Set the upper-right image to JPEG Maximum, the lower-left to JPEG High, and the lower-right image to PNG-24.

3. Carefully examine the PNG-24 image, comparing it to the two JPEG images. Some additional detail is preserved. You'll particularly notice this on the blouse and hair if you zoom in.

   Note the difference, however, in file size and loading time — more than six times as long to load as the high-quality JPEG image. Clearly, 118 seconds (nearly 2 minutes) is unacceptable for the minimal gain in quality for this image.

4. Click Cancel, and close the file without saving.

Not all documents saved out of Photoshop for the Web are 24-bit color. Often we'll want to save an image containing "flat" color, and a limited palette. When saving files with flat colors, we want to use the fewest possible colors and still maintain fidelity to the original image. Fewer colors mean a faster-loading file. When possible, we want to use the Web-safe palette so that the image will look the same under Windows as it does on a Macintosh.

Save a File in GIF Format

1. Open **Balloon Man.EPS** from the **SF-Adv Photoshop** folder. Make certain that Mode is set to RGB and Resolution to 72 ppi. Leave the dimensions at their defaults. Anti-aliased should be checked.

2. Select File>Save for Web.

3. Set the upper-right image to GIF, specify the Web palette, Colors: 32, No Dither. Set the lower-left image to GIF, Web palette, Colors: 16, No Dither. Set the lower-right image to GIF, Web palette, Colors: 8, No Dither.

4. Examine the differences in the images. Note especially how reducing the number of colors affects the gradients in his nose and hatband. The 8-color image also experiences some severe color shifts.

5. Select the lower-right image, and change it to Colors: 16, Diffusion Dither of 85%. This smooths out the gradients and adds no appreciable time to the loading time. With this image selected, click OK.

6. Save as "Balloon Man.GIF" to your **Work in Progress** folder. Close the file without saving.

While the Adaptive palette usually yields the most attractive results, the Web is not a color-controlled environment. Older monitors may not display 24-bit color, and the colors on the Macintosh are different from those in Windows. When it can't display the exact color specified, a browser will substitute a palette that works for the monitor being used. It will also dither the colors in the image. Dithering is placing pixels next to one another to simulate a different color.

Manage Files with a Range of Color

1. Open **Spectrum.PSD** from the **SF-Adv Photoshop** folder.

2. To have more control over how the image is converted, you first need to convert the image to Indexed Color Mode. This happens automatically when a file is saved as GIF. We're going to make some comparisons using the Save for Web function. Select File>Save for Web and choose the 4-up view.

3. For the upper-right, lower-left, and lower-right images, change the Settings to GIF Web Palette with Colors: Auto. Set the upper-right image with a 0% dither, lower-left image with a 75% Diffusion dither, and lower-right image with a 100% Diffusion dither.

When you set the diffusion dither, set the Settings switch to read [Unnamed].

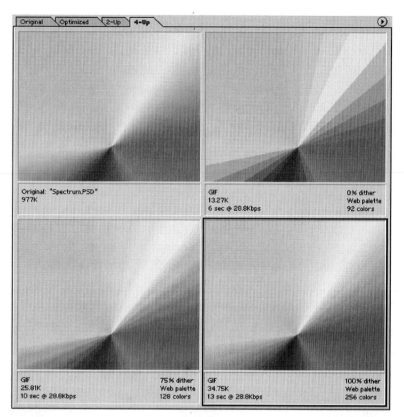

4. Notice that the image quality is tremendously improved, especially when using a 100% dither. However, we've also changed from a 6-second display time to a 13-second wait.

5. Select the image on the lower left. Change the setting to JPEG Medium. Clearly, this is our best choice. It looks better than any of the GIF solutions, is smaller, and loads faster, but we lose transparency. With continuous-tone images, you're much better off with lossy compression than with banding.

6. What if you need transparency and smoothness, and time is less important? Choose the PNG-24 output settings. Notice that the image is smooth and transparency is preserved. The loading time, however, is 34 seconds.

7. Click Cancel and close the file without saving.

Images Containing Transparency

As you have just seen, not all formats support transparency, and sometimes you have to make trade-offs when you use images containing transparency. When you use an image for print, you achieve transparency by including a clipping path with the image. Images saved for use on the Web, however, are another issue entirely.

While GIF and PNG images both support transparency, you may see a halo effect when the anti-aliased image is placed on a Web page. If you know the color of the Web page, a better solution is to use a matte, which can be used with GIF, PNG, and JPEG images, blending the image with the background color.

Save a File with Transparency

1. Open **Broadway.EPS** from the **SF-Adv Photoshop** folder. Make certain that Mode is set to RGB and Resolution is set to 100 ppi. Leave the dimensions at their defaults. Click on Anti-aliased.

   This logo comes in with a white background, which is not desirable for the background that we're going to lay it over.

2. Choose File>Save for Web. Adjust the image so that both feet are visible. For the upper-right selection, choose GIF . Make the color reduction algorithm Selective, Colors: 256, Diffusion Dither: 100%, and check the Transparency box. Leave the Web Snap at 0%.

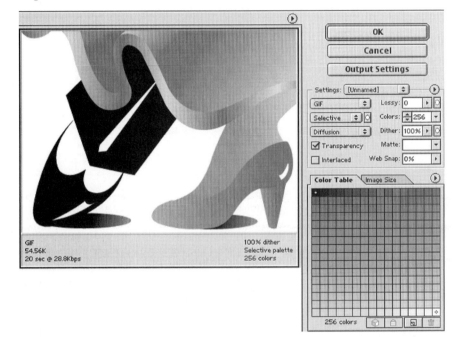

   What do you think will happen here? The matte color is white by default. The highlight on the woman's shoe and the mans' trousers would become transparent, as would the man's shoes.

   There's an easy solution to the problem. Click Cancel to exit the window.

3. With the Magic Wand tool, select the white background. Press Delete/Backspace to create a transparent background. Deselect.

   Now let's try some options.

4. Choose File>Save for Web. Set the upper-right, lower-left, and lower-right selections to the GIF specifications you set earlier. Adjust the position of the image as you did earlier. Zoom in so you can see the edge of the skirt and the transparent background. What will happen here? You'll see a white halo against the background of the Web page.

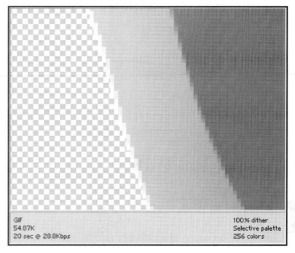

Halo effect viewed at 300%.

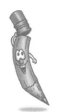

When selecting Web colors, the first two digits are Red, the second two are Blue, and the third two are Green.

5. Choose Matte: Other. Specify CCCCCC as the number in the Color Picker, and click OK.

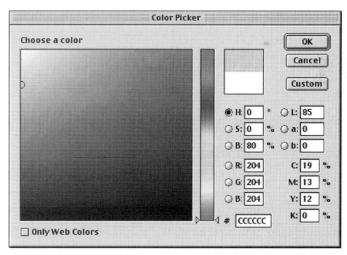

Notice that the former halo became the neutral gray of the Web page; it will blend cleanly with the background of the Web page.

6. In the lower-right image, change the settings to JPEG with Medium Quality, a Blur of 0, and a matte of CCCCCC.

7. Click on the JPEG image to select it (it will reproduce the most faithfully, and will display in the fastest time). Click OK, and save to your **Work in Progress** folder as "Broadway.JPG". Close the file.

Occasionally we hear that an RGB file can be saved as GIF, leaving the impression that it's somehow different from an indexed color GIF. Let's take a closer look at the process and its results.

Explore the Myth of RGB GIF

1. Open **Orange Slice.TIF** from the **SF-Adv Photoshop** folder. Check Image>Mode, and confirm that it is an RGB file.

2. Choose Save As>CompuServe GIF. You will receive the warning: "Some of this file's data will not be saved using the chosen format and options." The file is also being saved automatically as a copy. Click Save and save it to your **Work in Progress** folder.

3. The Indexed Color menu appears. It is obvious from this that whenever a file is saved as a GIF, the colors are indexed to a maximum of 256 colors.

4. Close the file without saving.

Summary

The Web palette is comprised of the 216 colors common to both the Macintosh and Windows environment. Using other colors, particularly in GIF files, will often result in the color being far off from what is intended.

It should be clear from the exercises we've completed that creating images for the Web is different from creating images for print production. Instead of exact color matches with infinitesimal nuances of color, we have a reasonable shot at an acceptable range of color, based upon the viewer's monitor settings and platform.

More important than exact color match is that pages load rapidly. It's important to pay attention to the details of numbers of colors in the palette, the resolution of the image, and the dimensions of the image. Remember, it's designed for screen resolution, so resolution greater than 96 ppi (on Windows-based systems; 72 ppi for Macintoshes) will be discarded. The standard is 72 ppi.

For print output, the standard is 1.5 to 2 times the value of the line screen, usually around 300 ppi. If images will be used both for print and for the Web, they should be manipulated at high resolution. A high-resolution RGB file should be saved in Photoshop format. Save a copy of the file at high-resolution in CMYK for print, and a copy at reduced resolution for the Web.

CHAPTER 16

WEB GRAPHICS WORKFLOW

CHAPTER OBJECTIVE:

To learn how to prepare images effectively for presentation on the Web. To become familiar with how to use Photoshop and ImageReady to create a workflow that optimizes graphics and incorporates automatically generated HTML code in the final product. In Chapter 16, you will:

- Learn about checking for browser effects and compression optimization.

- Discover how to create a navigation-bar image map, linking areas of the image to URLs.

- Become familiar with how to slice an image to achieve a minimum file size.

- Learn how to create switch images.

- Gain experience working with JavaScript rollovers.

PROJECTS TO BE COMPLETED:

- Just Shoot Me (A)

- Baby Shower Invitation (B)

- Retouching the Jones Family Portrait (C)

- The Fix Is In! (D)

- Makeover (E)

- Photomat (F)

Web Graphics Workflow

Adobe has included ImageReady 3.0 with Photoshop to handle many of the chores of preparing images for the Web. The criteria for use of images and graphics on the Internet are much different from those for print production. ImageReady focuses on image optimization and on generating sophisticated HTML (HyperText Markup Language) code for rollovers, image maps and animations that can be published from a Web server and viewed with any of the commonly available Web browsers.

Photoshop and ImageReady

ImageReady is not just another application — it is truly an extension of Photoshop. Adobe has invested considerable thought into the concept of maintaining a standard user interface among its graphic arts applications, and ImageReady is evidence of the success of this effort.

Integrated Workflow

ImageReady is tightly coupled with Photoshop, with each having a "JumpTo" button at the bottom of the application toolbox that seamlessly switches to the other program. The image is kept active in both, with updates from the previous program applied as you jump to the other program. Of course, changes made in each program are saved to the same file.

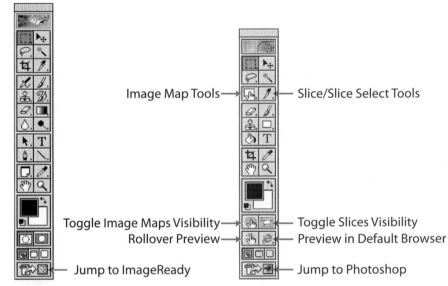

Image Map Tools → / ← Slice/Slice Select Tools

Toggle Image Maps Visibility → / ← Toggle Slices Visibility
Rollover Preview → / ← Preview in Default Browser
Jump to ImageReady
Jump to Photoshop

Similar Interface

Many of the tools and functions that have been covered in this course are also found in ImageReady. They perform the same functions in the same ways. Several specialized ImageReady tools have been added (Slice, Slice Select, Ellipse/Rectangle/Rounded Rectangle tools, Show/Hide Slices, and Jump to Photoshop). Image changes made and saved in Photoshop are updated when you jump back to ImageReady, and the update is maintained as a state in the ImageReady History palette so that it can be undone at any time.

Web Graphics

For years, Photoshop has been central to the creation of images for the Web; with the integration of ImageReady, Adobe has delivered a product that can apply all of the necessary adjustments to optimize Web graphics without the need for third-party software.

Minimize File Size

The smallest possible file size means that Web graphics will download quickly, even on a slow Internet connection. The trade-off is that image quality inevitably suffers as file size is reduced. Given a range of compression options, image quality degrades as more-compact image files are generated. The trick is to achieve the best compression while maintaining acceptable image quality. Accurate previews permit selection among compression and color-level options.

Checking for Browser Effects

Since there are differences between the display of Web graphics in Macintosh and Windows browsers, Photoshop and ImageReady provide for accommodating these differences in the Save for Web window. This allows you to compensate for the screen brightness differences when your graphics are displayed on these different systems. Graphics will look darker on a Windows display. Each time you select Standard Macintosh Color or Standard Windows Color, you can visualize how your graphics will appear.

2-Up and 4-Up Views

To help you select among the available degrees of compression, multiple views, called "LiveView" panels, provide side-by-side comparisons of the results. For the 4-up display, the original is shown with three optimized versions: the first uses the settings that you have selected and the other variations use settings selected by Photoshop. You can also modify these views to experiment with different settings.

Compression Optimization

Controls are included that permit selection of the type of Color palette and number of colors used for the GIF or PNG file, and the degree of JPEG or GIF lossy compression used. Other options can be selected to "snap" GIF colors to the 216 Web-safe Color palette.

Advanced Web Formats

Specialized tools handle tasks that otherwise require laborious and technically advanced manual image procedures coordinated with detailed and very stringent HTML coding. ImageReady reduces these tasks to a visual approach that can readily be mastered by even the most programming-challenged Web-site designer.

Once the Web effect has been saved, a separate HTML file is generated with the required code that can be copied and pasted directly into the HTML of a Web page.

Image Maps

An image can be assigned "hotspot" targets that will link to specified URLs when viewed in a Web browser. These hotspots can be rectangular, oval, or polygonal. When Save Optimized is chosen, HTML Options let you select either client-side or server-side image map coding. Image maps may be created using the Image Map tools or by using layers.

Use vertical guides to divide the image into 10 areas, 64 pixels each. The fixed-size selection marquee can be used to position the guides quickly and accurately. An alternative to the copy/ paste technique would use the fixed-size selection marquee to fill between the guides with black or red.

Usually the Home page of a Web site is located at the root or first level of the directory structure and is named index.htm/.html/ .asp, default.htm/.html/.asp, or welcome.htm/.html/.asp. Other pages can be represented by files at the same root level and are referenced by a relative URL that only need to cite the filename, not the entire Web-site address.

You could create an Action of Step 5 to help you create the background of the navigation bar.

Navigation-bar Image Map

1. Create a new document in ImageReady that is 640 pixels wide and 30 pixels high with a White background.

   For the background of the navigation bar, make a series of selections across the image, filling alternately with black and red. The following guidelines may be helpful, although there are different ways in which the background can be created. Change the Marquee Tool Options to a Fixed Size of 64 pixels wide by 30 pixels high.

2. Convert the background layer to a normal layer.

3. Make the foreground and background color swatches black (#000000) and red (#FF0000).

4. Fill the first 64 × 30 px-area with black.

5. Select Layer>Duplicate Layer, then Layer>Set Layer Position. Set the Offset to Horizontal: Current Position, 64 pixels.

6. Press "X" to exchange foreground and background colors and fill with red.

7. Continue with steps 5 and 6, alternating red and black until the bar is filled.

8. Starting with the upper layer, use Command/Control-E to Merge Layers down, one by one, until only Layer 0 remains. The following steps, using the Layer via Cut procedure can be applied to any image that you wish to use as an image map; clickable areas can be rectangular, circular, or polygon-shaped.

9. Select the first 64 × 30-pixel block in Layer 0, and choose Layer>New>Layer Via Cut. This produces and selects Layer 2.

10. Position a horizontal guide about 20 pixels from the top of the image. This will be the baseline for the button text. With the Type tool selected, position the cursor on the baseline in the center of the first button.

11. Use ATC Coconuts ExtraBold, 12 pixels, and set the anti-aliasing option to Crisp. Choose the type color from the Options bar. (In later steps, you will apply black type to the red buttons.) Type "HOME" centered on the navigation button.

12. Double-click the HOME type layer to display the Layer Options dialog box.

13. The Name field is filled in automatically by the type in the layer. Check Group with Previous Layer.

14. Select Layer 0, and choose Layer>New Layer-Based Image Map Area. Name the layer "Against the Clock", and link to the URL "http://www.againsttheclock.com."

Change the marquee back to normal or change its fixed size to 128 × 30.

15. Return to Layer 0, and select and choose Layer Via Cut for each of the remaining navigation buttons. Type the button name, and link the image-map URL (Uniform Resource Locator) for the remaining buttons as you did in steps 11–14.

- "NEWS" link to "news.htm"
- "SEARCH" link to "search.htm"
- "SUPPORT" link to "support.htm"
- "SHOP" link to "shop.htm"
- "FINANCE" link to "finance.htm"
- "GAMES" link to "games.htm"
- "HOW TO" link to "howto.htm"
- "E-MAIL" link to "mailto:info@againsttheclock.com?subject=Photoshop"
- "CHAT" link to "chat.htm"

Note that each button consists of two grouped layers with a notation as to the hyperlink.

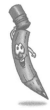

Use the Info palette to precisely position the segments.

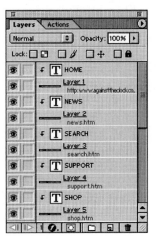

Press Command/Control-Shift-J to access Layer Via Cut.

16. If the Optimize palette is not already visible, select Window>Show Optimize. Choose GIF as the file type, and Web as the palette.

17. Click on the 4-up tab, and evaluate the views of the finished navigation bar. Note the different GIF options that offer a choice of file sizes and image qualities.

18. Select either the first or second version, and choose File>Save Optimized as "navbuttons.html" to your **Work in Progress** folder. Close the file.

The files saved are the JPEG image and the HTML code for the image map.

19. Check out the final GIF image map in a Web browser by dragging the HTML document to a browser icon or open window. If you move your cursor to one of the buttons, you will see the full path of the document.

The link, http://www.againsttheclock.com, can be viewed in the browser's status bar.

20. Look at the source code of the HTML file. Use either View Source in your Web browser, or open the HTML file with any text editor. This is the coding that ImageReady provides for you. The code between the *<!— ImageReady Slices (Navbuttons1.psd) —>* and the *<!— End ImageReady Slices —>* comment lines can be cut and pasted into an existing page or you can develop content within this page. When finished, close the file without saving.

You can cut and paste HTML source code into any Web page you create.

Slicing Images

The term slicing refers to the horizontal and/or vertical division of an image combined with the coding of a matching HTML table that reassembles the image when viewed in a Web browser. Slices can be resized, divided, merged, deleted, rearranged, and layered.

Slicing for Image Maps

Each slice can be assigned a Web link to a specified URL (Uniform Resource Locator), and provided with an ALT tag (the text displayed in non-graphical browsers) or with a JavaScript message that appears in the browser's status bar.

Slicing for Minimum File Size

Slices can be used to apply different format and compression options to different parts of the image, preserving full-color, high-quality JPEG detail in one part while making an adjacent area of flat color very compact using a lossy GIF with limited colors.

Slicing to Incorporate Animation

Animation effects can be embedded into a larger image by isolating the smaller area using slices. This will dramatically reduce the file size required for the combined image.

Slicing to Incorporate JavaScript Rollovers

The sophisticated coding required to create a "mouseover" or "onclick" Web effect is handled internally by ImageReady.

Slicing to Define a Text Area

A slice can be defined as "non-image" and contain text (and optionally, a background color) which is entered directly in the Slice palette.

The concept of this next exercise is to create a Web rollover image for each of the four presidential figures on Mt. Rushmore. When viewed in a browser, rolling the mouse over one of the presidential busts will switch the image to display an oval-shaped, soft-edged portrait with the individual's name.

Furthermore, since we are concerned about minimizing the download time for the Web and the image is dimensionally large, we will only save the faces as high-quality JPEGs; the rest of the surrounding image will be GIFs with a sharply-reduced color table.

Slice an Image

This concept can be used to identify mountains in a mountain range, to place corporate officers in a group setting, then isolate them, complete with bios, or to show an entire product line, then display individual products and prices when that product is selected.

1. In ImageReady, open the **Mt. Rush.TIF** image from your **SF-Adv Photoshop** folder. We will be isolating each of the presidents in separate slices.

2. Downsample the image to 400 pixels wide; check Constrain Proportions.

3. Save the file as "Mt. Rush.psd" in your **Work In Progress** folder.

4. Double-click on the Zoom tool to adjust the view to 100%, and adjust the window to see the entire image.

5. Double-click Layer 1 in the Layers palette. Rename the image layer "Mt. Rushmore".

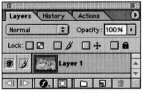

6. Choose the Slice tool (press "K") and drag a diagonal across George Washington's face. This will create a user-slice and four surrounding "auto-slices."

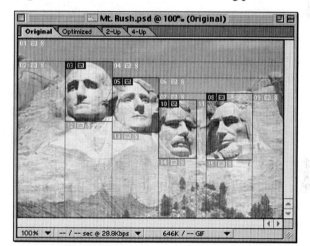

7. If the rectangle does not closely frame Washington's face, use the Slice Select tool ("A") to resize the slice.

8. Repeat the slice procedure with each of the remaining presidential busts.

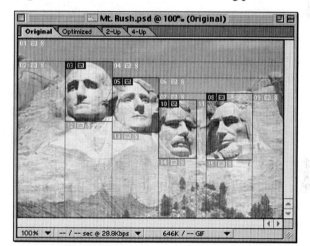

9. Save the file, and leave it open for the next exercise.

Assign Optimum Formats to Slices

1. With the document Mt. Rush.psd open, and the Slices Select tool chosen, choose All Slices from the Select menu, then choose View>Show>Deselect (uncheck) Slices.

2. Open Window>Show Optimize, and select GIF 32 Dithered. You may experiment with reducing the color table even more, but it may produce an unacceptable amount of tonal banding. This setting will control the characteristics and file size for the non-face slices.

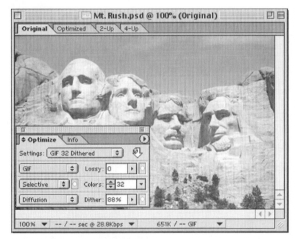

3. Select View>Show>Slices. Use the Slice Select tool ("A"), and click on the first bust image; and then, while holding the Shift key for multiple selections, click on the other three. Choose Hide Slices from the Slice menu (View>Show>Slices).

4. In the Optimize window, choose JPEG High to improve the quality of the presidential images. These settings, and the consequential larger file sizes, will be applied to the selected face slices only.

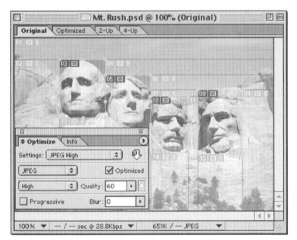

When you choose File>Save, the image is written out as a Photoshop (*.psd) document. Later we will choose Save Optimized, which will generate the multiple GIF and JPEG images, as well as the HTML-coded document.

5. Choose View>Show>Slices to deselect the slices. Select the 2-up display by clicking the tab to compare the optimized versions with the original.

6. Return to the original view.

7. Save and leave this file open for the next exercise.

Create Switch Images

1. With the document Mt. Rush.psd open, choose the Elliptical Marquee tool, and make a selection of Washington's bust.

2. Feather the selection by 10 pixels.

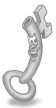

Press "M" to cycle to the Marquee tool, then press Shift-M to toggle among the marquee tools.

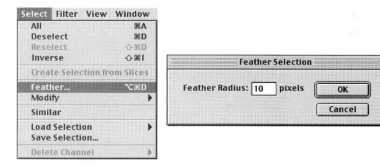

3. Create a New Layer Via Copy.

A switch image is the alternate form of the image that is displayed when a rollover is assigned.

If your Marquee tool is still set at a fixed size, return it to Normal.

4. Name the new layer "Washington". Turn off the layer visibility for the Mt. Rushmore layer, and move the Mt. Rushmore layer to the top of the layer stacking order.

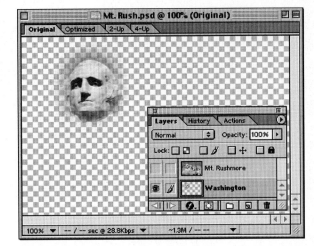

5. With the Type tool ("T"), select ATC Coconuts ExtraBold, 20 pixels, and position the cursor next to Washington's bust. Type the President's full name.

6. Apply a Drop Shadow effect to the name using the Layer Effects icon at the bottom of the Layers palette.

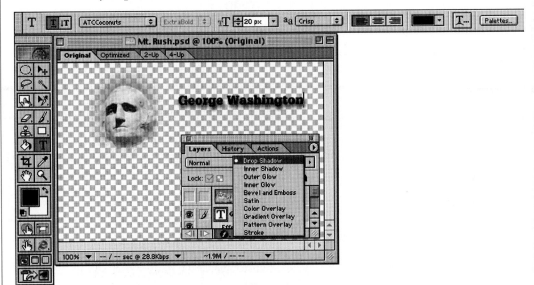

Remember to move the Mt. Rushmore layer to the top of the layer stacking order each time, and to select this layer before selecting Layer via Copy.

7. Turn on Mt. Rushmore layer visibility. Since the Washington layer is below the Mt. Rushmore layer, it cannot be seen.

8. Repeat the procedure to create switch images for each of the presidential images.

9. Save the file and leave it open for the next exercise.

After completing this exercise, try developing a secondary rollover with a text image that triggers an image change beside it.

JavaScript Rollovers

Images that switch when the cursor passes over them have become commonplace on interactive Web sites. Using layers in ImageReady, images can be combined as rollovers, automatically generating the complex HTML code for you. ImageReady can generate four types of rollovers:

- rollover (in the same location as the cursor)
- secondary rollover (in a different part of the page)
- rollover as a simple image swap or a complex animation
- rollover as a change in Layer visibility or other layer effects

Assign Rollovers

1. With the Mt. Rush.psd document open, check that the Mt. Rushmore layer is the top layer. If not, drag it to the top of the Layers palette.

2. With the Slice Select tool, click on Washington's bust, and select Window>Show>Rollover to activate the Rollover window. This shows the Washington slice as the Normal image view for our rollover.

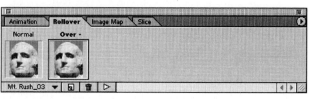

3. Click on the Create New Rollover State icon at the bottom of the Rollover window; an "Over-" state frame appears.

4. In the Layers palette, turn off visibility for the Mt. Rushmore layer, and make only the Washington (image) and George Washington (type) layers visible. This defines the rollover state.

5. Repeat for the other three rollovers.

6. To see how the rollover states will appear, click the Rollover Preview button near the bottom of the Tool palette, and position the cursor over each president's face.

7. Save the file.

8. To generate from the slices all of the separate images, the rollovers, and the HTML file with JavaScript and table code, choose File>Save Optimized. Be certain to select Format: HTML and Images. Name the file "MtRush.html".

9. Preview the rollover (File>Preview in>[then choose a browser on your computer]); or transfer the HTML file and the Images folder containing all the JPEG and GIF images to another computer that does have a Web browser installed.

10. Look at the JavaScript rollover code in the HTML file. It can be copied and pasted into your Web page. When finished, close the file without saving.

Summary

Preparing graphics for a Web workflow involves preplanning to achieve the result you desire. You can positively affect the file size by incorporating slices. These can be used to differentiate high- and low-resolution sections of the image, and can be used to create image maps and JavaScript rollovers. They can also be used to define a non-image area of the file.

ANIMATIONS

CHAPTER OBJECTIVE:

To learn how to prepare animations that will enhance Web sites. To use the features of Photoshop to speed production, and to understand that the number of steps needed to produce an animation may result in an unmanageable file for the Web. In Chapter 17, you will:

- Learn to build a cel-based animation.

- Discover the functions of Tweening between frames of an animation.

- Become familiar with how to animate a simple tweened object.

- Learn to add more complex elements to animations.

- Discover how to optimize images for the Web.

PROJECTS TO BE COMPLETED:

- Just Shoot Me (A)

- Baby Shower Invitation (B)

- Retouching the Jones Family Portrait (C)

- The Fix Is In! (D)

- Makeover (E)

- Photomat (F)

Animations

Simple Web animations are multi-framed GIF images that are displayed sequentially with specifications for the duration of each frame display and for looping. These GIF animations can be produced from one or more multilayered image files. Each layer, or layer change becomes a separate frame or animation "cel." Alternatively, frames can be imported from Apple QuickTime movies or QuickTime-compatible movie formats.

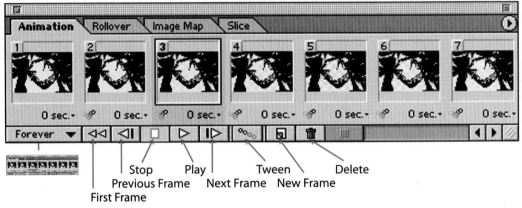

Animating objects on Web pages is important to holding the visitor's interest. However, as with everything else you have learned about Photoshop, too much of a good thing can be detrimental. Unless your business is animation, the animations on your Web page should be straightforward, and designed to enhance the point of your page — not to show how creative and innovative you can be at the expense of time and real estate.

Create a Simple Cel-based Animation

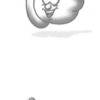

1. Open the document **Banana Boat BW.EPS** from the **SF-Adv Photoshop** folder in ImageReady. Click OK to accept the Rasterize default options.

2. In the Layers palette, drag Layer 1 to the New Layer icon at the bottom of the palette. This creates a copy of the initial layer.

3. Using your choice of tools, in the Layer 1 copy, color the banana and the "B" of the word banana a pastel color.

Double-clicking on the file will launch Photoshop. For these exercises, be certain to open the file from within Image Ready.

4. Repeat the layer copy using the modified layer.

5. In Layer 1 Copy 2, color the next letter with the same or a different color.

6. Continue making copies and adding colors to the logo in each successive layer until you have colorized the entire logo.

7. Remove layer visibility from all layers except the first black-and-white version of the logo.

8. Select Window>Show Animation. The first frame is already there. In the Animation window, add a second frame by clicking on the Duplicate Current Frame icon at the bottom of the Animation window.

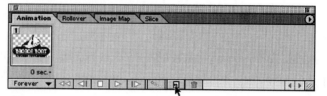

9. With the new frame selected, change layer visibility to display the next layer.

10. Continue adding frames to the animation, and assigning the display of the next layer in sequence.

11. Click on the Play button at the bottom of the Animation window to see how your animated logo appears.

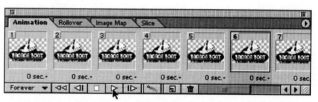

12. Use the Stop button, and change the Looping option from Forever to Once.

13. Select Window>Show Optimized. Choose GIF 32/Dithered from the drag-down menu. Select File>Save Optimized As, to save the animation as "Banana-Boat-BW.GIF" to your **Work in Progress** folder. You can view the file in a Web browser by dragging it to the browser window.

14. Close the Banana Boat BW.EPS file without saving.

Animation Transitions

In the simplest of animations, such as the cel-based animation that you created, one frame simply replaces another. For many effects, however, this would produce a very jerky movement that would be unacceptable.

Controls at the bottom of the Animation window include:

• *Selects First Frame*

• *Selects Previous Frame*

• *Stops Animation*

• *Plays Animation*

• *Selects Next Frame*

• *Tweens Animation Frames*

• *Duplicates Selected Frame*

• *Deletes Selected Frames*

The Animation palette can be used to generate — *tween* — additional frames of motion between two other frames. This works in two different situations: If a selection within a layer of a multilayered image is moved, intermediate positions of the selection can be generated by tweening. On the other hand, if animation cels are generated from separate layers, tweening generates a fade effect using the opacity of the two layers.

Transitions are controlled by determining what happens to the image on the first frame being tweened and by defining what happens during the tweening process. These parameters are established using two menus.

Frame Disposal

The drag-down Frame Disposal menu determines what happens to the current frame during a transition. There are three options:

- **Automatic.** This option discards the current frame if the next frame contains layer transparency. This is the default, and is desirable for many animations. This method must be used when optimizing images using the Redundant Pixel Removal optimization option.

- **Do Not Dispose.** This option preserves the current frame as the next frame is added, allowing the current frame to show through transparent areas of the next frame. To preview an animation accurately, using this option, you should use a browser.

- **Restore to Background.** This option deletes the current frame before the next frame is loaded. The current frame will not appear through transparent areas of the following frame.

Tweening Options

When creating frames that go between existing frames, ImageReady bases its actions on a variety of parameters that appear when you click the Tweening icon in the Animation palette.

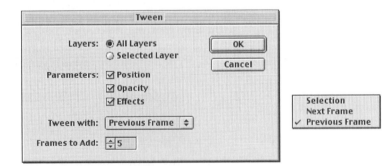

All Layers or the Selected Layer may be included in the metamorphosis. If Selected Layer is chosen, data from non-affected layers will be discarded in the tweened frames.

Specific parameters may be affected:

- **Position.** This parameter alters the content of the frame, spreading it evenly between the first and last frames of a tween.

- **Opacity.** This parameter alters the opacity of the frames, spreading the change evenly over the range of the tween.

- **Effects.** This parameter alters the settings of layer effects evenly over the range of the tween.

You cannot tween using discontiguous frames.

The Tween with drag-down menu is dependent on what frame or frames you have selected.

- If a single frame (other than first or last) is selected, you can choose to tween between the next frame and the previous frame.

- If the first or last frame is selected, you can tween with an adjacent frame or the first or last frame.

- If two contiguous frames are chosen, the tween will take place between the selected frames.

- If a number of contiguous frames are chosen, all frames in the selection will be included in the tweening action.

You can add up to 100 frames, but doing so would create a huge, unmanageable file.

Keep the Ball Rolling

1. In Photoshop, open the document **Ball.PSD** from your **SF-Adv Photoshop** folder.

2. Option/Alt-double-click on Layer 0 to access Layer Properties, and rename the layer "Ball".

3. Click the Add a Layer Style button at the bottom of the Layers palette to add a drop shadow to the Ball layer.

4. Click the Jump to ImageReady button in the Toolbox.

5. With the ruler visible, set vertical guides at 130, 220, 300, 370, and 440 pixels. Set horizontal guides at 75 and 150 pixels.

6. Open the Animation window. Click the New Frame icon in the Animation palette.

7. Drag the ball to center on the first vertical guide, with the bottom of the ball at the bottom of the page.

8. Select Edit>Transform, and rotate the ball somewhat.

9. With frame 2 selected, click the Tween icon, and accept the defaults.

10. Create a new frame and move the ball to center on the second vertical and first horizontal guide. Rotate the ball.

11. With frame 8 selected, Tween with the previous frame, accepting the defaults.

12. Create a new frame, dragging the ball to the third vertical guide, resting on the bottom of the window. Rotate the ball.

13. Tween frames 13 and 14.

14. Create a new frame, dragging the ball to center on the fourth vertical and second horizontal guide. Rotate the ball. Tween frames 19 and 20.

15. Create a new frame, dragging the ball to the fifth vertical guide, resting on the bottom of the window. Rotate the ball and tween frames 25 and 26.

16. Create a new frame, and drag the ball to the right of the page. Rotate the ball.

17. Click the Tween button, and change the Frames to Add to 7.

18. From the Looping Options drag-down menu, choose Once.

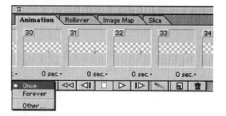

19. Create a new layer below the Ball layer. Allow it to default to the name "Layer 1". Fill the layer with a color of your choosing. Play the animation.

20. Save the file to your **Work in Progress** folder as "Bouncing Ball.psd".

21. Select the 4-up tab. Click on the last optimization option, and see if you can get an acceptable (in quality and in size) solution by changing the number of colors in the GIF image using the Optimize palette.

22. When you have a solution that works, choose File>Save Optimized As "Bouncing Ball.gif" to your **Work in Progress** folder.

23. Close the file without saving.

Some animations are much more complex than the one that we just created. See how much more effort is involved in creating this animation.

Laze Away the Day (and Night)

1. Open in ImageReady **Lazy Days.PSD** from the **SF-Adv Photoshop** folder.

2. Show the Layers and the Animation palettes, and rename the original layer "Hammock".

3. Create a new layer, and call it "Morning". Position it below the Hammock layer.

4. Select a shade of yellow (we chose FFFF66), and fill the layer with the color.

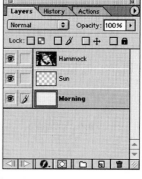

5. Add a frame to the animation.

6. Create a new layer below the Hammock layer and above the Morning layer. Call it "Sun".

7. Draw a circle that will eventually travel across the sky at the lower left of the frame, and fill it with a light yellow (we chose FFFFDD). Deselect.

8. Add a frame to the animation, and move the sun from the left side to the middle of the illustration above the hammock.

9. Add another layer just above the Morning layer, and call it "Noon". Select a shade of yellow just slightly darker than the sun (we chose FFFFAA). Turn off the Morning layer.

10. Control/Right-click on the second frame. This allows you to view the Disposal Method menu. Choose Do Not Dispose. This will blend the two frames to provide a smooth animation.

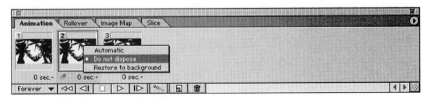

11. Click on the second animation frame and, from the Animation palette menu, select Tween. Use the default settings, except change Tween with to Next Frame. Click OK.

This generates the intermediate positions of the rising sun, simulating the rising morning sun. See how the project is coming along by clicking on the Play icon at the bottom of the Animation window, then click the Stop icon to move on. You can also move the animation one frame at a time.

12. Click on frame 8, the High Noon frame. Control/Right-click to ensure that the Disposal Method remains Do Not Dispose. Create a new frame. Drag the sun to the lower right of the frame, so just a portion of it is showing.

13. Choose a new foreground color. (We used FFDD99.) Create a new layer named "Dusk", and fill it with this color. Position it below the Sun layer.

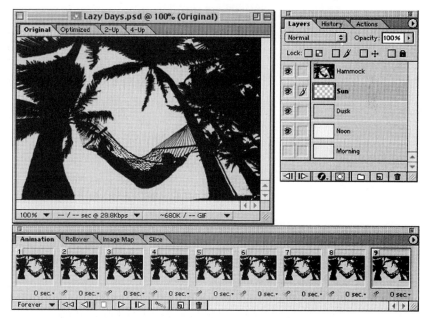

14. All the frames will fill with the Dusk layer. Shift-click on each of frames 1-8, then click on the Dusk layer's visibility icon to hide the layer for those frames.

15. Click on frame 8, and Tween between the frames. Use the default settings, except change Tween with to Next Frame. Click OK.

16. Click on the last frame in the Animation window, the one that shows the sun setting. Control/Right-click to ensure that the Disposal Method remains Do Not Dispose. Add a frame.

17. Now we have reached the end of the day. With the new frame selected, create a new layer beneath the Sun layer. Name this layer "Night". Turn off the Dusk layer.

18. Move the sun off the page at the lower right. Fill the night layer with black. Click (or Shift-click) on frames 1–14 and deselect the Night layer from the Layers palette.

19. Tween between the last two frames. This will generate a gradual change in opacity for each added frame, depicting nightfall.

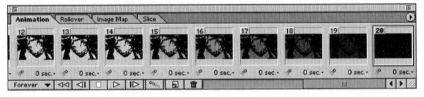

20. Click on frame 20, the Night frame. Tween with First Frame to create the dawn of a new day.

21. Play the animation. It should look fine, except the transition from dusk to dawn is too rapid. Click the Stop icon.

22. Notice that at the bottom of each frame is an indicator of the delay associated with the frame, "0 sec" by default. Choose frame 20, and click on the delay indicator to access a pop-up menu. Choose a 2 second delay, to give a sense of extended nighttime.

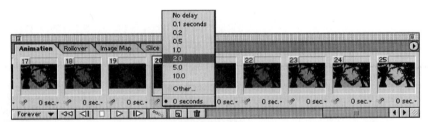

23. Play again. Make changes to experiment with the options, if you wish.

24. Click the 4-up tab, and note the file size and estimated download times. Pick the second GIF version, 100% dither, Selective palette, 128 colors. Save Optimized to your **Work in Progress** folder as "Lazy Days.gif", with the Images Only format selected.

25. Save Lazy Days.psd to your **Work in Progress** folder, and close.

The animation that we just created has 25 frames and occupies 350 to 413 KB, and takes 125 to 148 seconds to download at 28.8 Kbps — far too large for efficient downloading from a Web site. It would, however, be appropriate to use in a multimedia presentation.

Summary

You have created a variety of animations, ranging from a very simple cel-based animation to more complicated animations using the Tweening function. When you saved these optimized animations, you discovered that you can control both the quality and the speed of downloading of these Web-based images. Careful planning of your animation can result in an enhanced experience for visitors to Web sites you create. Animations that are simply thrown together, or serve little purpose (such as spinning mailboxes for a "mailto" item) can turn away potential e-customers.

PROJECT ASSIGNMENT #2

Assignment

The time has come to establish yourself as the creative image specialist you are. You are to assemble images representative of your best work for a multimedia presentation or on the World Wide Web.

Your Web page must contain sufficient information so visitors will be able to contact you and see the kind of work you do.

Your assignment is to incorporate striking images that show the full extent of your creative capability and your technical skills.

Ideally, use photos you have taken and enhanced. You can secure appropriate photographs from any source, but be sure to credit the source. Alternately, you can use the photos supplied in the SF-Adv Photoshop folder, or that you have saved to your Work in Progress folder. Be sure to adjust the resolution appropriately.

Applying Your Skills

To design the multimedia/Web presentation, you will need to use the following functions, methods, and features:

Create your design in Photoshop and ImageReady.

Consider using layer styles and remapping of color or grayscale images to enhance photos or photo presentations.

Explore the use of patterns, textures, and other special effects to enhance the presentation of your images.

As you bring together the components of your Web site, use the automation features to make your job easier and consistent.

When you select appropriate resolution for your images, take into consideration the time it takes each to display, so employ the Save for Web function. You will probably find it appropriate to slice images to control them more effectively.

Include at least one practical animation and one image with transparency in your presentation.

Specifications

The presentation should include a variety of image types. GIF, JPEG, and PNG images may be used for full-sized images, thumbnails, or animations, as appropriate.

The resolution of thumbnail images and full-size images for presentation only in the multimedia presentation/Web page should be 72 ppi; high-resolution images for downloading or viewing should be 300 ppi.

Use RGB as the color mode.

Included Files

You may use any image in your SF-Adv Photoshop folder or your Work in Progress folder. Using images of your own, if you have them, however, is a better solution. We encourage you to further enhance any image that you plan to place in the presentation.

Publisher's Comments

For this assignment, we recommend that you explore the Web and check out a number of photographers' or stock houses' pages to get ideas of how you would like to present your images. You may also want to show some before-and-after images, as we have done on the inside cover of this book, so people can see the magic you can work with your new skills.

CHAPTERS 9 THROUGH 17

In Chapters 9 through 17, we learned the value of the blur and sharpen filters, and how to use them effectively to enhance images or achieve special effects. We learned to remap colors and levels of gray. Working with layer styles, we were able to apply effects to type layers and regular layers, achieving dynamic results with minimal effort. We created tiles and learned to create a variety of textured backgrounds, combining different filters and techniques to achieve specific effects. We learned to use special effects using type, line art, and images. We found ways to speed our workflow and make it more consistent using Photoshop's automation features. We learned how to import files from vector-drawing programs, and to understand the file formats used for images on the World Wide Web. In addition, we used Photoshop and ImageReady to handle many of the chores necessary for preparing images for use on the Web, including automatically generating HTML and JavaScript. Finally, we learned to create cel-based and more complex GIF animations. After completing the discussions, exercises and projects, you should be able to:

- Use the blurring and sharpening filters to enhance images and create moods including the effect of motion, and to sharpen an image using Luminosity only, to minimize color shift.

- Create special effects by remapping colors and tones in an image, ranging from simple inversions of color and applying a gradient map to performing complex posterization of an image.

- Use layer styles to add striking effects to an image, such as drop shadows, embossing, and glows. You are also able to combine various styles to achieve compound layer effects that are editable.

- Produce patterns and textures for use with other images, or for creating striking backgrounds. You found that compounding effects, in conjunction with use of Hue/Saturation, produces dynamic results.

- Combine functions to achieve special effects using layers, channels, filters, and Liquify. You also know to keep track of your steps to make the effects repeatable.

- Employ the automation features to speed workflow and relieve the boredom of repetitive tasks, storing batch commands as droplets for later use.

- Create images for the Web while paying attention to details — numbers of colors in the color palette, resolution, and the dimensions of an image — and choosing the appropriate format in which the image should be saved.

- Work with a combination of Photoshop and ImageReady to produce documents for use on the Web, using image slicing to reduce file size and to create image maps that will be used in JavaScript rollovers.

- Produce animations that can be optimized, controlling both the quality and download speed for Web-based images, using ImageReady's tweening function to automate the preparation of intermediate images.

Project A: Just Shoot Me

Sometimes conditions conspire against your getting the shot you need for a project. Your client, a real estate developer, wants you to provide a strong image for a poster he plans to use to show points of local interest. Your image will be the dominant image of the poster. Unfortunately, budget, time constraints, traffic, and people walking in front of the camera made it impossible to set up the 4 × 5 camera and wait for conditions to be perfect for the shot you had planned. Getting any shot at all was akin to a guerilla operation.

This image was shot on a 35 mm camera on a solid tripod, which sets up quickly and whose wide-angle optics auto focus and auto exposure enabled you to work quickly. It is a good image from which to start your work. Since the shot is less than ideal for its final use, however, you will now optimize it, making it not only fit for publication, but bringing the quality up to where it could hold its own with any other professional photograph.

Optimize the Image

1. Open the file **Citrus Park.TIF** from the **SF-Adv Photoshop** folder. Begin by analyzing the image.

   Several problems with the photograph are at once apparent. The vertical lines are not straight. The color of the light under the awning is not attractive. Although the sky shows good detail, it is not the spectacular color we expect of strong architectural photographs, and the sky's overall contrast and color saturation also need improvement. Furthermore, the photograph would improve with enhancements — darkening the corners would bring more attention to the main entrance and lightening the sign in the fountain would make it much more readable and prominent.

Straighten Verticals   Change Color of Highlight   Make Sky Color More Dramatic

Darken Foreground   Light Up Sign   Improve Contrast and Overall Color Saturation

2. Double-click on the Background layer, and change its name to "Layer 0" or give it any other name to convert it to a normal layer.

3. The first task is to fix the vertical lines. Make sure that the rulers are showing. (Type Command/Control-R, or select View>Show Rulers.) Click and hold inside the vertical ruler, and drag a guide line onto your image. Position it near the vertical edge of the round tower for reference.

4. Press Command/Control-T to activate Free Transform. While holding the Command/Control key, move the upper-left handle of the image to the left. Allow time for the screen to redraw, and check the vertical lines against your guide. Adjust them as needed until the edge of the building is reasonably straight. Press Return/Enter. (The picture will look a little distorted during this process but will redraw smoothly as soon as you press Return/Enter to finish the adjustment.)

When taking pictures of buildings, photographers normally use an adjustable camera known as a "view camera." This instrument allows an upward view with no distortion, but it is large, slow, and awkward to use. Photoshop can be used to duplicate the perspective control of the view camera.

Next we will change the color of the light reflecting off the underside of the awning. Fluorescent lights often photograph as a yellow/green, especially when slide film is used. This color is often considered unattractive, so you will want to improve it. First you need to identify which colors are most affected by this color shift.

5. Add an adjustment layer for Hue/Saturation. Click OK to accept the default name. Select the Edit drop-down menu, and choose the Greens. Push the Saturation slider all the way to the right.

This oversaturates all of the greens, allowing us to see exactly where they appear in the image. Obviously, what we saw as green in the image is really caused by another color — a component of green.

6. Return the slider to the center. Try the same technique with the control for Yellows. It is apparent that our color problem lies here. Notice where yellow shows up throughout the image.

7. Set the Saturation slider back to the center. Switch to the hue slider, and move it to the left.

(Give the screen time to redraw — lots of calculations are being made.) As the color changes, you will see that eliminating the yellow/green cast on the awning also changes some of the other colors, but not to their detriment. (We think they look better with the warmer look.) When you like the color, click OK.

8. Next we'll turn our attention to the sky. Make sure the picture layer is active, and switch to channels. Select the blue channel. Use the Magic Wand, with its Tolerance set to 20, to select the Sky. Hold down the Shift key as you use the Magic Wand to select the sky on the other side of the building as well. This should work very well, needing little or no selection modification. Make any selection modifications you find necessary.

9. Select the RGB channel, and return to the Layers palette. With the picture layer highlighted, add an adjustment layer for Hue/Saturation, click Colorize, and adjust the Hue and Saturation sliders until you have a color you like. We chose a purple, as that is a common color for a night sky in the south.

If you take the time to look at each of the color channels, you will see that the blue channel has very little detail in the sky, making it ideal for this selection. Many time this is the case, saving the savvy Photoshop artist lots of time.

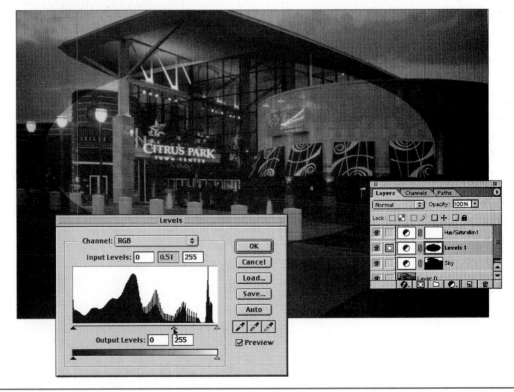

Notice how much better the image is starting to look. Now it's time to finish it up.

10. Make an oval selection around the center of the image, including the areas of most interest and detail. Invert the selection (Command/Control-Shift-I). Add an adjustment layer for Levels, and move the middle slider to the right to darken the edges of the image. It's OK to overdo this slightly, because you can adjust it later. Click OK.

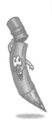

A selection on an adjustment layer masks the image beneath it.

11. Apply a Gaussian Blur of about 100 pixels to the adjustment layer mask, so the edge of the transfer is soft and barely noticeable. Click OK. Adjust the opacity of the adjustment layer until the effect is just what you want. Toggle the visibility icon for the adjustment layer on and off to see the effect.

12. The final step in the optimization of this image is to lighten up the Citrus sign in the fountain. Be sure you're working on the picture layer. Use the Magic Wand to select each of the letters, holding the Shift key as you add to your selection.

13. Add an adjustment layer for Levels. Name it "Citrus Sign". Move the midtone slider to the left until the letters look like they are lit from within. Click OK. Apply a small (1-2 pixel) Gaussian blur to the mask to smooth the edges, and you're finished!

Congratulations. You have taken a photo that represented the best quality that could be obtained under natural conditions and, through enhancements, created just what your client needs. A strong mall image will suggest that houses in this area are desirable as the real estate agent reaches out to potential residents.

Preparing Files for Output

Now that you have a Photoshop file, you need to prepare a file for the printer and other distribution. Save all files to your **Work in Progress** folder.

Prepare Files for RGB-savvy Printers

1. Choose File>Save As, and select TIFF from the Format drop-down menu. Save the file to your **Work in Progress** folder as "Mall_RGB.TIF".

2. Leave the file open for the next operation.

Prepare Files for Lithographic Printing

1. Flatten the image.

2. Convert to CMYK mode.

3. Adjust the PPI for appropriate screen frequency and size.

4. Select File>Save As. Check the As a Copy box, and save to your **Work in Progress** folder as "Mall_CMYK.TIF".

Prepare Files for the Web

1. From Image>Image Size, change the Resolution to 72 ppi.

2. Choose File>Save for Web, and select JPEG from the Settings drop-down menu. Save to your **Work in Progress** folder as "Mall.JPG".

3. Close the file without saving.

Project B: Baby Shower Invitation

Your boss's daughter is going to have a baby — her first — in less than a month. While the boss is going to do all the preparation for the shower itself, she doesn't want a mundane off-the-shelf invitation. Instead, she wants to grab attention, so more people will come.

The challenge is to take pictures of a number of babies, lift them out of their original settings, and seamlessly combine them into an attractive background photo. In the process, we'll deal with harsh lighting from flashbulbs and other-than-ideal available light conditions.

Needless to say, we're not going to print thousands of these invitations, but we will take advantage of technology that allows us to print from a few dozen to a few hundred.

Isolate the Object from the Background

1. Open **Baby Background.TIF** from the **SF-Adv Photoshop** folder. This picture will act as the background for the babies.

2. Open **Baby01.TIF** from the **SF-Adv Photoshop** folder.

   This cute baby is going to be the first picture that you place onto the "stage." There's only one problem: our little baby has to be isolated from the background. We will do this using the Magnetic Lasso tool. (This tool snaps to the edges of your image, allowing you to select the edges of your picture easily. The Magnetic Lasso tool is on the left side of the toolbar, under the standard Lasso tool. Click and hold the button, and the tool pops out.)

3. With the Magnetic Lasso tool, click somewhere along the edge of the baby. A starting anchor point appears. Slowly move your mouse around the edge of the baby. A series of anchor points appears and snaps to the outside of the baby image. When you reach the beginning, click on the starting point. The anchor points disappear, and "marching ants" appear instead.

4. Notice that the marching ants do not completely enclose the baby. We need to add and subtract some areas with the Lasso tool to obtain a good clean selection of the baby.

   Move around the image methodically, working from the top down, and add in all of the areas that the Magnetic Lasso tool missed. If you overselect an area, you can delete that area by holding down the Option/Alt key and drawing around the overselected spot.

5. The baby should now be completely enclosed by the marching ants. It is not critical that the selection is perfect — we will refine it later.

Create a Path

1. If the Paths palette is not already open, select Window>Show Paths.

2. Hold down the mouse button with your cursor over the little black triangle at the top-right side of the menu. Select Make Work Path. A dialog box appears. Select a Tolerance of 2.0 pixels, and click OK. A line appears around your picture. This line holds all the information you so carefully isolated a moment ago.

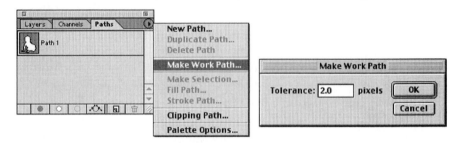

3. Let's give this line a name. Double-click on the Work Path box that has now appeared in the Paths palette. A dialog box appears. Accept the default name of "Path 2". Click OK. This new path will now be part of your image when you save it. Save this image to your **Work in Progress** folder with its new information.

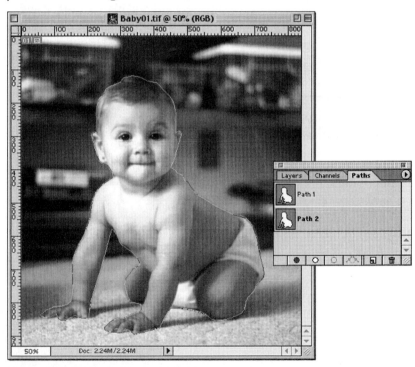

4. Once the picture has a path, that path can easily be changed into a selection. Click on the top-right black triangle, and choose Make Selection. Set the Feather Radius to 0 (zero), and check the Anti-aliased box. Click OK. A set of marching ants now appears around the image.

5. Position Baby Background.TIF and Baby01.TIF so that you can see both pictures. Be careful not to deselect the marching ants in the Baby01.TIF picture.

Once you have created your path, you can always refine it, if necessary.

6. Select the Move tool ("V"), and drag the baby over to the background picture. As you move the picture, a gray box appears around the background picture. This tells you that you are moving the picture correctly. Release the mouse. The baby now appears as Layer 1 on the background.

7. That Baby sure is large! Let's size him down a little so we have room for all the other babies. If you cannot see the Layers palette, select Window>Show Layers. Layer 1 should be the active layer.

8. In the Edit menu, select Transform, then select Scale. A set of white handles appears around your baby. Hold down the Shift key (to constrain the selection, and grab a corner handle. Slowly drag the handle toward the center of the picture. The baby begins to shrink. When you are satisfied with the size change, press the Return/Enter key. If you change your mind, undo (Command/Control-Z) the scale and try again.

9. If you zoom in, notice that the edges around the baby are too sharp. The baby needs to be blended into the background. We'll use the Eraser tool in Paintbrush mode to accomplish this.

   Select the Eraser tool. In the Options bar, select the soft brush in the second row, four over from the left (Soft Round 17 pixel). Set the Opacity to 50%. Zoom in to 150% over the area of the baby's hands.

10. The background color on the Tool palette should be white. Hold down the mouse button, and slowly erase around the edges where the hands and knees meet the water. A soft edge should appear. Be careful not to erase too many of the pixels — you are trying to create a natural feel.

Create a Layer Mask

1. You want the baby to appear to be in the water. We will accomplish this with a layer mask. Make certain that Layer 1 is still active. In the Layer menu, select Add Layer Mask, Reveal All. A white square appears in the Layers palette. Now select the Gradient tool, and choose Linear Gradient from the Options bar. For the effect to work, black must be the foreground color and white the background color on the palette. From the Gradient Picker, select Foreground to Transparent, Opacity at 100%.

2. Click somewhere below the baby's hands, and drag the line up to about the baby's elbow. The baby appears to blend into the water.

3. Let's blend the baby into the background a little more. Click on the picture of the baby in the Layers palette. Change the Opacity to 98%. This causes the baby to sit a little more into the background and makes the picture more realistic.

Create a Composite

1. Now let's bring the rest of those babies into the picture. Click the close box to Baby01.TIF, and save any changes. Open **Baby02.TIF** from the **SF-Adv Photoshop** folder. This picture will be added to the first picture.

    A path has been created for you in each of the baby pictures. You may use that path or create a new one for practice.

2. Convert the paths to selections, and drag the Baby02.TIF image to the Baby Background.TIF picture. Remember that there are now two layers plus the Background layer. Resize as necessary, and adjust the opacity to blend the baby into the background. Be certain that Layer 2 is active when you are making a layer mask.

3. When you have completed the above steps and are satisfied, click the close box for Baby02.TIF. Open **Baby03.TIF** from the **SF-Adv Photoshop** folder. Now we have a new problem. This baby is facing in the wrong direction. Let's fix that.

4. Make certain that Baby03.TIF's path is not active. From the Image menu, choose Rotate Canvas. Select Flip Horizontal. Notice that the path changes as well.

5. Our picture is a little dark compared to the others. Let's lighten him up using the Curves dialog box. Choose Image>Adjust>Curves. The Curves dialog box appears.

6. Select a point along the curve line, close to the center. Pull that line up slightly. The entire image lightens up. When you are satisfied with the results, click OK.

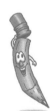

You can use the arrangement of babies that we used or create your own collage.

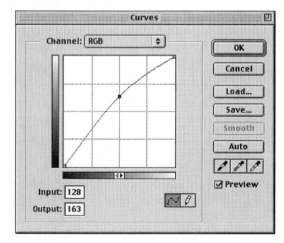

A number of the babies have hard lines, resulting from harsh shadows. Be sure to remove them with the Eraser. Experiment with different sizes and opacity.

Although merging layers makes the file smaller, it also makes it more difficult to move and edit individual components. Only merge when it is necessary.

7. Use the same process to place Baby03.TIF onto the page with the other babies.

    Let's take a look at the file size. Look at the button to the left of the picture window; the file has grown from its original size of 4.29 MB to about 9 MB. Each of those layers holds all of the pixel information plus the mask information for your picture. If you have lots of RAM, this is not a problem, but if you need to make the file smaller, Photoshop provides the means. It is called Merge, and it is a very powerful function.

8. Notice a visibility icon in the Layers palette. Click on the icon to turn off the Background layer. The babies look as if they are sitting on a checkerboard pattern.

9. Click on Layer 1. It should be the active layer. Hold down the mouse button with your cursor over the black triangle, and select Merge Visible. This makes your three babies one layer, but still keeps the Background layer separate. Click on the visibility icon to turn back on the Background layer.

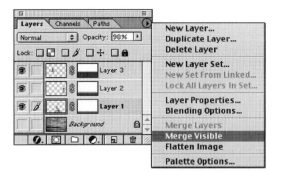

10. Save the image to your **Work in Progress** folder as "Invitation.PSD".

11. Open each of the remaining baby pictures, and place them all into the image. There are 14 different babies for you to place on the page. After every three or four pictures, merge the layers. Don't forget to save your image periodically.

Create the Type

Now that we have all of the babies in place, let's create some type for our invitation.

1. Choose the Type tool, and click on the bottom-left side of the image. Select ATC Island Bold, 60 pt., and type "Come to a Baby Shower". Let's make that type blue. With the Eyedropper tool, select a shade of blue from the sky.

2. Lets use a layer style to enhance the look of the type. In the Layer menu, select Layer Style>Satin. Make the following selections, or create an effect of your own. Set Blend Mode: Multiply, Opacity: 50%, Angle: 19°, Distance: 11 px., Size: 14 px., Contour: check Invert.

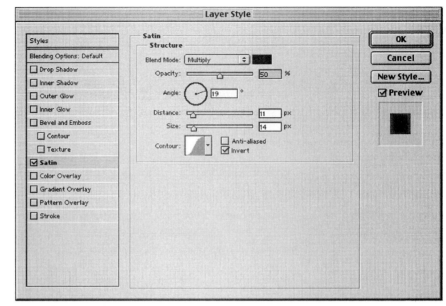

3. With the Layer Style dialog box still open, click the Drop Shadow box, then double-click the words "Drop Shadow." Add a shadow to help the type pop off the page. When you are satisfied with the results, click OK.

4. Use the Move tool to center the type on the invitation. Save the image before closing, or proceed to the next steps.

You have successfully placed 14 babies onto the background image, creating an interesting composite and an invitation to be remembered. In the process, you have overcome a number of challenges based on the inconsistencies of the original photographs.

Preparing Files for Output

Now that you have a Photoshop file, you need to prepare your file for the printer and other distribution. Save all files to your **Work in Progress** folder.

Prepare Files for RGB-savvy Printers

1. Choose File>Save As, then choose As a Copy, and select Photoshop from the Format drop-down menu. Name the file "PCC_RGB.PSD".

2. Close the file without saving.

Project C: Retouching the Jones Family Portrait

The Jones family contracted for this picture, taken on location at their home. Although it is an excellent photograph, there are several areas that need attention. This is often the case, when you have several people in the photograph, and small details you may not see through the viewfinder become major distractions when you see the image in print.

When you analyze the photograph, you'll note some distracting elements, such as the color of clothing and distortion in parts of the image. In addition, Gina, the woman on the right, holding the baby on the right, was unable to maintain a good pose due to the activity of a small child who was not really interested in having his portrait taken.

The photo will be placed on the family's Web page and will be used for a short-run greeting card.

Fix the Sweater

1. Open **The Joneses.PSD** from the **SF-Adv Photoshop** folder. Rename the background layer "Jones".

2. Use the Lasso tool to draw a rough selection around the sweater of the girl on the left. Don't worry about getting it close for now.

3. Add an adjustment layer for Hue/Saturation. Set it to colorize, and adjust the color by sliding first the Hue then the Saturation and Lightness sliders until the color of the sweater fits well with the overall color harmony of the group.

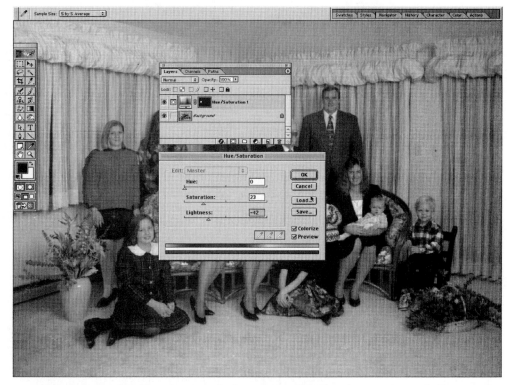

4. Select a soft-edged brush. Type "D" to set the default colors, and type "X" to toggle between foreground and background until black is the foreground color.

5. Make certain that the Hue/Saturation adjustment layer is active. Use the soft-edged black paintbrush to remove any color change that overlapped the boundaries of the sweater.

As you can see by the icon in the Layers palette, the color change takes effect wherever white pixels appear on the adjustment layer and not where the layer is filled with black. In this respect, adjustment layers work just like layer masks. If you make a mistake while editing the adjustment layer, type "X" to toggle to white, and paint over your error. In this way, the color of the sweater can be altered undetectably.

Podiatric Plastic Surgery

1. Make another loose selection with the Lasso tool — this time around the foot in the left foreground. Be certain to include some of the carpet along with the foot since it will be needed to cover the original one. Copy the selected area. (Did you remember to make Jones the active layer?)

2. Paste the foot onto its own layer. Name this layer "Foot" by Option/Alt-double-clicking the new layer. Reduce the Opacity of the layer to 50% to allow a view of the underlying image.

3. Type Command/Control-T to activate Free Transform. Hold down the Shift key to maintain proportion and resize the foot to be just a little smaller. (A little goes a long way here.) Rotate the layer a small amount to the right. Move the resized and rotated foot until it is in a natural position, and press the Return/Enter key. Return the Opacity to 100%.

4. Add a layer mask to the Foot layer. Use a soft-edged paintbrush and black and white paint to blend the edges until a natural look is achieved. (Be certain that the mask icon is active in the Layers palette when editing layer masks.)

5. Merge the layer with the Background layer.

Picture-Perfect Posture

1. Use the Lasso tool to draw a rough selection — this time around the legs of Mrs. Jones, the woman in the middle. Do not make a tight selection, because plenty of background will be needed for this step.

2. Copy and paste her legs to a new layer. Option/Alt-double-click this new layer, and name it "Legs". Reduce the Opacity to 50%. Using the Move tool, cover Gina's (the woman with the baby) legs with Mrs. Jones's legs. You can line them up by using the furniture as a guide.

3. Return the Opacity to 100%, and add a layer mask. You should be an old hand at this by now. Change back and forth between black and white, and change brush sizes as needed to achieve a natural-looking result.

Finish Up

1. Using the Oval Marquee tool, draw an oval around the group on the Jones layer. Inverse the selection.

2. Add an adjustment layer for Levels.

3. Move the midtone slider to the right. As you can see, this gives the effect of toning down the edges of the photograph in the same manner in which a custom printer tones down the edges in a darkroom. At this point the edge is far too sharp — apply a Gaussian blur to the levels layer to soften the edge.

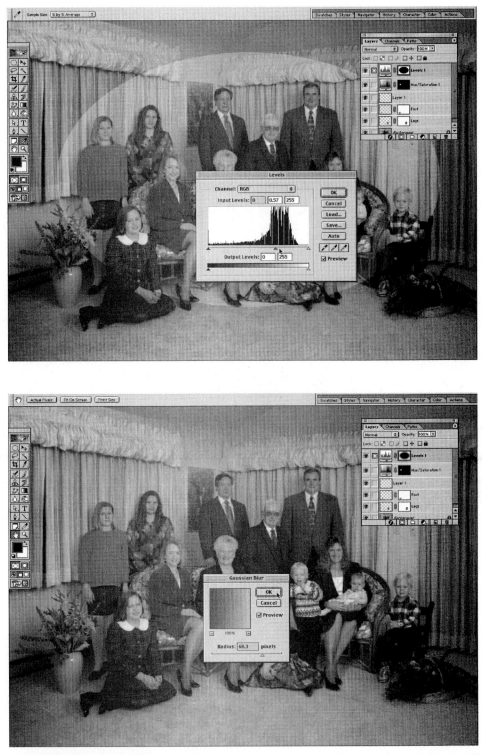

4. This levels layer should be at the top of the stack in the Layers palette so that it affects all the layers.

5. Add a new layer, name it "Spotting", and move it to the top of the stack.

6. Set the Clone Stamp tool to Use All Layers. Remove any dust spots, especially the one on the sweater. Since this file is sized to reproduce only at 3.5 in. × 5 in., there is not

enough resolution to retouch faces, and because of the small size, facial lines won't show very much. If this file were reproduced at 10 in. × 14 in., the file size would be about 100 MB and facial detail should be retouched.

7. Save the file to your **Work in Progress** folder as "The Jones.PSD". Close the file, or continue with the next section.

Preparing Files for Output

Now that you have a Photoshop file, you need to prepare a file for the printer and for other distribution. Save all files to your **Work in Progress** folder.

Prepare Files for RGB-savvy Printers

1. Choose File>Save As, and select TIFF from the Format drop-down menu. Name the file "Jones_RGB.TIF".

2. Leave the file open for the next operation.

Prepare Files for the Web

1. From Image>Image Size, change the Resolution to 72 ppi.

2. Choose File>Save for Web, and select JPEG from the Settings drop-down menu. You can choose from a variety of options and compare the results side by side. Choose the best compromise between size and image quality. Name the file "Jones.JPG".

3. Close the file without saving.

Notes:

Project D: The Fix Is In!

This image comes to us from the Veronica Cass School of Photographic Arts in Hudson, Florida, where it is used to teach both conventional and digital retouching. This project is quite typical of the type of work found in the world of retouching.

Your assignment is two-pronged. First, the image needs to be repaired (arms added, scratches removed, and a new background created). Secondly, the image must be colorized to recreate the hand-colored effect that was in vogue when the original was taken. This used to be a very labor-intensive process, but you have the tools and the skills to perform the task easily.

The image could be reproduced on disk or on a Web page to show off your work, or it could be printed using an RGB-savvy printer.

Retouch the Image

1. Open the file **Cop.TIF** from the **SF-Adv Photoshop** folder.

   Begin by analyzing the image. It is apparent that the scan was made from a copy of the original image. This was done to allow extra room for the arms and a larger background. It is a necessary step when you do conventional retouching since there is no way to add canvas as you can in Photoshop.

2. Choose the Pen tool. Although the Lasso tool has magnetic features, the standard Pen tool works best here due to the similarity of tone in areas of the background and foreground. We will also use the drawing capabilities of the Pen tool to add his missing arms.

3. Start at his shoulder and draw a path all the way around the cop. His slicked-down style haircut makes this job easier. Continue to draw the path where his arm should be. Don't panic if you can't draw well: just make several curves to suggest folds in the cloth.

The selection marquee keeps you from having to worry about drawing the edge of the coat since you can only paint inside the lines. It's like having a magic coloring book.

4. When your path is finished, double-click the Work path, and name it "Cop", then go to the bottom of the Paths palette and click on the dotted circle. This will turn your path into a selection. Click in the palette away from the path to turn it off. (If you forget to turn off the path, you will find a fine line where the path was.)

5. With the selection active on the Background layer, you are ready to paint in his arms. Feather the selection by about 1.5 pixels. Add a new layer on which to paint. Name it "Retouching". (The selection becomes active on this new layer.)

6. Select the Clone Stamp tool ("S" key) and, with the Use All Layers box checked, begin adding cloth to the area where his arms should be. Select a medium soft brush. Use as many different areas to from which to clone as possible, including the existing folds and seams to add detail and realism to your work.

7. At the same time, fix the damaged areas that fall inside the Selection Marquee. Don't worry about the area outside the selection: you will soon replace that with a new background.

   Take as much time as necessary to do a good job. When you are satisfied with your repairs, take a moment to toggle the visibility icon for the Retouching layer on and off to see just how much you have accomplished.

8. With the selection still active, rename the Background layer "Cop". Click the mask icon at the bottom of the layer palette to add a layer mask to the Cop layer. Add a new layer, and position it below the Cop layer. This will be part of your new background.

9. Type "D" to set the default colors to black and white. With the new layer active, select Filter>Render Clouds. Your new layer should be filled with Photoshop clouds.

10. Add another layer, and fill it with a linear gradient from dark at the top to white at the bottom. Blend the layers by adjusting the Opacity of whichever one is on top. Different effects can be achieved with different Opacity settings and by changing which one is on top. Experiment until you are satisfied.

11. Add a very small amount of noise to the topmost background layer, and give it a tiny (.2) Gaussian blur to match the grain pattern of the original.

One last trick before you begin to colorize. The badge is without detail because it has been copied too many times.

12. Use the Clone Stamp tool set at a low Opacity (20%) to add just a suggestion of detail from one of the uniform buttons. Don't add too much — just enough to make the viewer think he can see detail.

13. Merge the Retouching layer into the Cop layer. Save the image as "Cop.PSD" to your **Work in Progress** folder.

You'll want to save after every major step below, both as a matter of safe computing, and to avoid running out of RAM.

Colorize the Image

1. Select Image>Mode>RGB Color. Do not merge the image. Be certain that the Cop layer is active.

2. Option/Alt-click on the adjustment layer icon at the bottom of the Layers palette, and select Hue/Saturation. Check the Group with Previous Layer option, and give the layer an appropriate name. When the dialog box appears, check the Colorize box. Move the sliders until you have achieved a sepia tone. Click OK when you like the tone.

Don't worry about the sloppy edges. If you make the color too bright, you can always reduce the effect by lowering the Opacity slider for the adjustment layer. This is especially useful when adding color to the lips.

Hue/Saturation	
Edit: Master	OK
Hue: 30	Cancel
Saturation: 25	Load...
Lightness: 0	Save...
	☑ Colorize
	☑ Preview

3. Using the Lasso tool, loosely select the area around his hair. Add another Hue/Saturation layer, grouped with the previous layer. Adjust the sliders until you are happy with the hair color.

4. Reset the colors to default (black and white). (Type "D".)

5. Select a soft-edged brush. With black as the foreground color, paint on the Hue/Saturation layer to remove the sloppy edges. If you paint into the hair area, type "X" to switch foreground and background and paint over your mistake.

6. Use the same technique to colorize his lips and jacket. Each will have its own Hue/Saturation adjustment layer. When you have finished the jacket, use the black brush to remove the blue from his buttons and badge. (Don't forget his collar numbers.)

When you paint with white on the Hue and Saturation layer, you change the underlying pixels to the color specified in the adjustment layer.

7. When doing the eyes, follow the same technique, but colorize only the iris and pupil — they are very dark so the colorization will not be pronounced. Go to the very first (sepia tone) adjustment layer, and remove the sepia color in the whites of his eyes using the black soft-edged brush.

If you want to be thorough, you can go back to the eyes and remove the color from the pupil and highlights by using the soft-edged black brush on the adjustment layer that gives the eyes their color.

8. Duplicate the jacket adjustment layer. (Drag it to the new layer icon at the bottom of the Layers palette.)

9. Select Image>Adjust>Invert. At this point, the buttons and his face will all turn blue. Don't panic! Simply use the Marquee tool to select the area around his head, and fill with black, then deselect. (Be certain that you are still in the new adjustment layer.) That will remove the change from his face. Double-click the layer thumbnail to display the dialog box, and adjust the sliders to make the buttons and badge a nice brassy yellow.

10. Finally, choose the background layers. (Activate the one just below the Cop layer.) Add an adjustment layer for Hue/Saturation (do not click Link to the Previous Layer). Click Colorize, and decide on a color for your background.

You now have a completely editable version of the cop in color. By double-clicking on the various adjustment layers, you can change him to your heart's content, giving him any color hair, eyes, lips, jacket, and/or buttons. You can even alter his skin tone and the background. Good luck and happy pixel-pushing.

11. Save the image. Either close it or go on to the next section.

Preparing Files for Output

Now that you have a Photoshop file, you need to prepare a file for the printer and other distribution. Save all files to your **Work in Progress** folder.

Prepare Files for RGB-savvy Printers

1. Choose File>Save As, and select TIFF from the Format drop-down menu. Name the file "Cop_RGB.TIF".

2. Leave the file open for the next operation.

Prepare Files for the Web

1. From Image>Image Size, change the Resolution to 72 ppi.

2. Choose File>Save for Web, and select JPEG from the Settings drop-down menu. Name the file "Cop.JPG".

3. Close the file without saving.

Project E: Makeover

When you're in business, image isn't everything, but it certainly helps. This image will be used in a promotional piece for a real estate saleswoman.

Still images, especially when closely examined, show every line and flaw. Things that go unnoticed when speaking with an animated and lively person seem to take over and become far too noticeable when rendered by the sharp lenses of today's cameras.

Traditionally flaws have been painstakingly retouched by hand on the film negative. The resulting prints show an idealized version of reality. With the smaller negatives of today's cameras and the advent of digital cameras, retouching has largely become the task of the Photoshop artist. With this in mind, let's examine the image to see what needs to be done.

This grayscale image may be printed on business cards, appear in newspaper or local magazine ads, be displayed on signage, or placed on a Web page.

Retouch the Image

1. Open the file **Makeover.TIF** from the **SF-Adv Photoshop** folder. As always, begin by analyzing the image.

   Smoothing or eliminating facial lines, adding catchlights to her eyes, opening her left eye a fraction, smoothing skin texture, softening the hair, and closing the tiny gap that shows her teeth between her lips will have an amazing effect on this image. At the same time we can lighten her face and darken the background to call attention to the area in which we want the viewer to look. With a small amount of extra effort, we can even subtly reshape her jawline with Photoshop's Liquify feature.

Image courtesy of Rob/ Harris Productions, Tampa, Florida.

Type a right bracket (]) to make the brush larger and a left bracket ([) to make it smaller.

2. Create a new layer above the background, and name it "Retouching". This gives us a place to work without altering any of the original information. Choose the Clone Stamp tool (type "S"), and make the toolbar settings Mode: Normal, Opacity: 30%, Aligned, and Use all Layers. Choose about a 20-pixel brush.

3. Start with the two vertical lines between her eyes. Option/Alt-click just to the left of the line to load the brush. Click and drag over the area several times, watching as the line diminishes each time until it finally disappears completely. Reload the brush, as needed, to avoid tracks or other signs of retouching.

   Using the brush at a reduced opacity like this allows a much subtler approach. You may want to experiment a little here and set the mode to lighten. In this mode, only pixels darker than the source pixels are changed by the Clone tool. At times this can be a good way to work quickly since a somewhat larger brush can be used without contaminating areas that do not need to be changed. If you try this, remember that the tool is set this way since it may not work as you expect later.

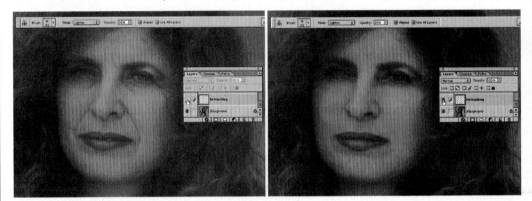

4. Continue to retouch the face, paying attention to the smile lines on either side of the mouth and the small bumps along the jawline and on the chin. Work also on the area under the eyes to remove bags and smooth tonality. Turn the visibility icon on and off to see your progress.

5. Take this opportunity to repair the slight gap in her lips that allows a tooth to show and fix her droopy left eye by cloning from her right eye. Line up the Clone tool, right on her pupil, and clone only enough to replace the iris and a bit of the upper lid. Use the airbrush and the smallest soft brush to add catchlights in her eyes.

   Avoid using too bright a tone for the catchlights. They should be the brightest tone on her face, as they are specular highlights, but they should retain tone and not go all the way to white. Try choosing some tone from a specular highlight on the rearview mirror. A little goes a long way here so be careful. You might want to add a new layer to test the catchlights and to give yourself the ability to adjust their opacity to your liking, then merge them down.

6. When you are satisfied with your retouching, type Command/Control-A to select all. Select Edit>Copy Merged (Command/Control-Shift-C), then Edit>Paste (Command/Control-V). This makes a new layer with the retouching merged into the background. It also leaves the old layers alone in case they are needed later. Name this new layer "Retouched Face".

7. Now we will attempt to reshape her jawline using the Liquify command. Select Image>Liquify (Command/Control-Shift-X). A new screen displays — take some time to explore it. We used the Shift Pixels tool at a Brush Size of 39 and Brush Pressure of 50.

   It is quite easy to overdo the subtle reshaping of the jawline. Practice several times until you get a feel for just how far to shift the pixels. Liquify can be a very powerful tool for reality-based retouching as well as a tool for caricature and cartoonlike effects. When you are satisfied with the results, click OK to apply them to your image.

8. Drag Retouched Face down to the new layer icon at the bottom of the Layers palette, and name the resulting copy "Soft Face". Blur this layer with a 9-pixel Gaussian blur. Reduce the Opacity of this layer to about 41%.

9. Add a layer mask. With a soft brush and black paint, bring back the sharpness of the eyes and lips. Set the brush to 50% Opacity, and see if that is enough to make you happy. If not, paint over the areas again. Toggle the visibility icon on and off to see the changes.

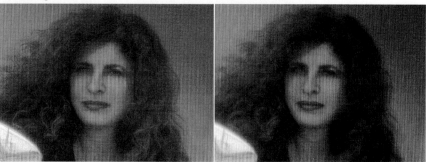

10. Next we will call attention to her face by making it brighter. Make an oval selection slightly larger than her face. Add an adjustment layer for Levels, and move the midtone slider to the left until the tone is where you want it. Click OK, and apply a Gaussian blur to the adjustment layer to soften the edge.

11. Command/Control-click on the resulting adjustment layer mask to load it as a selection. Inverse the selection, and add a new adjustment layer for Levels. This time move the midtone slider to the right to darken the area surrounding her face. The edge already is soft, but you can soften it more, if you want, by applying a Gaussian blur as before.

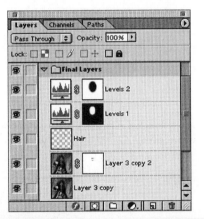

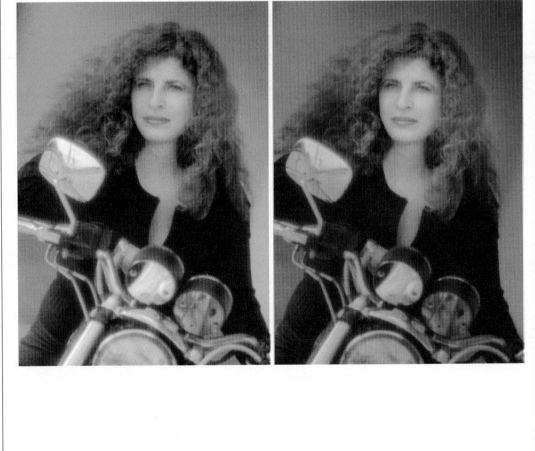

12. If you want to take this project one more step, arrange your layers into sets as shown by linking them and using the Layers palette Options menu.

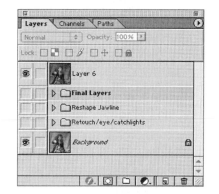

13. Add a new layer to the top of the stack in the Layers palette, turn on the Final Layers set, select all, copy merged, and paste a final layer at the top of the stack. You can toggle the visibility icon off and on to see the dramatic change made to the image.

14. Save the image to your **Work in Progress** folder for later use.

Congratulations! You've brought out the beauty of an already-attractive person by making small (but important) adjustments to her photograph. Careful attention to detail — and resisting the temptation to make large adjustments — have enabled you to modify the photograph and still keep its natural look.

Preparing Files for Output

Now that you have a Photoshop file, you need to prepare a file for the printer and other distribution. Save all files to your **Work in Progress** folder.

Prepare Files for RGB-savvy and CMYK Printers

1. Choose File>Save As, and select TIFF from the Format drop-down menu. Name the file "Makeover.TIF".

2. Leave the file open for the next operation.

Prepare Files for the Web

1. From Image>Image Size, change the Resolution to 72 ppi.

2. Choose File>Save for Web, and select JPEG from the Settings drop-down menu. Name the file "Makeover.JPG".

3. Close the file without saving.

Project F: Photomat

Now that you have a number of images in your portfolio, you want to show them off to best advantage. Placing the images in a presentation matte, with subtle shading and lighting, is a common way to present your images in their best possible light.

Having the product of your own imagination and skill hanging on your or someone else's wall is something of which you can be justifiably proud. This project will explore some ways to prepare your files so that when they are printed, they will be ready to frame and hang.

Here is an opportunity to show off all the skills you have learned. You will be able not only to create the matte that will frame your photos, but also to demonstrate your skills and creativity by choosing appropriate images to display.

Multi-opening Mat

1. Open a new RGB file the size that you would like to hang on the wall. In this case we will use 20 × 16 in. at 150 ppi.

   Most ink jet printers produce copies that look fine at 150 dpi. Printers capable of this larger-size format are becoming quite common at many GASPs and photo labs. Higher resolution is needed if you intend to print on one of the new breed of paper writers such as the Durst Lambda or the Kodak Pegasus. These machines use lasers or LEDs to expose photographic paper that is then processed in the same chemistry as any other photograph. These truly represent the highest-quality print currently available from digital files.

*A **GASP** is a Graphic Arts Service Provider — a company that has a substantial investment in high-resolution imaging equipment, and usually high-end scanners for input of the highest quality.*

Some functions we will perform in this project require a substantial amount of RAM. If you can't allocate at least 48 mb, do this project at a lower resolution.

New dialog box:

Name: Multi Mat   [OK]
Image Size: 20.6M   [Cancel]
Width: 20   inches
Height: 16   inches
Resolution: 150   pixels/inch
Mode: RGB Color

Contents
● White
○ Background Color
○ Transparent

2. Add a new layer above the Background layer, and fill it with a brown tone. Add noise using Filter>Noise>Add Noise — 12% to 15% Gaussian Monochromatic will do.

3. Select Filter>Distort>Shear, adjust the points as shown, and run the filter three to five times. Command/Control-F applies the last used filter again, as often as the user wishes.

4. Select Filter>Distort>Ripple, and set Amount: 100%, Size: Large. Apply the filter three to five times, until you see the burled-wood effect.

5. Add an adjustment layer for Curves, and add contrast as shown or until you like the appearance of the wood grain. We removed some red to give the burled walnut a more natural look. Option/Alt-click between the curves adjustment layer and the wood grain layer to be sure that the adjustment layer affects only the wood grain. (The adjustment layer offsets slightly to the right when this is done.)

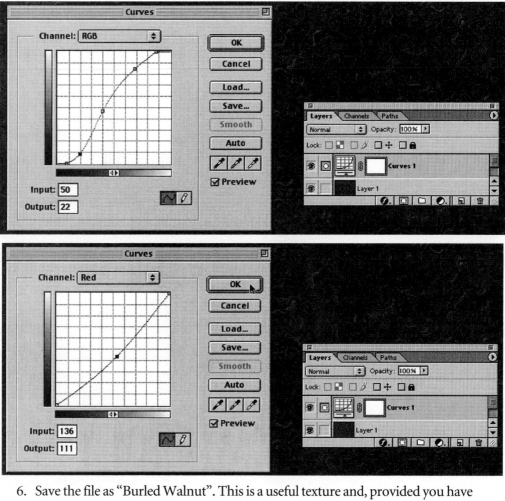

6. Save the file as "Burled Walnut". This is a useful texture and, provided you have enough room, is worth keeping for future use.

7. Select the Rounded Rectangle drawing tool. In the Options bar, choose Create Filled Region, set a Fixed Size of W: 4.5 in., H: 3 in. This allows for smooth rounded corners in our openings.

8. Create a new layer.

9. Draw three boxes. Use the Marquee tool to select and the Move tool to arrange them.

   You may find that using guides helps to position the boxes where you want them. (Click and drag guides onto your image from the rulers.)

   Feel free to place the boxes where you want them. The illustration shows just one possible arrangement.

10. We chose to place one vertical and two horizontal boxes per side in our arrangement. One efficient way to get the job done is to set up the first three boxes on one layer, duplicate the layer, and then move the boxes as a set. Note the guide lines.

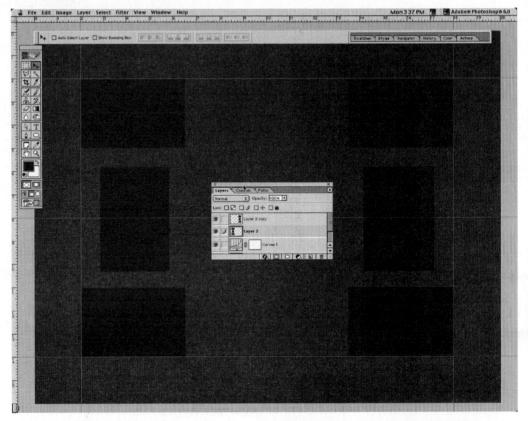

11. Command/Control-click on the layer that contains one set of boxes. Hold down the Shift key, and Command/Control-click on the layer that contains the other set of boxes. All of the boxes should have a selection marquee around them. Turn off the visibility icons on the layers containing the boxes.

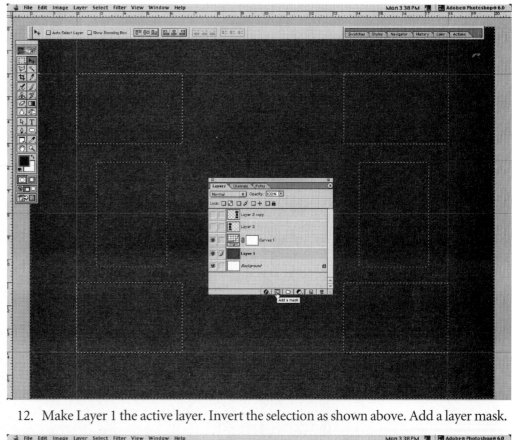

12. Make Layer 1 the active layer. Invert the selection as shown above. Add a layer mask.

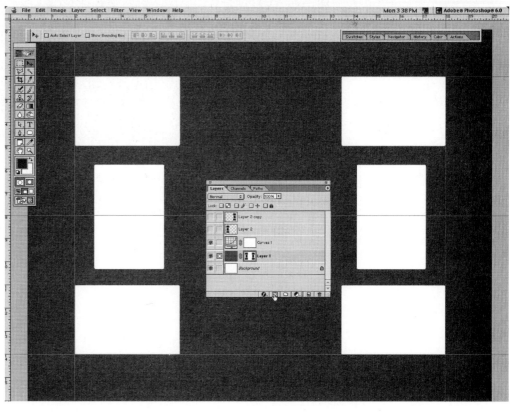

13. Double-click Layer 1. (This should be the layer with the wood grain and the layer mask.) When the Layer Style dialog box appears, choose Bevel and Emboss. Double-click on the words Bevel and Emboss, and set the resulting dialog box as follows.

In the Structure section, set Style: Inner Bevel, Technique: Chisel Hard, Depth: 100%, Direction: Up, Size: 18 px, Soften: 1px. In the Shading section, set Angle: 120°, Use Global Light: checked, Altitude: 30°, Anti-aliased: unchecked, Highlight Mode: Screen, Opacity: 56%, Shadow Mode: Multiply, Opacity: 38%.

Experiment with the controls here to create slightly different effects. When your satisfied with the effect, click OK.

14. Command/Control-click on the layer mask of Layer 1 to load a selection. Create a new layer below it, and fill the selection with black. Deselect and add a Gaussian blur of about 15 pixels. Use the move tool to position the resulting drop shadow slightly down and to the right to match the lighting on the bevels.

15. When you build a multi-opening mat, you often need to make additions. This elliptical opening could have been built with the flanking rectangular openings, but doing it now illustrates one way to modify an existing file.

    The center opening is to be an oval set to an aspect ratio of 5 in. × 7 in. Choose the Elliptical Marquee tool, and use the selection Options bar to create this easily.

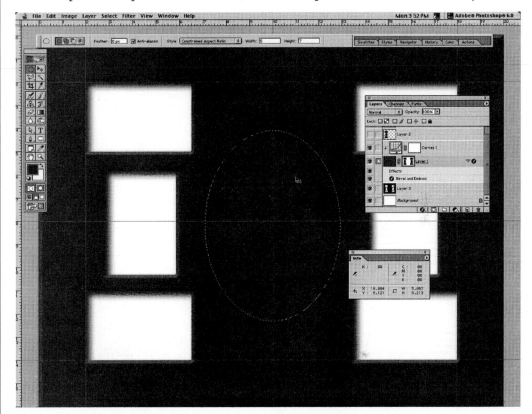

16. Be sure that the Layer 1 layer mask is the active layer, and fill the selection with black. The new opening appears with the Bevel and Emboss already applied by the styles layer. Keep the selection active, and switch to the layer that contains the shadows for the other openings. Move the selection slightly down and to the right, feather the selection about 30 pixels, and press the Delete/Backspace key. This should produce a new shadow effect that closely matches the other windows.

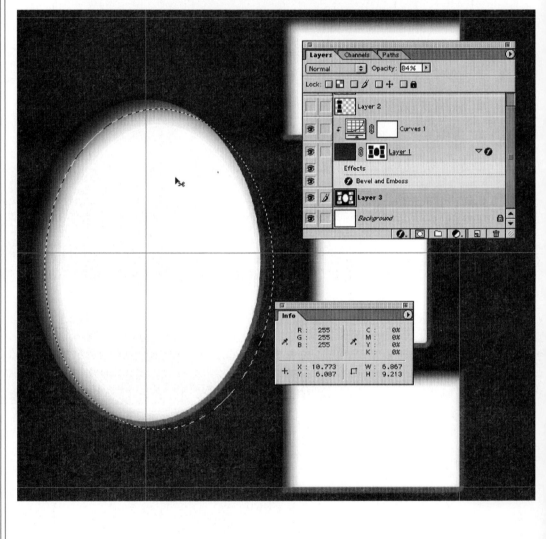

17. Double-click the Background layer, and click OK to make it a regular layer. Select all, and press Delete/Backspace — you should see the transparency checkerboard through the openings.

18. Copy and paste or drag your images into layers below the shadow layer. Select Edit>Transform>Scale to size the images to fit the openings.

Use the practice images supplied in your **SF-Adv Photoshop**>**Presentation** folder, or use some images of your own to make this project more personal. (The images provided are of various sizes and configurations to give you some practical experience.) You might well end up with a family heirloom.

19. If you want to carve type out of the surface of the wood, try this. Set the type in the normal manner. (We used ATC Margarita.) Command/Control-click on the type layer to load it as a selection, then turn off the type layer. Activate the layer that contains the wood texture. Copy and paste. The words do not show up because they are in register with the layer below. Double-click the new layer, and check Bevel and Emboss. Uncheck Use Global Light, and bring the light icon 180° around the circle. The words look as though they are carved from the wood. Experiment here to try different effects.

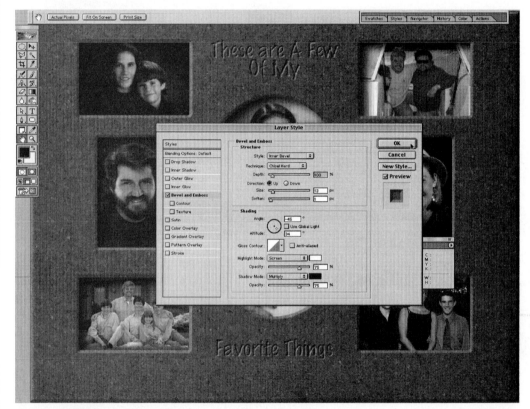

This is only one type of presentation technique. Hopefully it will give you some ideas. Many different textures can be generated and effects can mimic conventional display styles or be as creative as your imagination permits. If you can see it in your mind, the rest is just construction. Happy pixel-pushing!

Achromatic

By definition, having no color; therefore, completely black or white or some shade of gray.

Acrobat

This program by Adobe Systems, Inc. allows the conversion (using Acrobat Distiller) of any document from any Macintosh or Windows application to PDF format, which retains the page layout, graphics, color, and typography of the original document. It is widely used for distributing documents online because it is independent of computer hardware. The only software needed is a copy of Acrobat Reader, which can be downloaded free.

Adaptive Palette

A sampling of colors taken from an image, and used in a special compression process usually used to prepare images for the world wide web.

Additive Color Process

The additive color process is the process of mixing red, green, and blue light to achieve a wide range of colors, as on a color television screen. See Subtractive Color.

Adjacent Color

The eye will respond to a strong adjacent color in such a way as to affect the perception of the particular color in question. That is, a color having different adjacent colors may look different than it does in isolation.

Algorithm

A specific sequence of mathematical steps to process data. A portion of a computer program that calculates a specific result.

Alpha Channel

An 8-bit channel of data that provides additional graphic information, such as colors or masking. Alpha channels are found in some illustration or graphics programs, and are used in video production.

Anti-Aliasing

A graphics software feature that eliminates or softens the jaggedness of low-resolution curved edges.

ATM (Adobe Type Manager)

A utility which causes fonts to appear smooth on screen at any point size. It's also used to manage font libraries.

Background Eraser

This tool erases areas over which it is dragged to transparency.

Banding

A visible stair-stepping of shades in a gradient.

Bézier Curves

Curves that are defined mathematically (vectors), in contrast to those drawn as a collection of dots or pixels (raster). The advantage of these curves is that they can be scaled without the "jaggies" inherent in enlarging bitmapped fonts or graphics.

Bit (Binary Digit)

A computer's smallest unit of information. Bits can have only two values: 0 or 1. This can represent the black and white (1-bit) pixel values in a line art image. Or in combination with other bits, it can represent 16 tones or colors (4-bit), 256 tones or colors (8-bit), 16.8 million colors (24-bit), or a billion colors (30-bit). These numbers derive from counting all the possible combinations (permutations) of 0 or 1 settings of each bit: $2 \times 2 \times 2 = 16$ colors; $2 \times 2 \times 2 \times 2 \times 2 \times 2 \times 2 \times 2 = 256$ colors; $2 \times 2 = 16.8$ million colors.

Bitmap image

An image constructed from individual dots or pixels set to a grid-like mosaic. Each pixel can be represented by more than one bit. A 1-bit image is black and white because each bit can have only two values (for example, 0 for white and 1 for black). For 256 colors, each pixel needs eight bits (2^8). A 24-bit image refers to an image with 24 bits per pixel (2^{24}), so it may contain as many as 16,777,216 colors. Because the file must contain information about the color and position of each pixel, the disk space needed for bitmap images is usually quite significant. Most digital photographs and screen captures are bitmap images.

Bitmapped

Forming an image by a grid of pixels whose curved edges have discrete steps because of the approximation of the curve by a finite number of pixels.

Bleed

Page data that extends beyond the trim marks on a page. Illustrations that spread to the edge of the paper without margins are referred to as "bled off."

Blend

See Graduated fill.

Blind Emboss

A raised impression in paper made by a die, but without being inked. It is visible only by its relief characteristic.

Blow up

An enlargement, usually of a graphic element such as a photograph.

Brightness

1. A measure of the amount of light reflected from a surface. 2. A paper property, defined as the percentage reflection of 457-nanometer (nm) radiation. 3. The intensity of a light source. 4. The overall percentage of lightness in an image.

Burn

1. To expose an image onto a plate. 2. To make copies of ROM chips or CD-ROMs. 3. To darken a specific portion of an image through photographic exposure.

Byte

A unit of measure equal to eight bits (decimal 256) of digital information, sufficient to represent one text character. It is the standard unit measure of file size. (See also Megabyte, Kilobyte, and Gigabyte).

Calibration

Making adjustments to a color monitor and other hardware and software to make the monitor represent as closely as possible the colors of the final printed piece.

Calibration Bars

A strip of reference blocks of color or tonal values on film, proofs, and press sheets, used to check the accuracy of color registration, quality, density, and ink coverage during a print run.

Camera Ready

A completely finished mechanical, ready to be photographed to produce a negative from which a printing plate will be made.

Choke

See Trapping

Chroma

The degree of saturation of a surface color in the Munsell color space model.

Cromalin

A single-sheet color proofing system introduced by DuPont in 1971 and still quite popular in the industry. It uses a series of overlaid colorants and varnish to simulate the results of a press run.

Chromaticity Diagram

A graphical representation of two of the three dimensions of color. Intended for plotting light sources rather than surface colors. Often called the CIE diagram.

Cloning

Duplication of pixels from one part of an image to another.

CMS

See Color Management System

CMYK

Acronym for cyan, magenta, yellow, and black, the four process color inks which, when properly overprinted, can simulate a subset of the visible spectrum. See also color separation. Also refers to digital artwork that contains information necessary for creating color separations.

CMYK (Cyan, Magenta, Yellow, Black)

Acronym for the process colors cyan, magenta, yellow, and black (subtractive primaries) used in color printing. The letter K stands for "Key," although it is commonly used to refer to the Black ink that is added to the three colors when necessary. When printing black text as part of a four-color process, only the black ink is used. A four-color separation will have a plate for each of the four colors. When combined on the printed piece, the half-tone dots of each color give the impression of the desired color to the eye.

Color Balance

The combination of yellow, magenta, and cyan needed to produce a neutral gray. Determined through a gray balance analysis.

Color Cast

The modification of a hue by the addition of a trace of another hue, such as yellowish green, pinkish blue, etc. Normally, an unwanted effect that can be corrected.

Color Chart

A printed chart of various combinations of CMYK colors used as an aid for the selection of "legal" colors during the design phase of a project.

Color Control Strip

A printed strip of various reference colors used to control printing quality. This strip is normally placed outside the "trim" area of a project, as a guide and visual aid for the pressman.

Color Conversion

Changing the color "mode" of an image. Converting an image from RGB to CMYK for purposes of preparing the image for conventional printing.

Color Correction

The process of removing casts or unwanted tints in a scanned image, in an effort to improve the appearance of the scan or to correct obvious deficiencies, such as green skies or yellowish skin tones.

Color Gamut

The range of colors that can be formed by all possible combinations of the colorants of a given reproduction system (printing press) on a given type of paper.

Color Management System

A process or utility that attempts to manage color of input and output devices in such a way that the monitor will match the output of any CMS-managed printer.

Color Model

A system for describing color, such as RGB, HLS, CIELAB, or CMYK.

Color overlay

A sheet of film or paper whose text and art correspond to one spot color or process color. Each color overlay becomes the basis for a single printing plate that will apply that color to paper.

Color Picker

A function within a graphics application that assists in selecting a color.

Color Proof

A printed or simulated printed image of the color separations intended to produce a close visual representation of the final reproduction for approval purposes and as a guide for press.

Color Separation

The process of transforming color artwork into four components corresponding to the four process colors. If spot colors are used, additional components may be created containing only those items that will appear in the corresponding spot color layer. Each component is imaged to film or paper in preparation for making printing plates that correspond to each ink.

Color Sequence

The color order of printing the cyan, magenta, yellow, and black inks on a printing press. Sometimes called rotation or color rotation.

Color Space

Because a color must be represented by three basic characteristics depending on the color model, the color space is a three-dimensional coordinate system in which any color can be represented as a point.

Color Temperature

The temperature, in degrees Kelvin, to which a blackbody would have to be heated to produce a certain color radiation. (A "blackbody" is an ideal body or surface that completely absorbs or radiates energy.) The graphic arts viewing standard is 5,000 K. The degree symbol is not used in the Kelvin scale. The higher the color temperature, the bluer the light.

Color Transparency

A positive color photographic image on a clear film base that must be viewed by transmitted light. It is preferred for original photographic art because it has higher resolution than a color print. Transparency sizes range from 35mm color slides up to 8x10in. (203x254mm).

Colorimeter

An optical measuring instrument designed to measure and quantify color. They are often used to match digital image values to those of cloth and other physical samples.

Composer

Photoshop will use either the Single-line Composer, which composes every line using the parameters you have programmed into Preferences, or it will use the Every-line composer, which considers several lines when making hyphenation and justification decisions.

Composite proof

A version of an illustration or page in which the process colors appear together to represent full color. When produced on a monochrome output device, colors are represented as shades of gray.

Compression

A digital technique used to reduce the size of a file by analyzing occurrences of similar data. Compressed files occupy less physical space, and their use improves digital transmission speeds. Compression can sometimes result in a loss of image quality and/or resolution.

Continuous Tone

An image such as an original photograph in which the subject has continuous shades of color or gray tones through the use of an emulsion process. Continuous tone images must be screened to create halftone images in order to be printed.

Contrast

The relationship between the dark and light areas of an image.

Copyright

Ownership of a work by the originator, such as an author, publisher, artist, or photographer. The right of copyright permits the originator of material to prevent its use without express permission or acknowledgment of the originator. Copyright may be sold, transferred, or given up contractually.

Creep

The progressive extension of interior pages of the folded signature beyond the image area of the outside pages. Shingling is applied to correct for creep.

Crop Marks

Printed short, fine lines used as guides for final trimming of the pages within a press sheet.

Cropping

The elimination of parts of a photograph or other original that are not required to be printed.

Custom printer description file

A file containing information specific to a type of output device; used in conjunction with a standard PPD file to customize the printing process.

DCS (Desktop Color Separation)

Acronym for Desktop Color Separation, a version of the EPS file format. DCS 1.0 files are composed of five PostScript files for each color image: cyan, magenta, yellow, and black file, plus a separate low-resolution FPO image to place in a digital file. In contrast, DCS 2.0 files have one file that stores process color and spot color information.

Default

A specification for a mode of computer operation that operates if no other is selected. The default font size might be 12 point, or a default color for an object might be white with a black border.

Densitometer

An electronic instrument used to measure optical density. Reflective (for paper) and transmissive (for film).

Desktop

1. The area on a monitor screen on which the icons appear, before an application is launched. 2. A reference to the size of computer equipment (system unit, monitor, printer) that can fit on a normal desk; thus, desktop publishing.

Desktop Publishing (DTP)

Use of a personal computer, software applications, and a high-quality printer to produce fully composed printed documents. DTP is, in reality, an incorrect term these days. In the early days of Macintosh and PostScript technology, the term Desktop Publishing inferred that the materials produced from these systems was somehow inferior (as opposed to professional publishing). Now, the overwhelming majority of all printed materials - regardless of the quality - are produced on these systems, up to and including nationally famous magazines, catalogs, posters, and newspapers

Die line

In a digital file, the outline used to mark where cutting, stamping, or embossing the finished printed piece will occur. Uses to create a particular shape, such as a rolodex card.

Digital

The use of a series of discrete electronic pulses to represent data. In digital imaging systems, 256 steps (8 bits, or 1 byte) are normally used to characterize the gray scale or the properties of one color. For text, see ASCII.

Digital Camera

A camera which produces images directly into an electronic file format for transfer to a computer.

Digital Proofs

Digital proofs are representations of what a specific mechanical will look like when output and reproduced on a specific type of printing press. The difference with a digital proof is that it is created without the use of conventional film processes and output directly from computer files.

Dingbat

A font character that displays a picture instead of a letter, number or punctuation mark. There are entire font families of pictographic dingbats; the most commonly used dingbat font is Zapf Dingbats. There are dingbats for everything from the little airplanes used to represent airports on a map, to telephones, swashes, fish, stars, balloons - just about anything.

Disk Operating System (DOS)

Software for computer systems that supervises and controls the running of programs. The operating system is loaded into memory from disk by a small program which permanently resides in the firmware within the computer. The major operating systems in use today are Windows95 and WindowsNT from Microsoft, the Macintosh OS from Apple Computer, and a wide range of UNIX systems, such as those from Silicon Graphics, SUN Microsystems, and other vendors.

Dithering

A technique used in images wherein a color is represented using dots of two different colors displayed or printed very close together. Dithering is often used to compress digital images, in special screening algorithms (see Stochastic Screening) and to produce higher quality output on low-end color printers.

Dot Gain

The growth of a halftone dot that occurs whenever ink soaks into paper. This growth can vary from being very small (on a high-speed press with fast-drying ink and very non-porous paper) to quite dramatic, as is the case in newspaper printing, where a dot can expand 30% from its size on the film to the size at which it dries. Failure to compensate for this gain in the generation of digital images can result in very poor results on press. Generally speaking, the finer the screen (and therefore, the smaller the dot) the more noticeable dot gain will be.

Downloadable Fonts

Typefaces that can be stored on disk and then downloaded to the printer when required for printing.

DPI (Dots Per Inch)

The measurement of resolution for page printers, phototypesetting machines and graphics screens. Currently graphics screens use resolutions of 60 to 100 dpi, standard desktop laser printers work at 600 dpi, and imagesetters operate at more than 1,500 dpi.

Drop Shadow

A duplicate of a graphic element or type placed behind and slightly offset from it, giving the effect of a shadow.

Drum Scanner

A color scanner on which the original is wrapped around a rotary scanning drum. See Scanner.

DSC

Acronym for the Adobe Document Structure Conventions, designed to provide a standard order and format for information so applications that process PostScript, such as PressWise, can easily find information about a document's structure and imaging requirements. These conventions allow specially formatted PostScript comments to be added to the page description; applications can search for these comments, but PostScript interpreters usually ignore them. TrapWise requires that the PostScript in incoming files is formatted using conventional DSC comments, so certain functions may not work properly if the file is not DSC-conforming.

Duotone

The separation of a black-and-white photograph into black and a second color having different tonal values and screen angles. Duotones are used to enhance photographic reproduction in two-three-or sometimes four-color work. Often the second, third, and fourth colors are not standard CMYK inks.

Dye

A soluble coloring material, normally used as the colorant in color photographs.

Dye Transfer

A photographic color print using special coated papers to produce a full color image. Can serve as an inexpensive proof.

Electrostatic

The method by which dry toner is transferred to paper in a copier or laser printer, and liquid toners are bonded to paper on some large-format color plotters.

Elliptical Dot Screen

A halftone screen having an elliptical dot structure.

Embedding

1. Placing control codes in the body of a document. 2. Including a complete copy of a text file or image within a desktop publishing document, with or without a link (see Linking).

Emulsion

The coating of light-sensitive material (silver halide) on a piece of film or photographic paper.

EPS

Acronym for encapsulated PostScript, a single-page PostScript file that contains grayscale or color information and can be imported into many electronic layout and design applications.

EPS (Encapsulated PostScript)

Acronym for file format used to transfer PostScript data within compatible applications. An EPS file normally contains a small preview image that displays in position within a mechanical or used by another program. EPS files can contain text, vector artwork, and images.

Export

To save a file generated in one application in a format that is readable in another application.

Extension

A modular software program that extends or expands the functions of a larger program. A folder of Extensions is found in the Macintosh System Folder.

Faux

When creating type, Photoshop allows you to artificially make letters bold or oblique. This is called "faux bold" and "faux italic." You should always use real bold and italic when it is available.

Fill

To add a tone or color to the area inside a closed object in a graphic illustration program.

Film

Non-paper output of an imagesetter or phototypesetter.

Filter

In image editing applications, a small program that creates a special effect or performs some other function within an image.

Flat Color

Color that lacks contrast or tonal variation. Also, flat tint.

Flatbed Scanner

A scanner on which the original is mounted on a flat scanning glass. See Scanner.

Flexographic printing

A rotary letterpress process printing on a press using a rubber plate that stretches around a cylinder making it necessary to compensate by distorting the plate image. Flexography is used most often in label printing, often on metal or other non-paper material.

Font

A font is the complete collection of all the characters (numbers, uppercase and lowercase letters and, in some cases, small caps and symbols) of a given typeface in a specific style; for example, Helvetica Bold.

Four-color Process

See Process Colors

FPO

Acronym for For Position Only, a term applied to low-quality art reproductions or simple shapes used to indicate placement and scaling of an art element on mechanicals or camera-ready artwork. In digital publishing, an FPO can be low-resolution TIFF files that are later replaced with high-resolution versions. An FPO is not intended for reproduction but only as a guide and placeholder for the prepress service provider.

Frame

In desktop publishing, (1.) an area or block into which text or graphics can be placed; (2.) a border on .

G (Gigabyte)

One billion (1,073,741,824) bytes (230) or 1,048,576 kilobytes.

Gamma

A measure of the contrast, or range of tonal variation, of the midtones in a photographic image

Gamma Correction

1. Adjusting the contrast of the midtones in an image. 2. Calibrating a monitor so that midtones are correctly displayed on screen.

Gamut

See Color Gamut

GASP

Acronym for Graphic Arts Service Provider, a firm that provides a range of services somewhere on the continuum from design to fulfillment.

GCR (Gray component replacement)

A technique for adding detail by reducing the amount of cyan, magenta, and yellow in chromatic or colored areas, replacing them with black.

GIF - Graphics Interface File

A CompuServe graphics file format that is used widely for graphic elements in Web pages.

Global Preferences

Preference settings which affect all newly created files within an application.

Glyph Scaling

Photoshop will automatically scale individual letters in order to achieve appropriate hyphenation and justification.

Graduated fill

An area in which two colors (or shades of gray or the same color) are blended to create a gradual change from one to the other. Graduated fills are also known as blends, gradations, gradient fills, and vignettes.

Grain

Silver salts clumped together in differing amounts in different types of photographic emulsions. Generally speaking, faster emulsions have larger grain sizes.

Graininess

Visual impression of the irregularly distributed silver grain clumps in a photographic image, or the ink film in a printed image.

Gray Balance

The values for the yellow, magenta, and cyan inks that are needed to produce a neutral gray when printed at a normal density.

Gray Component Replacement

See GCR

Grayscale

1.An image composed in grays ranging from black to white, usually using 256 different tones of gray. 2. A tint ramp used to measure and control the accuracy of screen percentages on press. 3. An accessory used to define neutral density in a photographic image.

Greeking

1. A software technique by which areas of gray are used to simulate lines of text below a certain point size. 2. Nonsense text use to define a layout before copy is available.

Grid

A division of a page by horizontal and vertical guides into areas into which text or graphics may be placed accurately.

Group

To collect graphic elements together so that an operation may be applied to all of them simultaneously.

GUI

Acronym for Graphical User Interface, the basis of the Macintosh and Windows operating systems.

Gutter

Extra space between pages in a layout. Sometimes used interchangeably with Alley to describe the space between columns on a page. Gutters can appear either between the top and bottom of two adjacent pages or between two sides of adjacent pages. Gutters are often used because of the binding or layout requirements of a job — for example, to add space at the top or bottom of each page or to allow for the grind-off taken when a book is perfect bound.

Hairline Rule

The thinnest rule that can be printed on a given device. A hairline rule on a 1200 dpi imagesetter is 1/1200 of an inch; on a 300 dpi laser printer, the same rule would print at 1/300 of an inch.

Halftone

An image generated for use in printing in which a range of continuous tones is simulated by an array of dots that create the illusion of continuous tone when seen at a distance.

Halftone Tint

An area covered with a uniform halftone dot size to produce an even tone or color. Also called flat tint or screen tint.

High Key

A photographic or printed image in which the main interest area lies in the highlight end of the scale.

High Resolution File

An image file that typically contains four pixels for every dot in the printed reproduction. High-resolution files are often linked to a page layout file, but not actually embedded in it, due to their large size.

Highlights

The lightest areas in a photograph or illustration.

History Brush

A tool that allows you to paint to a specific state in the History palette.

HLS

Color model based on three coordinates: hue, lightness (or luminance), and saturation.

HSV

A color model based on three coordinates: hue, saturation and value (or luminance).

HTML (HyperText Markup Language)

The language, written in plain (ASCII) text using simple tags, that is used to create Web pages, and which Web browsers are designed to read and display. HTML focuses more on the logical structure of a page than its appearance.

Hue

The wavelength of light of a color in its purest state (without adding white or black).

Hyperlink

An HTML tag directs the computer to a different Anchor or URL (Uniform Resource Locator). The linked data may be on the same page, or on a computer anywhere in the world.

Hyphenation Zone

The space at the end of a line of text in which the hyphenation function will examine the word to determine whether or not it should be hyphenated and wrapped to the next line.

Imaging

The process of producing a film or paper copy of a digital file from an output device.

Imagesetter

A raster-based device used to output a computer page-layout file or composition at high resolution (usually 1000 - 3000 dpi) onto photographic paper or film, from which to make printing plates.

Import

To bring a file generated within one application into another application.

Imposition

The arrangement of pages on a printed sheet, which, when the sheet is finally printed, folded and trimmed, will place the pages in their correct order.

Indexed Color Image

An image which uses a limited, predetermined number of colors; often used in Web images. See also GIF.

Indexing

In DTP, marking certain words within a document with hidden codes so that an index may be automatically generated.

Inline Graphic

A graphic that is inserted within a body of text, and may be formatted using normal text commands for justification and leading; inline graphics will move with the body of text in which they are placed.

Intensity

Synonym for degree of color saturation.

Jaggies

Visible steps in the curved edge of a graphic or text character that results from enlarging a bitmapped image.

JPG or JPEG

A compression algorithm that reduces the file size of bitmapped images, named for the Joint Photographic Experts Group; JPEG is a "lossy" compression method, and image quality will be reduced in direct proportion to the amount of compression.

Kelvin (K)

Unit of temperature measurement based on Celsius degrees, starting from absolute zero, which is equivalent to - 273 Celsius (centigrade); used to indicate the color temperature of a light source.

Kerning

Moving a pair of letters closer together or farther apart, to achieve a better fit or appearance.

Key (Black Plate)

In early four-color printing, the black plate was printed first and the other three colors were aligned (or registered) to it. Thus, the black plate was the "key" to the result.

Keyline

A thin, often black border around a picture or a box indicating where to place pictures. In digital files, the keylines are often vector objects while photographs are usually bitmap images.

Kilobyte (K, KB)

1,024 (2^{10}) bytes, the nearest binary equivalent to decimal 1,000 bytes. Abbreviated and referred to as K.

Knockout

A printing technique that represents overlapping objects without mixing inks. The ink for the underlying element does not print (knocks out) in the area where the objects overlap. Opposite of overprinting.

L*a*b

The lightness, red-green attribute, and yellow-blue attribute in the CIE Color Space, a three-dimensional color mapping system.

Layer

A function of graphics applications in which elements may be isolated from each other, so that a group of elements may be hidden from view, locked, reordered or otherwise manipulated as a unit, without affecting other elements on the page.

Leading ("ledding")

Space added between lines of type. Usually measured in points or fractions of points. Named after the strips of lead which used to be inserted between lines of metal type. In specifying type, lines of 12-pt. type separated by a 14-pt. space is abbreviated "12/14," or "twelve over fourteen."

Letterspacing

The insertion or addition of white space between the letters of words.

Library

In the computer world, a collection of files having a similar purpose or function.

Ligatures

Ligatures. When this type option is selected, Photoshop will substitute the ligature (for example, ffi would be rendered using the ligature ffi). Ligatures are used when Open Type fonts are available.

Lightness

The property that distinguishes white from gray or black, and light from dark color tones on a surface.

Line Art

A drawing or piece of black and white artwork, with no screens. Line art can be represented by a graphic file having only one-bit resolution.

Line Screen

The number of lines per inch used when converting a photograph to a halftone. Typical values range from 85 for newspaper work to 150 or higher for high-quality reproduction on smooth or coated paper.

Linking

An association through software of a graphic or text file on disk with its location in a document. That location may be represented by a "placeholder" rectangle, or a low-resolution copy of the graphic.

Lithography

A mechanical printing process used for centuries based on the principle of the natural aversion of water (in this case, ink) to grease. In modern offset lithography, the image on a photosensitive plate is first transferred to the blanket of a rotating drum, and then to the paper.

Lossy

A data compression method characterized by the loss of some data.

Loupe

A small free-standing magnifier used to see fine detail on a page. See Linen Tester.

LPI

Lines per inch. See Line Screen.

Luminosity

The amount of light, or brightness, in an image. Part of the HLS color model.

LZW

The acronym for the Lempel-Ziv-Welch lossless data- and image-compression algorithm.

M, MB (Megabyte)

One million (1,048,576) bytes (220) or 1,024 Kilobytes.

Macro

A set of keystrokes that is saved as a named computer file. When accessed, the keystrokes will be performed. Macros are used to perform repetitive tasks.

Magic Eraser

This tool converts solid colors within a tolerance range to transparency with a single click.

Mask

To conform the shape of a photograph or illustration to another shape such as a circle or polygon.

Masking

A technique that blocks an area of an image from reproduction by superimposing an opaque object of any shape.

Match Print

A color proofing system used for the final quality check.

Mechanical Dot Gain

See Dot Gain

Medium

A physical carrier of data such as a CD-ROM, video cassette, or floppy disk, or a carrier of electronic data such as fiber optic cable or electric wires.

Megabyte (MB)

A unit of measure of stored data equaling 1,024 kilobytes, or 1,048,576 bytes (1020).

Megahertz

An analog signal frequency of one million cycles per second, or a data rate of one million bits per second. Used in specifying computer CPU speed.

Menu

A list of choices of functions, or of items such as fonts. In contemporary software design, there is often a fixed menu of basic functions at the top of the page that have pull-down menus associated with each of the fixed choices.

Metafile

A class of graphics that combines the characteristics of raster and vector graphics formats; not recommended for high-quality output.

Metallic Ink

Printing inks which produce gold, silver, bronze, or metallic colors.

Midtones or Middletones

The tonal range between highlights and shadows.

Misregistration

The unwanted result of incorrectly aligned process inks and spot colors on a finished printed piece. Misregistration can be caused by many factors, including paper stretch and improper plate alignment. Trapping can compensate for misregistration.

Moiré

An interference pattern caused by the out-of-register overlap of two or more regular patterns such as dots or lines. In process-color printing, screen angles are selected to minimize this pattern.

Monochrome

An image or computer monitor in which all information is represented in black and white, or with a range of grays.

Montage

A single image formed by assembling or compositing several images.

Neutral

Any color that has no hue, such as white, gray, or black.

Neutral density

A measurement of the lightness or darkness of a color. A neutral density of zero (0.00) is the lightest value possible and is equivalent to pure white; 3.294 is roughly equivalent to 100% of each of the CMYK components.

Noise

Unwanted signals or data that may reduce the quality of the output.

Non-reproducible Colors

Colors in an original scene or photograph that are impossible to reproduce using process inks. Also called out-of-gamut colors.

Normal Key

A description of an image in which the main interest area is in the middle range of the tone scale or distributed throughout the entire tonal range.

Notes

The Notes and Audio Annotated Notes tools allow you to attach comments to an image.

Nudge

To move a graphic or text element in small, preset increments, usually with the arrow keys.

Object-oriented art

Vector-based artwork composed of separate elements or shapes described mathematically rather than by specifying the color and position of every point. This contrasts to bitmap images, which are composed of individual pixels.

Offset

In graphics manipulation, to move a copy or clone of an image slightly to the side and/or back; used for a drop-shadow effect.

Old Style Numbers

When this type option is selected, Photoshop will substitute the old style number for the regular numbers (for example, 769 would be rendered 769). Old Style numbers are used when Open Type fonts are available. NOTE: Use these numbers from the Minion SC font.

Opacity

1. The degree to which paper will show print through it. 2. Settings in certain graphics applications that allow images or text below the object whose opacity has been adjusted, to show through.

OPI

1. Acronym for Open Prepress Interface. 2. A set of PostScript language comments originally developed by Aldus Corporation for defining and specifying the placement of high-resolution images in PostScript files on an electronic page layout. 3. Incorporation of a low resolution preview image within a graphic file format (TIF, EPS, DCS) that is intended for display only.

Toolbar

This toolbar automatically displays in the menu bar area of your Photoshop window, revealing the options available for the tool in use.

Output device

Any hardware equipment, such as a monitor, laser printer, or imagesetter, that depicts text or graphics created on a computer.

Overlay

A transparent sheet used in the preparation of multicolor mechanical artwork showing the color breakdown.

Overprint

A printing technique that lays down one ink on top of another ink. The overprinted inks can combine to make a new color. The opposite of knockout.

Overprint Color

A color made by overprinting any two or more of the primary yellow, magenta, and cyan process colors.

Overprinting

Allowing an element to print over the top of underlying elements, rather than knocking them out (see Knockout). Often used with black type.

Page Description Language (PDL)

A special form of programming language that describes both text and graphics (object or bit-image) in mathematical form. The main benefit of a PDL is that makes the application software independent of the physical printing device. PostScript is a PDL, for example.

Palette Well

An area in Photoshop's menu bar to which often-used palettes may be stored for quick and easy access.

Pantone Matching System

A system for specifying colors by number for both coated and uncoated paper; used by print services and in color desktop publishing to assure uniform color matching.

PCX

Bitmap image format produced by paint programs.

PDF (Portable Document Format)

Developed by Adobe Systems, Inc. (and read by Adobe Acrobat Reader), this format has become a de facto standard for document transfer across platforms.

Perspective

The effect of distance in an image achieved by aligning the edges of elements with imaginary lines directed toward one to three "vanishing points" on the horizon.

PICT/PICT2

A common format for defining bitmapped images on the Macintosh. The more recent PICT2 format supports 24-bit color.

Pixel

Abbreviation for picture element, one of the tiny rectangular areas or dots generated by a computer or output device to constitute images.

PMS

See Pantone Matching System

PMT

Photo Mechanical Transfer - positive prints of text or images used for paste-up to mechanicals.

Positive

A true photographic image of the original made on paper or film.

Posterize, Posterization

The deliberate constraint of a gradient or image into visible steps as a special effect; or the unintentional creation of steps in an image due to a high LPI value used with a low printer DPI.

PostScript

1. A page description language developed by Adobe Systems, Inc. that describes type and/or images and their positional relationships upon the page. 2. An interpreter or RIP (see Raster Image Processor) that can process the PostScript page description into a format for laser printer or imagesetter output. 3. A computer programming language.

PPD

Acronym for PostScript Printer Description; device-specific information enabling software to produce the best results possible for each type of designated printer.

PPI

Pixels per inch; used to denote the resolution of an image.

Primary Colors

Colors that can be used to generate secondary colors. For the additive system (i.e., a computer monitor), these colors are red, green, and blue. For the subtractive system (i.e., the printing process), these colors are yellow, magenta, and cyan.

Printer fonts

The image outlines for type in PostScript that are sent to the printer.

Process colors

The four transparent inks (cyan, magenta, yellow, and black) used in four-color process printing. See also Color separation; CMYK.

RAM

Random Access Memory, the "working" memory of a computer that holds files in process. Files in RAM are lost when the computer is turned off, whereas files stored on the hard drive or floppy disks remain available.

Raster

A bitmapped representation of graphic data.

Raster Graphics

A class of graphics created and organized in a rectangular array of bitmaps. Often created by paint software, fax machines, or scanners for display and printing.

Raster Image Processor (RIP)

That part of a PostScript printer or imagesetting device that converts the page information from the PostScript Page Description Language into the bitmap pattern that is applied to the film or paper output.

Rasterize

The process of converting digital information into pixels at the resolution of the output device. For example, the process used by an imagesetter to translate PostScript files before they are imaged to film or paper. See also RIP.

Reflective Art

Artwork that is opaque, as opposed to transparent, that can be scanned for input to a computer.

Registration

Aligning plates on a multicolor printing press so that the images will superimpose properly to produce the required composite output.

Registration Color

A color designation that prints on all four or more printing plates and is used to create alignment, or registration marks.

Resolution

The density of graphic information expressed in dots per inch (dpi) or pixels per inch (ppi).

Retouching

Making selective manual or electronic corrections to images.

Reverse Out

To reproduce an object as white, or paper, within a solid background, such as white letters in a black rectangle.

RGB

Acronym for red, green, blue, the colors of projected light from a computer monitor that, when combined, simulate a subset of the visual spectrum. When a color image is scanned, RGB data is collected by the scanner and then converted to CMYK data at some later step in the process. Also refers to the color model of most digital artwork. See also CMYK.

Rich Black

A process color consisting of sold black with one or more layers of cyan, magenta, or yellow.

ROM

Read Only Memory, a semiconductor chip in the computer that retains startup information for use the next time the computer is turned on.

Roman Hanging Punctuation

With the Roman Hanging Punctuation option selected, certain characters will be placed to the left or right of the escapement of a text frame, "hanging" into the margin.

Rosette

The pattern created when color halftone screens are printed at traditional screen angles.

RTF

Rich Text Format, a text format that retains formatting information lost in pure ASCII text.

Rubylith

A two-layer acetate film having a red or amber emulsion on a clear base used in non-computer stripping and separation operations.

Saturation

The intensity or purity of a particular color; a color with no saturation is gray.

Scaling

The means within a program to reduce or enlarge the amount of space an image will occupy by multiplying the data by a scale factor. Scaling can be proportional, or in one dimension only.

Scanner

A device that electronically digitizes images point by point through circuits that can correct color, manipulate tones, and enhance detail. Color scanners will usually produce a minimum of 24 bits for each pixel, with 8 bits each for red, green, and blue.

Screen

To create a halftone of a continuous tone image (See Halftone).

Screen Angle

The angle at which the rulings of a halftone screen are set when making screened images for halftone process-color printing. The equivalent effect can be obtained electronically through selection of the desired angle from a menu.

Screen Frequency

The number of lines per inch in a halftone screen, which may vary from 85 to 300.

Screen Tint

A halftone screen pattern of all the same dot size that creates an even tone at some percentage of solid color.

Shape Layer

A special vector layer is created whenever the special Shape tools are used.

Shape Tools

These vector-based tools include the Rectangle, Rounded Rectangle, Ellipse, Polygon, Line, and Custom Shape tools. They allow you to create and edit vector shapes in Photoshop.

Sharpness

The subjective impression of the density difference between two tones at their boundary, interpreted as fineness of detail.

Silhouette

To remove part of the background of a photograph or illustration, leaving only the desired portion.

Slice and Slice Select Tool

Allows you to create and edit user-defined slices of an image for creation of Web graphics.

Snap-to (guides or rulers)

An optional feature in page layout programs that drives objects to line up with guides or margins if they are within a pixel range that can be set. This eliminates the need for very precise, manual placement of an object with the mouse.

Specular Highlight

The lightest highlight area that does not carry any detail, such as reflections from glass or polished metal. Normally, these areas are reproduced as unprinted white paper.

Spot Color

Any pre-mixed ink that is not one of or a combination of the four process color inks, often specified by a Pantone swatch number.

Stochastic Screening

A method of creating halftones in which the size of the dots remains constant but their density is varied; also known as frequency-modulated (or FM) screening.

Subtractive Color

Color which is observed when light strikes pigments or dyes, which absorb certain wavelengths of light; the light that is reflected back is perceived as a color. See CMYK and Process Color.

Tagged Image File Format (TIFF)

A common format for used for scanned or computer-generated bitmapped images.

Tint

1. A halftone area that contains dots of uniform size; that is, no modeling or texture. 2. The mixture of a color with white.

Tracking

Adjusting the spacing of letters in a line of text to achieve proper justification or general appearance.

Transfer Curve

A curve depicting the adjustment to be made to a particular printing plate when an image is printed.

Transparency

A full color photographically produced image on transparent film.

Transparent Ink

An ink that allows light to be transmitted through it.

Trapping

The process of creating an overlap between abutting inks to compensate for imprecise registration in the printing process.

TrueType

An outline font format used in both Macintosh and Windows systems that can be used both on the screen and on a printer.

Type 1 Fonts

PostScript fonts based on Bézier curves encrypted for compactness that are compatible with Adobe Type Manager.

Type Family

A set of typefaces created from the same basic design but in different weights, such as bold, light, italic, book, and heavy.

UCR (undercolor removal)

A technique for reducing the amount of magenta, cyan, and yellow inks in neutral or shadow areas and replacing them with black.

Undertone

Color of ink printed in a thin film.

Unsharp Masking

A digital technique performed after scanning that locates the edge between sections of differing lightness and alters the values of the adjoining pixels to exaggerate the difference across the edge, thereby increasing edge contrast.

Varnish Plate

The plate on a printing press that applies varnish after the other colors have been applied.

Vector Graphics

Graphics defined using coordinate points, and mathematically drawn lines and curves, which may be freely scaled and rotated without image degradation in the final output. Fonts (such as PostScript and TrueType), and illustrations from drawing applications are common examples of vector objects. Two commonly used vector drawing programs are Illustrator and FreeHand. A class of graphics that overcomes the resolution limitation of bitmapped graphics.

Vignette

An illustration in which the background gradually fades into the paper; that is, without a definite edge or border.

Visible Spectrum

The wavelengths of light between about 380 nm (violet) and 700 nm (red) that are visible to the human eye.

Warped Text

The appearance of the text itself can be distorted through bending and distorting the text horizontally and vertically. The Create Warped Text button is located in the Text Options tool bar.

White Light

Light containing all wavelengths of the visible spectrum.

White Space

Areas on the page which contain no images or type. Proper use of white space is critical to a well-balanced design.

Wizard

A utility attached to an application or operating system that aids you in setting up a piece of hardware, software, or document.

WYSIWYG

An acronym for "What You See Is What You Get," (pronounced "wizzywig") meaning that what you see on your computer screen bears a strong resemblance to what the job will look like when it is printed.

NOTES